THE GRUMPY GARDENER

THE GRUMPY GARDENER

An A to Z Guide from
the Galaxy's Most Irritable
Green Thumb

STEVE BENDER

Southern Living Garden Editor

Oxmoor House.

Senior Editor: Katherine Cobbs

Project Editor: Melissa Brown

Design Director: Melissa Clark

Illustrator: Michael Witte

Assistant Production Director: Sue Chodakiewicz

Assistant Production Manager: Diane Rose Keener

Copy Editor: Susan Emack Alison

Indexer: Carol Roberts

Fellows: Hailey Middlebrook, Kaitlyn Pacheco, Matt Ryan, Hanna Yokeley

ISBN-13: 978-0-8487-5313-9

Library of Congress Control Number: 2017950175

First Edition 2017

Printed in the United States of America

10 9 8 7 6 5 4 3 2 1

We welcome your comments and suggestions about Time Inc. Books.
Please write to us at:

Time Inc. Books

Attention: Book Editors

P.O. Box 62310

Tampa, Florida 33662-2310

Time Inc. Books products may be purchased for business or
promotional use. For information on bulk purchases, please contact
Christi Crowley in the Special Sales Department at (845) 895-9858.

DEDICATION

To my saintly wife, Judy, who saved humankind by taking me off its hands; parents Edward Sr. and Mary Alice; sons Tom, Matthew, Brian, and families; brothers Ed and Chris; cats Ketchup and Jean-Luc; incredible colleagues at *Southern Living*, especially Gene Bussell who coined the moniker, "Grumpy Gardener;" and legions of adoring fans who rightly treat Grumpy's every word as gold.

CONTENTS

INTRODUCTION

Y ou are an extraordinary person. So many trivial matters compete for your attention—world peace, climate change, job stress, marital accord, budget woes, choosing the perfect wine for dinner—yet you have conquered the clamor and opened the one book written this century that can bring you hours of joy, fulfilment, and enlightenment every day. Why, you're probably feeling better this very moment, knowing that the knowledge to be imparted on the following pages will place you in the gardening elite. As Shakespeare noted in Hamlet, "'Tis a consummation devoutly to be wished."

I realize, however, that someone out there may shrink at the prospect of joining an elite. "I'm not worthy!" goes the lament. "I'll never know enough." Let me reassure you. This book is a compilation of articles, blog posts, essays, and answers to reader questions, all with the basic goal of helping both novice and veteran gardeners have a nice yard that pleases them. Empowering beginners has always been a hallmark of *Southern Living*. We live like you—well, except for the cave people in Arkansas, we're not into that—and face the same challenges that make life rewarding and infuriating at the same time. It's what makes me Grumpy.

Many people ask why they don't see more of my garden in *Southern Living*. Truth is it's because it's not as pretty as the ones that you do. It lacks a pigeonnier, for one thing—so embarrassing. A koi pond, Victorian glass greenhouse, Chihuly glass, sugar kettle, outdoor shower, and carriage house are missing too. My neighbors don't cut their grass. My roof has asphalt shingles. I collect antique glass insulators and display them proudly on our deck. And the garden has gnomes. Judy and I love hanging with our gnomies.

Would it shock you to learn that not every plant succeeds for Grumpy? Of course it would, but it's true. I cannot grow a decent tomato. Apples rot on the tree. Moth orchids do not rebloom. My lawn has weeds. Voles eat my hostas and toad lilies. Stinking squirrels dig up my annuals. Tea scales encrust my camellias. Evil violets smother my luxurious moss lawn. Black gunk slathers the leaves of my gardenia. My fiddleleaf fig looks like it's been strangled. My clivia shames itself with puny, stunted blooms. My sago palm rotted from too much water. I've dosed a sick beautyberry with nitrogen, iron, manganese, sulfur, magnesium, and calcium, yet it remains horribly chlorotic. I can grow pothos and snake plant quite well, however. There's that.

Gardeners often feel guilty when a plant dies. They feel they have failed in a public and most humiliating way. "Nothing grows for me!" they wail. "I kill every plant I touch." Wait a minute. Did they ever stop to consider that perhaps they were not at fault? Maybe that wimpy plant would have ascended to The Big Compost Pile in the Sky no matter what. Possibly a sinister critter, bug, or fungus murdered it in cold sap. Plants die. It's a hard truth, but one all gardeners must face. I encourage readers to reverse their thinking. Think of a plant's death in a positive way. If every plant you ever stuck in the ground lived, pretty soon every inch of your available gardening space would be consumed. You'd be sentenced to gaze at a stupefyingly boring, static landscape day after day. But when plants die, they present us with the opportunity to try something new and perhaps better. (Really, who needs another Knockout rose?)

In this A to Z Guide to Gardening, among other things we're going to talk about some really dumb things that gardeners do, like butcher crepe myrtles, scalp their lawns, put down rubber mulch, grow things that look like marijuana, set loose invasive plants, and crank chainsaws while up in a tree. We're going to pan a slew of awful plants no one should grow, such as golden euonymus, Chinese privet, Bradford pear, and mimosa. We're going to take righteous revenge on loathsome pests like squirrels, moles, voles, and deer that devour our best laid plants. You will understand why they call me "The Grumpy Gardener."

Take no prisoners. Lock and load.

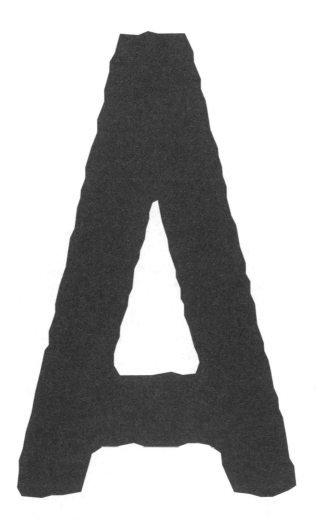

AFRICAN VIOLET TO AZALEAS

AFRICAN VIOLET

Nowadays, being given an African violet is akin to receiving your AARP membership card. It means you're old, maybe on death's door. Once the most popular of all flowering houseplants, the African violet remains practically unknown to Generation X, Generation Y, "Star Trek: The Next Generation," millennials, and anyone who uses a smartphone to turn on their AC and dishwasher from another state.

But before you dismiss African violets as "grandma plants," you might want to consider whether dear, old Meemaw ever flew in space. (Note: This does not include her unfortunate encounter with hard cider at the county fair.) African violets have. The EverFloris series resulted from seeds that spent six years in space, courtesy of the Space Shuttle. When the seeds returned and were sown, exciting mutations appeared. These space plants grow 50 percent bigger than normal. They display clusters of 20 blooms rather than the usual 5 to 7, and blooming is continuous. They also sing "Shine on, Harvest Moon," whenever there is a harvest moon. That's pretty special stuff.

Thus, the near disappearance of African violets from our homes is hard to explain. They aren't difficult to grow. They aren't expensive. And they bloom for a long time. They boast an amazing variety of flower shapes, sizes, and colors. Flowers may be single, semidouble, or double, and some flaunt fringed or ruffled petals. Color runs the gamut from blue, purple, lavender, red, pink, magenta, white, bicolors, and even green. Perhaps it was the green flowers that turned people off. Or the fact that they do need light and water to live, which doesn't fit in with today's active lifestyles.

African violets don't need direct sun to bloom well. In fact, they don't like it. What they want is 16 hours of bright, indirect light each day and 8 hours of complete darkness at night. A plant that is leggy, stretches, and never blooms isn't getting enough light. Of course, they're not going to get this much natural light in summer, so grow lights become a necessary supplement.

Aha! I think we've discovered the problem! The vast majority of grow lights used today are employed by the medical marijuana industry. If people notice grow lights in your home, they might assume the worst and turn you in. Have you ever seen what shameful things sheriff's deputies do to African violets mistaken for marijuana? On a more positive note, more and more marijuana growers are adding African violets to their greenhouses for a delightful splash of color. Grumpy approves.

If you'd like to follow their example, use well-drained potting soil that's formulated for African violets. Water from the bottom instead of the top. No, that doesn't defy the law of gravity like the moon's inexplicable failure to crash down on Buenos Aires. Just set the pot in a saucer filled with water for as long as it takes for the soil at the top to become moist, and then dump out the extra water. Or use one of those nifty self-watering pots that also call 911 if you fall and can't get up. Each time you water, mix in a bloom-booster fertilizer formulated for African violets, such as 14-12-14. Let tap water stand out overnight to allow the chlorine to evaporate and the liquid to assume room temperature.

Get with it, young Grumpians! Most of the folks who used to grow African violets assumed room temperature years ago. Our floral future rests with you.

AGAVE

ony Avent, owner of the famous Plant Delights Nursery in North Carolina, has no use for political correctness. Hence, he makes no apologies for the extensive selection of agaves in his catalog. Terrific when used as accents or in combination with plants of contrasting texture, agaves combine large, fleshy, straplike leaves and tall, unearthly bloom spikes. Trouble is most kinds feature leaves with sawtooth edges, vicious needles on the leaf tips that would do Vlad the Impaler proud, or both. Thus, the possibility exists that a careless gardener could rip his hand to shreds or in the words of my mother, "put your eye out." (Although I have never met anyone who did, mothers always warn about this even as they blissfully watch their kids leap from the garage roof onto a trampoline.) This does not bother Tony.

Mr. Avent believes that agaves are necessary to purify the human gene pool. In other words, the more people who answer the call to nature's blood bank by fatally spearing themselves on agave spines means fewer people passing on their oafish, lamebrain genes to the next generation. Survival of the fittest. Grumpy understands.

Tony's catalog doesn't try to hide anything from a safety-first public. The names of various selections

ASK GRUMPY

Out of Africa

Q. Will African violets grow in my yard outdoors like wild violets do?
—Tawny

A. Well, they will if you live in their native homelands of Tanzania and eastern Kenya. Outside of the tropics, African violets will turn to goop with the first frost. Even though both plants you mention are called "violets," they aren't related. African violets belong to the genus *Saintpaulia*, while our native violets belong to the genus *Viola*.

clue you in immediately. 'Shark Bite.' 'Eye Scream.' 'Bed of Nails.' 'Purple Heart.' I'm surprised there isn't one called 'Euthanasia' or 'Suppurating Puncture Wound,' but maybe they're in the works.

Dozens of species are native to southwest Texas, Mexico, and Central America. Of the two most familiar to the average Joe or Jose, one is century plant (*Agave americana*), a familiar sight along the south Atlantic and Gulf coasts. The common name comes from the widely held belief that it blooms only once every hundred years. The branches' spike of yellow blooms is truly spectacular, standing 30 feet tall or more. Like other agave species, the mother plant dies after blooming and produces offshoots that form new plants. Good luck seeing these bloom unless your name is Dorian Gray.

The other famous agave is the blue agave (*Agave tequilana*), source of the magical elixir called tequila. *(Uno mas, por favor!)* Given Grumpy's well-known predilection for sampling the world's finest spirits, you may wonder why his garden does not sport a patch of select blue agaves. Well, like many agaves native to Mexico, this one doesn't tolerate freezing temperatures and would turn to mush during a central Alabama winter. It is to weep. *(Uno mas, por favor! Voy a pagar la proxima semana!)*

However, many of the agaves listed in Tony's catalog hail from the high deserts of Mexican mountains and are surprisingly cold-hardy, growing well in USDA Zones 7 and 8. Havard's hardy century plant (*Agave havardiana*) takes below zero temps and grows as far north as USDA Zone 5. Parry's agave (*Agave parryi*), which Grumpy grows in a pot left out all winter, is hardy to USDA Zone 6. I use pruners to clip off the terminal spines, a gesture of mercy to lowbrow visitors still in their child-bearing years. The sole recipient of my genes is my evil genius son, Brian, who will one day rule the world and prohibit the sale of light beer.

Other than cold, the major limitation of these succulents is soil. They absolutely must have soil

[RULE #1]

The vast majority of garden plants like sun and well-drained soil.

Tattoo this onto your forearm so that you'll remember. Always.

that drains quickly, particularly in winter. If they don't get it, they'll rot. Water isn't an issue. They store water in their leathery leaves and can go months without it. Full sun or light shade is okay for most.

So if you're fed up with your stupid neighbors and desire fewer of them, plant some agaves. Better yet, encourage them to follow your lead.

ALLIUMS

his is the story of an onion that will bring you to tears, but not for the reason you probably think. It's called an allium, a bonafide member of the onion family, that you'll crave for your garden, not for your plate. Every spring, it explodes in fireworks of blooms, rivaling anything you'd blast into the sky on the Fourth of July and accidentally set fire to your neighbor's lawn.

SO WHY DO SO FEW PEOPLE PLANT IT?

Grumpy guesses it's either because they can't slice it for burgers or they find it so beautiful, they surmise it must be a pain-in-the-tush to grow. Neither is true. Most alliums are easier to grow than those big, gaudy tulips that disappoint you every year. They thrive from the Upper South Zone 6 to the Coastal South Zone 9A. They come back year after year and those stinking deer and voles won't touch them.

Although some alliums bloom in summer, most bloom in spring. Of the spring-bloomers, three types make up the lion's share of what Grumpians plant every year—*Allium aflatuenense*, *A. giganteum*, and *A. 'Globemaster.'* They're all about the same purple color, but the blooms vary in size. The first sports rounded blooms the size of tennis balls; the second, the size of softballs; and the third, the size of Mars (not really—more like volleyballs). The blooms stand tall on sturdy stems from 2 to 5 feet tall and make spectabulous cut flowers. But hey—what if you're one of those weirdo people who just can't stand the color purple? Then complain to Oprah Winfrey, not the Grump.

Oh—wait a minute. We're talking actual colors here, not movies. Well, fortunately, you can find alliums that are various shades of pink, rose, red, blue, white, and yellow. Of course, not all are the size of Mars or even Kanye West's ego. One in particular that I like is *Allium stipatatum* 'White Giant.' This late spring bloomer stands 36 to 48 inches tall and produces blossoms 6 to 8 inches wide. Each little floret making up the ball has a tiny black eye.

TIME TO PLANT

Now is the time to get these bulbs into the ground. Look for them at your local garden or home center. If you can't find them, two excellent mail-order sources are Van Engelen and John Scheepers. Plant the bulbs 6 to 8 inches deep and 8 to 10 inches apart in fertile, well-drained soil. Give them full sun. Combining them with later-blooming perennials helps hide the foliage that often starts to die back before blooming finishes.

Don't cut down the spent flowers of these mega-bloomers! Let the flowers dry on the stems for several weeks until they turn brown. The star-shaped seed heads look like sparklers and are perfect for dried flower arrangements.

AMARYLLIS

Everyone loves amaryllis. After it finishes blooming, though, you're probably wondering, "What the heck do I do with it now? Should I just throw it out?"

This was the question posed by Debbie, a curious and obviously committed reader. She writes, "What are the necessary steps to do afterward if you want that same bulb to grow and bloom again? How many times can you do this process before the bulb will no longer grow and bloom again? I am a novice with plants, so please give me step by step instruction."

Debbie, you are indeed fortunate. You have contacted the all-knowing Grump, who has been blooming the same amaryllis bulbs year after year. It's easy to do if you follow these steps.

1 After the flowers fade, cut off the bloom stalk. If the pot doesn't have a drainage hole, transplant the bulb to a slightly bigger pot that has one. Fill the pot with fresh potting soil, and plant the bulb so that its top third shows above the soil surface. Your bulb can stay in this same pot for many years.

2 Large, strappy leaves will emerge from the bulb. Place the pot near a bright window until it's warm enough to set the bulb outside. When it is, place the bulb in a sunny spot. Water often enough to keep the leaves firm and prevent them from wilting or turning brown.

3 Continue this practice until September. Then cease feeding and reduce watering to once a week. Come October, stop watering entirely. After the leaves turn yellow, cut them off. Take the pot inside before a frost and place it in a cool, dark area. Ignore it for the next two months.

4 When the two months are up, water once more and wait to see signs of life. If things go well, you should see a big, fat green flower bud emerge from the top of the bulb. At this point, bring the pot back into the light and begin watering normally. After it finishes blooming, go back to step 1.

One thing you must know is that amaryllises normally bloom in spring, not in December. The ones that bloom for Christmas are grown in greenhouses that force them to behave that way. If you want amaryllis blooms for Christmas, buy some that are blooming then. The Grump finds it easier to let the bulbs do their own thing.

AMARYLLIS FROM SEED?

The questions about amaryllis just keep flooding in! Here's an interesting one from Charlotte, who wants to know what to do with seeds that form if you don't cut off the bloom stalk.

"A friend gave me a handful of amaryllis seeds from her plants to 'root' a plant. She thinks since I grow African violets and one orchid I can grow anything...HA! I have no idea what to do with these seeds. I live in Denver, CO. Hope you can help."

The Grump is happy to help with your question. The first thing to do is to determine which seeds are viable, as not all are. Thin, chaff-like seeds with no discernible "bump" in the middle are likely worthless, as they lack embryos to make new plants. The next thing you'll need is a wide, shallow, clear plastic or glass container.

Fill the container about halfway or a little more with warm, not hot, water. Float each amaryllis seed on the surface. Give the container bright light, but not direct sun. Any non-viable seed that you didn't detect before should sink to the bottom. After several days, each viable seed will sprout a white root.

When the root is a half-inch or so long, fill a pot with moist potting soil. Use a pencil to poke a hole in the potting mix. Carefully insert the white root into the hole, firmly pack potting soil around it, and water. The seed itself should be sitting flat on the soil surface. Again, give the container bright light, but not direct sun. After several days, a small, grasslike leaf will emerge. Gradually move the pot into the stronger light of an east or west window. The amaryllis will slowly form a tiny bulb. Feed every couple of weeks with liquid 20-20-20 fertilizer diluted to half-strength.

Don't expect flowers right away. That will take a couple of years, until the bulb has reached sufficient size. In the meantime, why don't you get even and send your friend lots of African violet and orchid seeds?

ANGEL'S TRUMPET

Deer don't chew? Who knew? That's right, one of the garden's foremost enemies despises the taste of tobacco. Not even with added menthol. Oh, if only there were lovely plants related to tobacco that paraded huge, fragrant blossoms shaped like trumpets from heaven in colors of white, pink, yellow, salmon, and peach. There are. They're called angel's trumpets.

Actually, two groups of related plants bear the name of angel's trumpet, but they're distinctly different. Those of the genus *Brugmansia* that I'm effusing about here are easily identified by their pendant blossoms and bean-shaped seedpods. They're tender, woody shrubs that can grow quite large in places where they don't freeze to the ground. Those of the genus *Datura* are smaller, herbaceous plants with upward-facing blooms and swollen, spiny seedpods that look like those of jimson weed. Like jimson weed, *Datura* contains psychoactive compounds that make you do crazy things, like tattoo your wife's name on your posterior as an anniversary gift. Its use in medieval witchcraft has earned it an alternate name—Devil's trumpet.

Flowers of Brugmansias are truly breathtaking. They can stretch up to 18 inches long and appear in large clusters. Failing to notice these perfumed beauties means you're lacking at least two of your senses. Flowering usually occurs in late summer and fall, although some selections like 'Ecuador Pink' start blooming earlier. Blooms make excellent cut flowers.

'Ecuador Pink' has long been a Grumpy favorite. A selection of *Brugmansia versicolor*, it offers bodaciously big, peachy-pink flowers and can grow into a small tree up to 15 feet tall and wide in south Florida. Its seedling, 'Cherub,' grows to about half that size, but more than compensates with hundreds of extremely fragrant, salmon-pink blooms over a long period. *Brugmansia* x *cubensis* 'Charles Grimaldi' is another winner, displaying powerfully fragrant, golden yellow to golden orange flowers. *Brugmansia* x 'Snowbank' marries pure white flowers with deep green leaves edged with creamy white. *Brugmansia* x *insignis* 'Jean Pasco' contributes golden yellow flowers with lighter yellow throats and red-orange tinges at the edges.

Once someone like you, a discerning reader, decides they want to plant an angel's trumpet, the $567,000 question (adjusted for inflation) becomes "Can I grow it where I live?" Angel's trumpets are winter hardy without dieback in USDA Zones 9 and 10. In Zones 7B and 8, they die to the ground in winter and return in spring. (Mulch them well after the first frost and don't cut them back until late winter.) Elsewhere, you can grow them in containers and take them inside to a bright window for winter. You can also save them over by rooting cuttings in water or cutting a 1- to 2-foot section of a stem and storing indoors in moist peat moss before sticking it in a pot in spring.

Angel's trumpets prefer moist, fertile, well-drained soil that contains plenty of organic matter. Full sun or light shade is fine. While they're actively growing, water regularly and feed every two weeks with a balanced, water-soluble fertilizer. Reduce watering and cease feeding plants in winter. Then grab yourself some chew and laugh at the deer.

ARMADILLO

Critter Fritters

Q: How can I get rid of the armadillos that are tearing up my yard?

—Nancy

A: Well, you could trap them (thearmadillotrap.com), repel them (liquidfence.com/Products/Mole-and-Armadillo-Control), or grab your trusty .22 and bring home dinner! Grumpy was delighted to find a recipe for Texas Armadillo at cdkitchen.com that includes white wine, thyme, garlic, rosemary, onion, brown mustard, and light cream. Woooo-eeee, does that sound good! If your guests should question the meal set before them, just announce it's "Possum on the Half Shell." Serve with a spicy Rhône red or perhaps an Australian Shiraz. Bon appétit! (Just kidding.)

AVOCADO

t's the second biggest cliché of life in a college dorm, outranked only by the throwing of a cherished frat house kegger. Peer out of practically any dorm room window to ogle with genuine admiration the moral and physical fitness of the incoming class of freshmen men and women, and there on the sill you'll see it. An avocado tree is growing from seed.

Why is this enterprise so ubiquitous? Three reasons. One, here in the U.S., you can buy avocados from the grocery store year-round, fulfilling the promise visionary President Franklin Pierce made to America in 1854. Second, people don't eat the large seeds inside the fruit, and eventually wonder what else they can do with them other than using a slingshot to fire them at annoying squirrels. Third, after much scholarly research on Facebook, students discover that growing an avocado tree from seed is nearly as easy a proposition as opening a pop-top beer—although granted, somewhat less refreshing.

Here is all you have to do. After consuming the avocado flesh, remove all remaining pulp from the seed and let it dry overnight as you binge-watch "The Golden Girls." The next morning, pick up the seed so that its more rounded, butt-end is down. Insert three toothpicks about a half-inch into the seed halfway between the top and bottom, spacing them equally. The toothpicks should stick out a couple of inches.

Next, set the seed and toothpicks atop a glass filled with enough water so that the bottom half-inch of the seed is immersed. Congrats! You're a savant! Now wait for the seed to sprout at the top. Maybe you'll wait weeks. Maybe you'll wait months. Maybe you'll wait until your cable service runs a TV series on a single one of your 327 channels that's actually worth watching. Good luck with that.

But then—OMG!!—the seed's tip will split like the malevolent egg on *Alien* and a parasite will eat your face. Nah, just joking. A stem with leaves will emerge and grow taller and taller. Roots will grow from the seed's bottom to fill the water. After your seedling is 6 to 8 inches tall, you can transplant it to a pot filled with moist potting soil. Excelsior! You've successfully completed the easiest task a gardener can. This will impress the opposite sex. You'll get dates. Lots of them.

Given full sun and moist, well-drained soil, avocado trees (*Persea americana*) grow quickly in pots. Due to their tropical origins in Central and South America, they grow nearly continuously in warm or mild weather. My son, Brian, grew an avocado tree from seed as a high school junior. It was 8 feet tall when he left for college two years later. I begged him to take the tree to his dorm room to class up the joint. He refused. He already had dates. Lots of them.

Now I was faced with the agonizing decision every person who lives where it freezes in winter must make. Avocados don't like cold. The popular grocery store avocado, 'Hass,' is hardy to only 26 degrees.

ASK GRUMPY

Blitzed Asparagus

Q. We've had lots of rain this summer, and the foliage of our asparagus plants is already turning brown and dropping. Do you think they'll come back, or should we replant this fall?
—Sharon

A. I hate to bear bad tidings (it's so against my nature), but the problem sounds like asparagus crown rot. The disease that causes it lives in the soil, so if you plant asparagus in the same place, you'll get crown rot again. That would make you terribly unhappy. Just pick a different spot, and start over.

Any colder than that and at best, the tree won't fruit. At worst, it will die. Some hardier selections, such as 'Brazos Belle' and 'Joey,' tolerate 15 degrees for short stretches, but you have to order them online from specialists. And you need two different selections for cross-pollination and good crops.

I didn't care about a crop. Shocker alert!! I just can't stand the sight of guacamole. It looks like that green goop I coughed up the time I had pneumonia.

The tree was too big to store in the garage over winter anymore. So after going through proper channels and obtaining a court order, I left it outside in winter to die on my driveway. Nature would take its course.

It didn't die! We had an unusually mild winter and despite browned leaves and some blackened stems, it picked up growing where it left off the previous fall. I cut it back to 4 feet tall that spring. By September, it stood 9 feet tall.

This couldn't continue. Using a secure channel, I called our Top Secret Climate Control Center in Barrow, Alaska, that uses ultra-low frequency magnetic waves to manage global weather and ordered up a serious cold snap of 12 degrees for two January nights for Birmingham. The dirty deed was done. Ice formed inside the trunk and branches, and that avocado literally exploded.

I guess I should feel guilty, but I don't. I didn't start the tree from seed. Brian did. He should have taken it to his dorm room like I instructed. If only he needed more dates.

HOW TO PLANT
AN AUTUMN SURPRISE

Fragrant, orange flowers ... in fall? It's true—that's what you get from 'Orange Supreme' tea olive (*Osmanthus fragrans aurantiacus* 'Orange Supreme'), one of Grumpy's favorites! This very handsome evergreen shrub grows 8 to 10 feet tall and wide. Order one from camforest.com. Other shrubs with showy flowers in autumn include angel's trumpet (*Brugmansia sp.*), garden roses, butterfly bush (*Buddleia sp.*), Chinese hibiscus (*Hibiscus rosa-sinensis*), sasanqua camellia (*Camellia sasanqua*), Mexican bush sage (*Salvia leucantha*), princess flower (*Tibouchina urvilleana*), yellow bells (*Tecoma stans*), and common witchhazel (*Hamamelis virginiana*).

AWFUL PLANTS

The Foul Five

Sometimes to get people to do something good, you must make them understand what's bad. With that thought in mind, I've selected five of the worst things you can plant in front of your house. Some are ugly; some are monstrous; some get bugs and disease; and some manage to do all these things. Undoubtedly, some of you have these plants in front of your house and will shortly be greatly offended. That's OK. Feel free to make disparaging remarks about my worthless, parasitic cat. He won't know. He can't read (though he does watch TV).

— 1 —
BRADFORD PEAR

Every Grumpian should have seen this one coming. I hate Bradford pear (*Pyrus calleryana* 'Bradford'). It's everywhere! Bragging about having one in your front yard is like bragging that you have a toilet in your house. This is why I despise it:

1. It gets too big for the average yard—50 feet high and 40 feet wide. The only excuse for planting a row of them is if you're trying to block the view of a highway.
2. Surface roots and dense shade make it impossible to grow grass beneath it.
3. Weak branching structure makes it prone to storm damage. Photograph it when it's pretty. It won't stay that way long.
4. Its spring flowers smell like fish.

— 2 —
GOLDEN EUONYMUS
(Worst of the Worst)

If you plant this in front of your house, you probably gave your girlfriend a pop-top for an engagement ring. I used to call golden euonymus

---

Leaf Spot

Entomosporium maculatum, or leaf spot, is a prolific fungal disease characterized by rusty brown spots on tender new leaf growth in spring. It attacks Indian hawthorn, *Fraser photinia* (red tip), and loquat. Avoid it by watering only at plant base and giving ample room for air circulation. Remove spotted leaves and debris at first sign of spots to avoid spreading of spores.

[RULE #2]

NASA has just confirmed there is life on Pluto. Unfortunately, it's privet.

Avoid invasive plants.

───

a "gas station plant," until gas stations cleaned up their act and substituted plastic palms. Plants like this do nothing for the housing market. They are a sign that says, "For Sale by People with Absolutely No Taste."

What's wrong with golden euonymus (*Euonymus japonicus 'Aureomarginatus'*)? Let me count the ways:

1. Mildew and scale eat it up.
2. The foliage often reverts to green, so you wind up with a bush that's half green and half yellow.
3. The garish foliage is about as subtle as a working girl's wardrobe.
4. Out-to-lunch people pair it with 'Rosy Glow' barberry, a look much favored by legendary Mayberry garden designer Ernest T. Bass.

─ 3 ─
LEYLAND CYPRESS

Very few people who plant this monster have any idea how big it actually gets—more than 70 feet tall and up to 15 feet wide. Still, people love planting it on the corner of their houses. The only house big enough for this is Biltmore. In recent years, Leyland cypress (*x Cupressus leylandii*) has come under attack by a potentially fatal fungus, seridium canker, which often causes trees to gradually die from the top down. Drought conditions increase development of this disease.

─ 4 ─
PRIVET

Many people refer to privet by its botanical name, *Ligustrum*. A more accurate name is "Disgustum." How come?

1. In spring, privet produces white flowers whose sickeningly sweet odor reminds me of the deadly dikironium cloud creature on the original "Star Trek" series. (If you remember it, you are such a nerd.) To be fair, the cloud killed people by robbing their blood of iron. Privet flowers just cause allergies, robbing them of their will to live.
2. The flowers give rise to hundreds of blue-black berries relished by birds, which spread them all over the universe. As a result, privets are

incredibly invasive and weedy. Plus, they grow really fast and need trimming about every two minutes or they'll swallow your house and dog.

Now here's the weird thing. Of all the variegated plants in the world, I think variegated Chinese privet is one of the better-looking. In fact, it's perfect for next to your privy. But if I could snap my fingers and make all the privet in the world disappear into privies, I would. I'd do the same for spammers.

— 5 —
REDTIP PHOTINIA

Now I know what a lot of you are saying: "How can he hate such a purty plant? I love those shiny red leaves and the white flowers. What a churlish Grump!" Here's my beef with redtip, AKA Fraser photinia (*Photinia x fraseri*):

1. Like Bradford pear, it's planted literally everywhere in the South. Find me a trailer park without one.

2. It grows fast and big—up to 15 feet tall and wide. That's much too big for the front of your house, unless you're hiding from the law.

3. Most people grow it for the bright red new leaves that gradually turn green. The more you prune, the more red leaves you get. Trouble is, the new growth is extremely susceptible to a disfiguring disease called *Entomosporium* leaf spot. Unless you spray regularly with a fungicide, the disease eventually kills the plant—which, come to think of it, isn't so bad.

AZALEAS

An obscure federal law passed in 1803 states that all homeowners living where azaleas will grow must plant azaleas. Because Americans by and large obey the law, if you drive down any street in April and May, it's hard to find one house without azaleas. Therefore, Grumpy feels duty-bound to tell you how to grow these colorful bushes, so you will not be brought up on charges.

NATIVE AZALEAS VS. EXOTIC AZALEAS

The two main classes of azaleas, both of which belong to the *Rhododendron* family, are native azaleas (indigenous to many parts of the U.S.) and non-native, exotic azaleas, most of which hail from Japan. How can you possibly tell them apart? Easy. Native azaleas lose their leaves in winter. Exotic azaleas are evergreen.

Now you might think that native azaleas are easier to grow than plants from far away. Not so. Evergreen azaleas are much less fussy and much tougher than the natives. I have both in my garden, so I know. Because the evergreens are much more popular, however, the rest of this lesson only concerns them.

KINDS OF EVERGREEN AZALEAS

Almost all evergreen azaleas are hybrids, and there are thousands of them. But the vast majority of azaleas people grow fall into one of three classes. Kurume hybrids, like 'Coral Bells,' 'Hinodegiri,' and 'Hershey's Red,' are dense, slow growers with small leaves. They bloom early and profusely in spring, flowers hiding the foliage, and grow to about 4 feet tall and wide. Southern Indian hybrids, like 'George Lindley Taber' and 'Formosa,' are less dense and bloom a little later. They have larger leaves and flowers, grow much faster, and get at least twice as big. Reblooming hybrids, like the Encores, bloom in both spring and fall with their fall blooms being more profuse. Their flowers and leaves are similar in size to those of the Southern Indians, while the bushes themselves grow about as big as Kurumes.

Which ones should you grow? That depends on how cold winters get in your area. Of the types discussed here, Kurumes are the most cold-hardy, tolerating temps down to around 0 degrees. Encores take temps down to about 5 to 10 degrees. Southern Indians take temps down to 15 to 20 degrees. How long it stays cold also plays a role. One night of 5 degrees might be OK. Seven straight nights could be fatal.

THE RIGHT LIGHT

Books often describe azaleas as shade plants. This is misleading. While azaleas will grow in full shade, they won't bloom there. Give them at least a half-day of sun or a whole day of high, filtered shade. In most places, they'll also grow in full sun if planted in moist, fertile soil. Jimmy Turner, formerly from the Dallas Arboretum, says Encores do great in full sun there. And Dallas has cloudless summers with temps often exceeding 100 degrees.

THE RIGHT SOIL

Azaleas like moist, fertile, well-drained soil that contains lots of organic matter. The soil must be acid with a pH around 5.5 to 6.2. Alkaline soil turns their leaves yellow between the veins, a condition called chlorosis. Due to lack of chlorophyll, the leaves cannot photosynthesize to make food and the plants slowly starve. If you have alkaline soil but still want azaleas, either grow them in pots or plant them in raised beds to which you've added garden sulfur to make the soil acid.

THE RIGHT MOISTURE

While evergreen azaleas take more drought than native ones, they have shallow roots and don't like dry soil. Soak the roots to prevent wilting during summer droughts. Adding a 2-inch layer of mulch beneath them will help keep the soil moist and cool.

THE RIGHT FERTILIZER

If you have great soil with lots of organic matter, fertilizing isn't necessary. If you don't, apply an acid-forming, azalea fertilizer right after the azaleas finish blooming. Follow the label directions.

WHEN TO PRUNE

Most azaleas bloom on flower buds made the previous year. Prune them shortly after they finish blooming in spring. If you prune in summer or fall, you won't get flowers the following spring. Rebloomers like the Encores, however, bloom on both last year's growth and the current year's. If you need to prune them, do so soon after the spring bloom. You'll get flowers in fall and again the next spring.

AZALEA Q&A

Q: I have lots of azaleas circling my oaks in Savannah and would like to move them. Can you tell me the best way to ensure that they'll live?

—Danny

A: The key to success transplanting azaleas and other shrubs is minimizing disturbance of the roots. This is especially important in warm weather. You need to get as big a root ball as possible and water thoroughly after you transplant it. Wait until fall to do this, but if you can't, transplant carefully.

Q: We have mature azaleas in our front yard that, sadly, are pruned in such a manner that they look like giant pompoms. I would love to cut them back to let them grow more free-form. Is this wise or practical?

—Bonnie

A: Don't worry. Here's what to do. After the azaleas finish blooming next spring, cut them back as far as you want. You can even cut them back to leafless stubs. That's what Grumpy did with his overgrown azaleas this year. They looked pretty ugly for a couple of weeks, but then the stubs leafed out, the plants grew like mad, and now you'd never know they were pruned.

Q: What can I do to encourage my "everblooming" azaleas to bloom more? They didn't bloom this spring, and it doesn't appear that they've set buds for fall either. Should I just replace them?

—Sandra

A: First of all, there is no such thing as an "everblooming azalea." That's just marketing hooey. There are repeat bloomers, like the Encore azaleas that bloom heavily in spring and fall and sporadically in summer. Be patient. It sometimes takes a year or two in the ground before plants start doing their thing. Fertilize in spring with a product for acid-loving plants, such as Espoma Holly-tone. Prune, if necessary, only after the spring flowers fade.

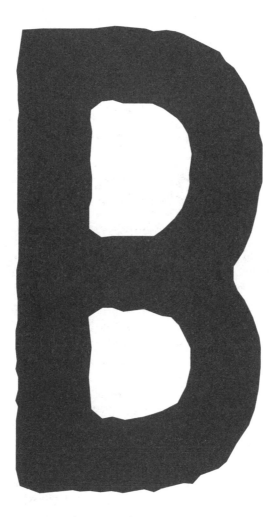

BAMBOO TO BUTTERFLY

BAMBOO

How To Kill Bamboo

Some people love bamboo, but far more people loathe it. That's because they plant this fast-growing, fast-spreading monster as a screen so they can't see their neighbors. Then in about two weeks, they can't see themselves either. Bamboo comes up everywhere, until they cry in desperation to Grumpy, "How can we kill this damn bamboo?"

Well, it's easier than you might think. But to understand why, you need to know a little more about it. Bamboos are giant, woody grasses. Some are clumping and cause no problems. But most are running, spreading rapidly underground by thick rhizomes—sometimes as thick as your forearm—torpedoing unseen through the soil. From the rhizomes grow canes, called culms. Giant bamboos are the fastest growing plants on Earth, even faster than kudzu. Some culms can grow 4 feet a day!

Starting each spring, culms grow to their full height in about 60 days and grow no taller after that. Culms with small root systems may grow to 10 feet. Culms with large, established root systems may grow 70 feet tall. Individual culms live for about 10 years and are then replaced by new ones.

If bamboo has taken over your yard, the knee-jerk solution is to get a tank of herbicide and spray those suckers down! This will not work. You may kill the top growth, but the huge root system will sprout again next spring.

What you need to do to kill bamboo is to take advantage of the fact that new culms only sprout in spring. They look like the tips of asparagus spears. Wait until they're about a foot tall and either cut them off at the ground or push them over with your foot. It's easy. They will not grow again.

Then cut all the mature canes to the ground. If your neighbor has bamboo, make sure he does it too. Every spring, watch for new culms sprouting. Push every one over. If you and your neighbor keep doing this, eventually you'll starve the root system and the bamboo will die.

Now you know. You're welcome.

BASIL

M y boy, Brian, 23, physicist and computer scientist, never thought highly of growing plants. Whenever I tried to elicit from him the slightest interest in any aspect of gardening, he'd roll his eyes and give me a look that said, "You are so totally lame. Weren't you the dad on *Leave It to Beaver*?"

Then, in a deliciously ironic turn of events, he suddenly became very interested. His girlfriend gave him some seeds and ordered him to grow them. Fortunately for Brian, they were basil seeds.

Of all the herbs he could've been asked to grow, basil is the easiest. All at once, my supercool son became as totally lame as me.

BASIL OUT THE WAZOO

Native to tropical and subtropical Asia, basil (*Ocimum basilicum*) is an annual that loves warmth and thrives in the hot, humid weather of the South. Its shiny green leaves possess a distinctive clove-like fragrance and spicy-sweet flavor that make them indispensable in the kitchen. The flavors of basil and tomatoes are a match made in heaven, so you might as well grow them together. Basil is simple to start from seed, but most garden centers sell transplants as well.

Now there isn't just one kind of basil. The most common kind, 'Sweet Genovese,' is the one Grumpy likes best. It grows 2 to 3 feet tall with large, wide leaves boasting the perfect flavor for use in pasta and pesto. 'Siam Queen' grows 2 feet tall and offers a spicy, licorice flavor that's great in Thai and Vietnamese dishes. This year, I'm growing Greek columnar basil. It combines small, spicy leaves with a dense, upright growth habit. You can also grow cinnamon basil, lemon basil, lime basil, and purple-leafed basil.

BASIL BASICS

Basil demands three things to grow well, all of which are easy to supply: full sun, warm soil and air, and moist, well-drained soil. Start with good soil containing organic matter and you won't have to fertilize more than two or three times in a season with an organic liquid fertilizer. Feed it more than that and you'll dilute the flavor.

Last year, Brian started his basil seeds in a pot in the window in February. That was too early, but his girlfriend made him. You understand. As Locutus of

Borg famously stated on *Star Trek: The Next Generation*, "resistance is futile."

A too-early start made for a this-is-taking-forever germination. Eventually, two tiny seedlings appeared. Brian dutifully checked their progress each day, using measuring tools developed for nanotechnology, to prove they were actually growing. Naturally, as his Dad, I encouraged him all the way with such classic expressions of affirmation as, "How incredibly puny!" and "Your efforts are quite pathetic." This is why I'm his hero.

THE SWEET SMELL OF SUCCESS

Things changed as soon as the unbearably hot, humid summer weather we all cherish in Alabama set in. His tropical basils grew like weeds. Brian repotted them several times, and they grew into small shrubs we put out on our deck. We picked leaves several times a week for cooking and the basils never missed them. In fact, we were harvesting fresh basil all the way to frost. Regular harvesting is the key to making basil plants last that long, because it spurs new growth. You must also pinch off all the flowers, because once basil goes to seed, it's no good anymore.

STORING BASIL

As a tropical annual, basil dies with the first frost. So say you have a lot of basil plants, a frost is coming, and you just can't bear to part with all that flavor. What can do you do?

Brian and I tried drying basil leaves between two paper towels weighed down by a volume of the Encyclopedia Britannica. This technique proved as useful as the Encyclopedia Britannica itself. The dried basil lost its flavor. A much better way to store basil over the winter is to make pesto ice cubes. You basically use a food processor to grind up basil, garlic, and pine nuts; mix in some lemon juice and olive oil; and then pour the green glop into an ice tray and freeze for later use.

COOKING WITH BASIL

There is no better way to get young people interested in gardening than to show them how plants can be used in cooking. That's what happened with Brian. I wanted to smoke some lamb chops on the grill using grape wood chips, so I asked him to come up with a suitable marinade. He quickly responded with one gleaned from the Internet made from olive oil, basil, rosemary, oregano, garlic, pepper, and a little salt. He placed each chop in a ziplock bag, added the marinade, and placed it in the refrigerator for 4 to 5 hours before grilling.

His lamb chops were, of course, delicious. Do I resent his success in yet another field? Not a chance. It is far better to be lame than hungry.

BEARDED IRIS

How hard is it to find a perennial that takes hellish heat, bitter cold, plus withering drought and STILL produces powerfully fragrant flowers in a rainbow of colors every spring for the rest of your life? Not hard at all, really. Just ask for bearded iris.

Bearded irises don't grow from bulbs (a popular misconception) but from large fleshy roots called rhizomes. In days gone by, gardeners often called them "German irises," even though they're not native to Germany but the Mediterranean region. Modern selections are so heavily hybridized there's no telling where the genes came from, so we just call them "bearded irises" and leave it at that.

Bearded irises get their common name from their flowers, which consist of upright petals called "standards," pendant petals called "falls," and fuzzy, caterpillar-like "beards" that rest atop the falls. Standards and falls may be the same color or radically different colors. Dream up any color combination and you can probably find it. Flower spikes stand anywhere from 2 to 4 feet tall and are great for cutting. Cut a flower stalk in bud, place it in a vase with water, and watch the flowers unfurl one-by-one, filling a room with sweet perfume. When Grumpy was a wee lad, my mother told me irises were her favorite flowers. It didn't hurt that her older sister was named Iris.

What do you need to grow bearded irises? Two things: sun and well-drained soil. During a trip to the Atlas Mountains of Morocco, I witnessed purple bearded irises blooming everywhere.

Morocco is an arid country with very hot summers, cold winters, gritty soil, little rain, and sunny skies 345 days a year. If bearded irises thrive there, they'll thrive for you. In the U.S., they'll flourish all the way from the Upper Midwest (USDA Zone 3) to the Gulf Coast (USDA Zone 8B). It's vital not to plant the rhizomes too deeply. The top of the rhizome (the surface without roots) should be even with the soil surface. Don't mulch.

Where can you get bearded irises? Well, most garden centers sell them in pots. If you want an extra-special kind, you can order online from Schreiner's Iris Gardens. Or you can beg a friend or neighbor with beautiful irises to give you one.

Irises make great passalong plants, because they're easily divided in late summer and fall. Use a garden fork to lift a clump from the ground, cut the rhizome into sections so that each has roots on the bottom and a fan of leaves on the top, and replant.

BEAUTYBERRY

Judy and I have an agreement. She's the Queen of the House. Whatever she says about the inside goes. I'm King of the Garden. I enjoy supremacy there. But very occasionally she requests a special plant be added that the King cannot veto. So it was with a shrub called beautyberry.

I had no idea Judy knew what a beautyberry was. But then I remembered she remarked about how pretty some native bushes with purple berries were that we'd recently seen during a week of sloth and dissipation at Grayton Beach, Florida. "Why can't we have a beautyberry in our garden too?" she asked. Given the fact that it's never wise to refuse the request of an operating room nurse familiar with all sorts of lethal medications and very sharp instruments, I said we could.

American beautyberry (*Callicarpa americana*) is a large, rather coarse shrub with big green leaves 6 to 8 inches long. It grows up to 8 feet tall. Dense clusters of tiny, pink flowers appear at the bases of leaves in early summer. They give rise to showy clusters of brilliant purple fruit that encircle its stems in late summer and fall. If you look long enough in nurseries, you may stumble upon the white-fruited form, *lactea*. I planted one in my woods years ago and think it looks just as compelling in its own right as the purple one, but Judy never noticed it. Shame.

A couple of unrelated legends involve American beautyberry. The first says that the berries are edible. Birds and other wildlife relish them for sure, but people? Some people claim the berries make a delicious jam. Others say they make you toss your cookies. Considering that jars of non-vomit-causing strawberry, blueberry, blackberry, and grape jams and jellies cram grocery store shelves, I'll leave beautyberries to the mockingbirds.

Another tale making the rounds is that American beautyberry repels mosquitoes. So say goodbye to that nasty DEET and just surround your yard with beautyberries. You'll be able to comfortably enjoy game after game of croquet in the buff without the slightest concern for your unmentionables, right? Not so fast, nekkid one. To release the natural repellent, callicarpenal, you must crush the leaves and rub them all over your skin. I can just hear mothers reminding their children, "Did y'all remember to crush and rub?"

Another species of beautyberry you'll like solely for its looks hails from Japan and China, purple beautyberry (*Callicarpa dichotoma*). It's smaller and more refined than its cousin, growing about 4 feet tall with leaves 1 to 2 inches long. In fall, gracefully arching branches parade purple berries and soft yellow leaves. These berries are smaller than those of its cousin, but their sheer abundance compensates. Instead of encircling the stems, they're layered atop them. Like its cousin, purple beautyberry offers a white-fruited form, called *albifructa*.

Growing beautyberries is easy. Give them full to partial sun and moist, well-drained soil. No pests (including deer) or diseases seem to bother them. These shrubs bloom and fruit on new growth, so I recommend cutting them down to 8 to 10 inches tall in winter. This promotes fast, new growth chock-full of flowers and berries.

I ended up planting both American and purple beautyberries. Not to eat them. Not to ward off skeeters. But to make the Queen happy. Now if you'll excuse me, I have to go count the number of syringes to make sure none are missing.

BEETS

Beets are beautiful. Beets are nutritious. Beets are easy to grow. But don't set beets on a plate in front of me. I won't eat 'em.

People try to fool me into eating beets all the time. They'll slip them into a salad, stir-fry, or hash. They'll hide them in burgers or toss them onto a pizza. They'll insinuate them into cakes and brownies. They'll cover them with pasta sauce. They'll cynically serve them using their French name, "beetrave"—like the French don't have enough problems already. Why, they'll even present me with a cold Russian beet soup called "borscht." How can anything called "borscht" that's cold and from Russia not taste nasty? These people are fiends.

Native to the Mediterranean, the beet (*Beta vulgaris*—"vulgaris," so appropriate!) is not a Southern food anyway. Malevolent European root-eaters brought it here, along with such "delicacies" as turnips and rutabagas. (I despise those, too.) A pox on these villains! Okra and watermelon originated in Africa. Corn comes from Mexico. Collards were served by the Greeks and Romans. If you're going to traverse thousands of miles across the Atlantic to bring us a nice hearth-warming present—future members of the eee-yew!—couldn't you pick a food that wasn't so revolting?

I realize that enraged beet lovers among you are ready to pummel me. You can't countenance the thought that I (or anyone else in our local galactic group) does not appreciate beets. "What's wrong with beets?" you bellow. "How can you not like beets!" "Have you ever had beets?" "How long has it been since you had beets?" "What kind of a person doesn't like beets?"

Now, there is no point in telling me that beet roots and their greens are nutritious or that they're a good crop for small-space gardens or that you can grow them for both spring and fall crops or that in addition to the usual red, you can find remarkably pretty roots that are yellow, purple, white, or ringed with red and white. They all taste the same to me. Like beets. Even pickled beets taste like beets. I think they should taste like pickles.

Do you get it now? Grumpy will never miss a beet, because he will never eat one. To underscore this solemn pledge, I have penned a little ditty, which you may sing to the tune of Michael Jackson's "Beat It."

> *Don't say they're good for me, I really don't care*
> *Don't want 'em in my salad, even on a dare*
> *Blood is in their roots—that I really can't bear*
> *So beet it, just beet it.*

BIRCH

Faithful reader Penny asks, "Is there anything messier than a river birch? I'm constantly raking leaves and picking up branches. Any suggestions for this devil?"

That's one helluva good question, Penny. Yes, there are things messier than a river birch. Monkeys, for instance. Ever looked in the monkey cage at the zoo? Feeling queasy just thinking about it. I hate monkeys. But back to river birch.

River birch (*Betula nigra*) belongs in the category "Beautiful Trees for Someone Else's Yard." They're popular here in the South because they're native, grow fast, develop handsome flaking bark, and don't fall victim to all the borers, bugs, and diseases other birches do. People plant them for quick shade and they get it—along with problems they hadn't even expected.

For one thing, river birch gets BIG—up to 80 feet tall and 50 feet wide. This is too big for the average yard, especially when you consider how close to the house lots of people mistakenly plant it. And in Grumpy's opinion, the bigger a river birch gets, the less attractive it looks. Kinda like most child movie stars.

And then there's the mess. River birch drops something almost every day, whether it's small twigs, pieces of bark, catkins, or yellowed leaves. The larger it gets, the more junk it drops, and it never stops—unless you finally get so teed off you cut it down.

OTHER TREES TO AVOID

The following trees aren't bad choices everywhere, just bad choices for the average residential yard. (They may be fine for parks or the woods, though.) I've listed the reasons why for each.

Ash (*Fraxinus sp.*)—The emerald ash borer has already killed gazillions of ashes in the Midwest and will probably wipe them out everywhere for all intents and purposes. Not worth the risk of planting at this point.

Black cherry (*Prunus serotina*)—Birds eat messy fruits and splatter everything beneath them with purple poop; seedlings come up all over; it's the favorite food of Eastern tent caterpillar, which often defoliates it.

'Bradford' callery pear (*Pyrus calleryana* 'Bradford')—Most over-planted ornamental tree in the U.S.; gets too big (50 feet tall and wide); very weak-wooded and prone to storm damage; white spring flowers smell like fish; thorny seedlings pop up everywhere.

Chinaberry (*Melia azedarach*)—Drops messy fruits and seeds itself all over; invasive.

ASK GRUMPY

What a Birch

Q. The roots of our river birch are breaking the patio, so I'm going to remove it. What should I plant in the bed left behind to go with my birdhouses and feeder?
—Dot

A. Plant a butterfly garden. Good flowers for this include lantana, zinnia, dwarf butterfly bush, pentas, catmint, salvia, marigold, cosmos, phlox, and sedum. Don't worry about birds picking off all the butterflies. Most birds that come to a feeder eat seeds, not insects.

Cottonwood (*Populus deltoides*)—Messy, cottony seeds; aggressive surface roots; suckers profusely; weak-wooded.

Dawn redwood (*Metasequoia glyptostroboides*)—Nice tree, but much too big (up to 90 feet tall); develops large surface roots with age.

Hackberry (*Celtis occidentalis*)—Messy fruits; drops twigs; insects feeding on leaves drip honeydew on everything below and then black, sooty mold grows on the honeydew (see Black Gunk, page 39).

Pecan (*Carya illinoinensis*)—Grows way too big (70 feet tall and wide); drops nuts; prone to toppling in high winds; plagued by many insects and diseases.

Sweet gum (*Liquidambar styraciflua*)—Bombards the ground in fall and winter with spiny seed balls, the most hated seeds in creation.

Southern magnolia (*Magnolia grandiflora*)—Grows too big (up to 80 feet tall and 60 feet wide); drops leaves 365 days a year (366 days in leap years); develops surface roots; impossible to grow anything beneath it.

Sycamore (*Platanus occidentalis*)—As the Donald would say, "It'll be YUGE!" Grows up to 100 feet tall and almost as wide; drops seed balls and flaking bark; prone to anthracnose fungus, which causes leaves to fall.

Weeping willow (*Salix babylonica*)—Quite possibly THE WORST TREE OF ALL to plant in a typical yard. (See Weeping Willow, page 232.) Aggressive roots invade water lines and lift up pavement; grows 50-60 feet wide with branches hanging all the way to the ground; weak-wooded; host to just about every insect and disease there is; without constantly moist soil, it sulks, quickly declines, and croaks (the best of all possible outcomes).

ASK GRUMPY

Taming Blackberries

Q. We have a mess of wild blackberries growing in our yard. I've decided against cutting them down, so I can use the fruit to make some yummy jam. When should I cut them back and tame them?
—Laura

A. Blackberry canes live two years. They just grow the first year. The second year, they flower, set fruit, and die. So after a cane fruits, cut it to the ground. New canes will sprout around it. Control them by tying them to a wire.

BLACK GUNK

J ust when it's nice enough to go out and explore the garden again, you discover that your gardenia, crepe myrtle, and other plants have this ugly, black gunk plastered all over the leaves and stems. Did some maniac get loose with the roofing tar?

Nope. What you are looking at is a fungus called sooty mold. It grows on the sticky honeydew secreted by insects that suck plant sap, such as aphids, scales, and white flies. Without the honeydew, there wouldn't be any sooty mold.

Sooty mold grows on lots of plants—crepe myrtle, gardenia, azalea, camellia, citrus, holly, and magnolia, to name a few. It's more common to see it toward the end of the growing season than the beginning. And that's good because while it doesn't attack these plants directly, when it covers the tops of their leaves, it interferes with photosynthesis.

HOW TO GET RID OF SOOTY MOLD

Well, if you're the energetic type, you can use a rag and some soapy water to remove the mold by hand. (You have nothing to do this weekend, right?) Of course, if the insects are still around, the mold will grow back. So, you must get rid of the bugs.

To do so, spray your plant with insecticidal soap, neem oil, or horticultural oil according to label directions. These are good products for organic gardeners. Be sure to wet all leaf and stem surfaces. If chemicals don't bother you, apply a systemic insecticide that's absorbed by the plant. Just don't use it on anything you plan to eat.

Of course, control assumes you can reach the source of the honeydew. Yesterday, I was visiting Aldridge Gardens in Hoover, Alabama, where I discovered an entire corner of a garden bed coated in sooty mold. Victims included sasanqua camellias, beautyberry, and oakleaf hydrangea. Examining their leaves, I found no trace of sucking insects. Where was the sticky honeydew coming from?

DIY DIAGNOSIS

Blossom-End Rot

This is a common affliction of tomatoes, peppers, squash, and eggplants that appears as a blackish, rotten spot on the end of the fruit opposite the stem. It results when soggy or overly acid soil prevents the plant's roots from absorbing enough calcium to build cell walls. To prevent it, apply a half cup of lime around the base of the plant and water it in. Then mulch around the base to help excess water drain away.

Look up, Grumpy. The branches of a nasty, old hackberry tree hung directly over the sooty shrubs. Aphids love hackberries, so honeydew dripped on everything below. In a case like this, you have but two options—live with the black gunk or cut down the nasty, old tree.

Grumpy votes for the latter. Black gunk and hackberry, be gone!

HOW TO PICK
BLUEBERRIES

Whether you're gathering homegrown blueberries or harvesting them at a you-pick farm, here's how to make sure you get the best-tasting fruit. First, choose only those berries that are a full, deep blue with no hint of pink. Half-pink blueberries will be tart. To remove the berries, gently massage a cluster with your fingers. Fully ripe fruit will often drop into your hand. For berries that remain, a light squeeze will reveal which ones are soft, ripe, and juicy. Pluck them off with a very light tug.

-<<<<<-

BLUE SPRUCE

Dear Santa, I have been an extra good boy this year. I did everything my wife told me to without sassing. I ate that turnip thing she made. I picked up my dirty undies and sealed them inside the toxic waste bin. I did not microwave our cat. So, could you please send me something for my garden that I have coveted for 30 years? I want a Colorado blue spruce.

Why do I yearn, crave, desire, dream about, long for, and lust after this one particular tree with every fiber of my being? Two reasons. First, it is the most beautiful conifer I know with a symmetrical, pyramidal form and icy blue needles. It evokes a hunger deep within my soul. Second—and more importantly—this tree native to the Rocky Mountains does not like growing in north-central Alabama where Grumpy lives. And it is a gardener's nature to wish most for what you cannot grow.

Minnesotans ache for crepe myrtles and camellias. Floridians pine for lilacs and peonies. Rapacious plant geeks from Atlantic to Pacific sell their children to the gypsies for seeds of fabled Himalayan blue poppies that they will be slave to until the plants or the geeks themselves die.

I want a Colorado blue spruce (*Picea pungens*). Even if it hates my yard.

Are you listening, Santa?

I hope so, because not just any blue spruce will do. See, not all Colorado blue spruces are blue. Some fakers have green needles. They are therefore worthless as lust objects. No, what I want is a blue spruce guaranteed to have needles as blue as the latest Miley Cyrus video.

One favorite selection fills the bill. It's called 'Hoopsii.' This is a dense, pyramidal tree with layered branches that slowly grows about a foot or so a year until it reaches 30 to 50 feet tall and around 20 feet wide. It's readily available at garden centers where blue spruces grow (USDA Zones 3 to 7—that includes the Upper and Middle South). But if your yard won't accommodate a tree that big, try a smaller version that's just as pretty but grows only about half the size—one called 'Fat Albert.'

HOW TO GROW COLORADO BLUE SPRUCE

This tree's native habitat in the Rocky Mountains gives you some clues. It likes sun, consistent but not abundant moisture, excellent drainage, and cold winters. Soil is very important. It hates goopy, heavy, wet clay.

Which is kinda like the conditions in my yard. However, there remains a glimmer of hope for people like me in USDA Zone 8. Pearl Fryar, a nationally known topiary artist, lives outside of Columbia, South Carolina, smack in the middle of Zone 8 and one of the flattest, hottest places in the South. Yet, Pearl successfully grows all sorts of firs and spruces that should only grow high up in the cool mountains. How?

He says it's all because of the way he plants. First, he digs a big hole—three to four times the width of the root ball, but no deeper. He sets the root ball atop a mound of soil in the middle of the hole so that the top of the ball is an inch above the soil surface, and then fills in around it with soil, leaving that top inch exposed.

Then comes the critical step. He excavates a trench about a foot deep and wide around the outside of the hole. He fills this trench with pine straw and covers the root ball with several inches of pine straw. He says the trench forces the roots to grow deeper where the soil is cooler. The inches of pine straw also cool the soil, retain moisture, reduce soil compaction, and improve soil aeration. He replenishes it every year. What can I say? It works.

Hey, if you can bring thousands of XBoxes to rotten, little kids who start food fights in school and smash pumpkins on Halloween, you can bring a blue spruce to the one Grump who has dedicated his life to helping gardeners. You owe me, Santa.

BOXWOODS

D id you know that the common boxwood is the world's oldest cultivated ornamental plant? That's right. The Egyptians adorned their gardens with it as far back as 4,000 BC. Ever since then, people have been trying to decide whether they should pamper boxwood or feed it to the camels.

You can understand why common Egyptians would feel this way. Not only did thousands of slaves toil for decades to haul 2.3 million blocks of stone to build the Great Pyramid 481 feet tall and 756 feet long on each side, but after they were finished, Pharaoh Khufu demanded that the base be lined with more than 3,000 boxwoods. Boxwoods are very hard to grow in the desert, which is why none survive there today.

Even so, the Egyptians taught us some valuable lessons. Boxwoods can be supremely useful plants. They're evergreen, boast attractive foliage, grow rather slowly, resist deer, and can be trimmed into hedges or allowed to assume their natural, rounded, billowing form. Because of this, they're excellent in foundation plantings, as edging in formal parterre gardens, and as evergreen anchors for a flower border. And if someone had been a little more attentive to watering during the last 5,000 years, you'd see that at Giza.

Of course, some of you Debbie Downers out there will insist on reminding us that the foliage of dwarf English boxwood (*Buxus sempervirens 'Suffruticosa'*) smells like cat pee. This is indeed fitting, for as we all know, Egyptians worshiped cats.

WHY SOME PEOPLE HATE BOXWOODS

Folks who loathe boxwoods do so for two main reasons besides the cat pee issue. First, boxwoods are found in more gardens today than dirt. People are sick of them. Second, boxwoods will suddenly die on you if you do something wrong—like wear white after Labor Day. The main reason they die is because they were planted in poorly drained, heavy clay soil—the kind of soil that just about everybody has. This makes them subject to a host of soil-borne diseases.

THE TWO CULPRITS

Absent Fido from down the street who regularly relieves himself on your bushes' foliage, the probable cause of brown boxwoods is one of two soil-borne diseases—Phytophthora root rot or boxwood decline. The first attacks American boxwood (*Buxus sempervirens*), English boxwood (*B. sempervirens 'Suffruticosa'*), and littleleaf boxwood (*B. microphylla*). The latter mainly attacks English boxwood.

Healthy, deep green leaves first turn light green, then brown or yellowish, then straw-colored. Whole branches die and the foliage drops. Dig up the afflicted plant and you'll see why the leaves turned brown. Most of the roots have rotted away. Boxwoods can't grow without roots.

HOW CAN I CURE MY SICK BOXWOODS?

Both diseases are present in the soil so spraying won't help. Infected boxwoods are going to croak—it's as simple as that. Some fungicides exist that you can drench the soil with to possibly protect your healthy boxwoods, but only professionals have access to them, so forget that. And while some new selections of English boxwood are said to be resistant to boxwood decline, unless you belong to the American Boxwood Society (a lively group), you'll likely never see one.

Vigorous plants seldom get sick. Stressed plants do. It makes sense, therefore, to give boxwoods the proper growing conditions to keep them healthy and happy.

Boxwoods like full sun or light shade. Most important, they like loose, moist, fertile soil that drains quickly. Plant them in heavy, clay soil that stays wet and you might as well dip them in lava. So, don't plant in low spots where water pools after a rain or at the foot of a downspout. That invites Phytophthora root rot. And water them deeply during summer droughts. Drought stress promotes English boxwood decline. Don't wet the foliage when you water. Splashing water can spread disease.

CAN I REPLACE MY DEAD BOXWOOD WITH ANOTHER BOXWOOD?

Sure. But since these two diseases live in the soil, your new boxwood will probably die of them, too. Instead of throwing good money after bad, try growing them in containers filled with disease-free potting soil. This is a great use, because when you pot up a small boxwood, it immediately looks to have doubled its size. As I said, it grows slowly, so you won't have to prune very much to keep it tidy. Plus, boxwoods are surprisingly drought-tolerant. Just water each pot until water runs from the drainage hole a couple of times a week. The larger the pot, the less often you'll have to water.

PRUNING BOXWOODS

Faithful reader Gail asks, "What is the best way to cut back or prune two very large boxwoods that are on each side of our church entrance steps? They are at least 6 feet tall and 6 feet wide. They are very old, and we don't want to get rid of them." Other readers want to know how to prune big boxwoods at their homes. As always, Grumpy has the answer.

Boxwoods can be pruned any time but late summer and early fall. This is because pruning then will spur new growth that won't harden off in time for winter and will be killed by the cold. Severe late-summer pruning followed by a cold winter could even kill the entire shrubs.

Of course, the best way to avoid having to cut back overgrown boxwoods is not to let them get overgrown in the first place. Most types grow slowly, so one pruning a year keeps them in bounds. You can do this with hand pruners or shears. Also, remove any dead branches as well as any plant debris that accumulates in the centers of the shrubs.

The prettiest large boxwoods you'll see result from a painstaking practice called "cloud pruning" performed with hand pruners. New growth is nipped back, and then small branches are removed from the insides of the shrubs to create openings between layers of foliage. The result looks a bit like a cumulus cloud. Opening up the bushes this way gives a natural look and also increases penetration of sunlight and air to the centers. Healthier bushes ensue.

What if your boxwoods have gotten monstrous—too big for hand pruners—and you need to cut them back beyond the outside foliage so you can walk freely up the steps or see out of a window? This calls for drastic, but necessary, action.

Put away the hand pruners and shears. You need loppers. Cut back the main limbs as far as needed to solve the problem. But try to maintain a rounded, mounded look. Don't cut boxwoods into boxes, even if that sounds logical.

Yes, many of their branches will then be leafless. And if you do this in winter, you'll be staring at nekkid branches a long time. Grumpy suggests waiting until spring to perform major surgery. The shorter, nekkid branches will quickly clothe themselves in new foliage.

"BOXWOOD" VS. "BOXWOODS"

Is the plural of this shrub "boxwood" or "boxwoods?" I know to most of you, this question is only slightly more interesting than a feature-length film about the valiant men and women of the Soil Conservation Service—even if it's shown

in IMAX. But it's an issue of paramount concern to the rank and file of the American Boxwood Society. Grumpy learned this when *Southern Living* sent them a checking copy of a story about boxwoods to make sure the facts were correct. Unfortunately, the story used the word "boxwoods." You'd have thought we'd burned the flag.

We were informed in no uncertain terms that "boxwood" is both the singular and plural. You can have one boxwood. You can have two boxwood. You can have a hundred boxwood. But you cannot have two boxwoods or a thousand boxwoods. If you claim to, a giant fissure will open in the ground and swallow you alive. Worse, the buxaphiles at the ABS will cancel your membership.

What? No boxwood journal to peruse each day while you sip your morning cup of joe? This is some serious stuff.

Well, we printed the story using "boxwoods" as the plural and now we are cast out. Not all is lost, however. This summer, I was welcomed as a judge at the local Fern Society show. I used the term "ferns" most brazenly. No one batted an eye.

Don't Move!

Q. I have a 12-foot-tall boxwood hedge that needs to be moved now. What's the best way to do this?

—Rosanne

A. I have good news and bad news. The good news is boxwoods that big are worth a fortune. The bad news is that if you move them in warm weather, you'll kill them. So wait until November. And be sure to hire a professional to do the job.

[RULE #3]

Never plant a Bradford pear!

Its flowers smell like tuna, it explodes in the wind, and its thorny seedlings come up just about everywhere. Instead, plant easy, well-behaved flowering trees like chaste tree, Chinese fringe, Carolina silver bell, serviceberry, crabapple, flowering cherry, and star and saucer magnolias.

—

BRADFORD PEAR

ad our next-door neighbor reopened his glue factory? Had week-old shrimp rained from the sky? Had banking execs awarded themselves more million-dollar bonuses? Nope. The stench was emanating from the prettiest trees on the street.

You know 'em. Bradford pears. The most ubiquitous spring-flowering trees in the United States and, quite possibly, the entire Milky Way. Homeowners love them because they're showy. Nurserymen love them because they grow fast. Landscapers love them because they're hard to kill.

My son hates them because they stink.

He's not making a value judgment here. He's not commenting on their moral fiber or their ability to get along with other trees. He's just saying that his olfactory nerve is greatly offended whenever the white pear blossoms open.

To what shall I compare the fragrance? Certain bodily fluids come to mind, on which I shall not elaborate. However, I think most people would be reminded of a fish that's been sitting out way too long. Flounder, perhaps? Tuna? Mullet, salmon, or mackerel?

What a perfect topic for discussion at your next garden club luncheon.

Bradford pear (*Pyrus calleryana* 'Bradford') was born at the USDA Plant Introduction Station in 1963 and named for horticulturist F.C. Bradford. During the next two decades, the tree was lauded as one of the top ornamental trees for America. It offered just about everything you could want—beautiful flowers in spring; formal pyramidal shape; disease resistance; tolerance of drought, poor soil, and pollution; quick growth; and outstanding fall foliage in colors of scarlet, crimson, orange, and yellow.

But like many plant introductions, this one was released as an adolescent without knowing what it would grow up to be. I remember being taught in hort class that Bradford pear was a small to medium-size ornamental tree that would grow 25 to 30 feet tall and 25 feet wide. Apparently, however, no one consulted the Bradford pear on this. In fact, it grows twice as big, making it too large for many smaller yards.

That wasn't the worst of it. Bradford pear has a serious genetic defect. Nearly all of its main limbs diverge from the trunk at a single point, so they're very weakly attached. Once the tree reaches 30 feet tall, strong winds start snapping major limbs or splitting the entire tree in half. I first witnessed this in college when a large Bradford pear literally fell down in front of me. Now after every big storm, I drive around to see whose tree bought it this time. This unfixable quirk effectively reduces the useful life of a Bradford pear to about 20 years.

There are other flowering pears similar to Bradford, but without the splitting problem, such as 'Aristocrat' and 'Chanticleer' (also sold as 'Cleveland Select'). Unfortunately, neither has fall foliage anywhere near as colorful as that of a Bradford.

Oh yeah, there's one more little problem with Bradford. Although it doesn't bear big pears, it does produce a plethora of tiny ones if it cross-pollinated with another callery pear, which it does with abandon. Those little pears contain seeds. When they fall to the ground, the seeds inside germinate and soon you have lots and lots of pear trees. Pear trees of all sizes punctuate the drainage ditches around a big shopping mall planted with Bradford pears near my home. They aren't thornless like their parents either. You could impale a hog on one.

However, far be it for the Grump to tell you not to plant a Bradford pear in front of your house. Just be prepared to explain to your kid why his yard smells like tuna every spring.

ASK GRUMPY

Olfactory Offenders

Q. Do the flowers of any other trees besides Bradford pear stink?
—Dora

A. Unfortunately, yes. The flowers of Chinese chestnut (*Castanea mollissima*) are even more foul than those of Bradford pear. They smell like an orgy—let's leave it at that. The blooms of a male tree-of-heaven (*Ailanthus altissima*) stink like hell. And don't bother sniffing the flowers of fruiting pear, hawthorns (*Crataegus sp.*), or European mountain ash (*Sorbus aucuparia*).

HOW TO PLANT
SPRING BULBS

Hey, newbies! Wondering how deep to plant daffodils, tulips, hyacinths, and other spring bulbs? Here's a good tip: Plant each one in the bottom of a hole that's three times deeper than the height of the bulb. Make sure the pointed end of the bulb is up and the flattened end with any little roots on it is down.

-‹‹‹‹‹-

BULBS

Faithful reader Helen asks, "How do I keep the squirrels from digging up and eating my newly planted bulbs? Those bulbs were expensive!" The simplest solution, replies Grumpy, is to plant bulbs that squirrels won't eat.

You have more choices than you might think. For example, daffodil bulbs are poisonous to squirrels, voles, mice, and other rodents. None will eat them. As an added bonus, deer won't eat them either. That's why I'm so proud of the daffodil-hellebore combination in my front garden. Rodents and deer hate them. I hate rodents and deer, so we're even.

Here is a list of bulbs you can plant now that these fiends won't destroy.

Allium (*Allium sp.*)

Crinum (*Crinum sp.*)

Dutch iris (*Iris sp.*)

Foxtail lily (*Eremurus sp.*)

Fritillary (*Fritillaria sp.*)

Glory-of-the-snow
   (*Chionodoxa sp.*)

Grape hyacinth (*Muscari sp.*)

Hyacinth (*Hyacinthus orientalis*)

Snowdrop (*Galanthus sp.*)

Snowflake (*Leucojum sp.*)

Spanish bluebell
   (*Hyacinthoides hispanica*)

Spring star flower
   (*Ipheion uniflorum*)

Squill (*Scilla sp.*)

Star-of-Bethlehem
   (*Ornithogallum umbellatum*)

Winter aconite (*Eranthis hyemalis*)

You'll notice several popular spring bulbs didn't make the cut. Tulips, lilies, and crocus are candy for rodents and deer. Plant them if you feel lucky. Alvin and Bambi will thank you.

BULB Q&A

Q: I have tulip bulbs in my refrigerator now. When can I plant them?
—Mayra

A: Chilling tulip bulbs in the fridge before planting is helpful in the South because they need 8 to 10 weeks of temps below 45 degrees to bloom well. If they don't get it, the flowers will have either short stems or no stems at all. Just avoid storing the bulbs in the refrigerator door between the mustard and mayo. Grumpy came home last week and caught his teenage son making a tulip sandwich. Bottomless Pit will eat anything!

Q: I left my daffodil bulbs in the refrigerator until this April. Should I plant them or throw them out?
—Fern

A: First, let me ask you. What were you thinking? What was SO IMPORTANT from October to New Year's Day that you couldn't take a half-hour to plant a couple dozen bulbs? This, I have to say, is shameful. You can go ahead and plant now if you feel guilty, but your bulbs are probably goners. Buy and plant new bulbs this fall and never do this again!

Q: My daffodils haven't bloomed in two years. I plan to dig them up and move them. Do you think they'll bloom again?
—Claudia

A: There's no way to be certain, but start by giving them the conditions they like when you transplant. Plant the bulbs 4 to 6 inches deep and 6 inches apart in well-drained soil where they'll get plenty of sun. Add 1½ teaspoons of Espoma Organic Bulb-tone 3-5-3 fertilizer to each hole when planting.

BUTTERFLY 101 for BROWN THUMBS

You desperately want beautiful flowers in front of your house all summer long and yet you haven't acted. You're not an expert, after all, and what if you pick the wrong flowers and they die pathetically and the neighbors snicker and you feel like a total loser? Fear not, faithful reader! Once again, Grumpy will save you. Here are six easy-to-grow flowers that will bloom nonstop from now until frost and attract clouds of butterflies too.

— 1 —
ANGELONIA

For spiky summer flowers resembling snapdragons, you can't do better than angelonia. This tropical American native grows 18 to 24 inches tall and offers orchid-shaped blooms in colors of purple, blue, lavender, red, pink, or white. It loves heat and sun, has no pests, is great for cutting, and does well in gardens or containers. Because of its upright habit, it makes a great combination with many other flowers in your garden.

— 2 —
COSMOS

Cosmos (*Cosmos bipinnatus*) vie with zinnias for the title of easiest flowers to start from seed. These annuals can grow up to 8 feet tall (although 4 to 6 feet is more the norm) with 3- to 4-inch flowers in colors of pink, rose, lavender, purple, or crimson that are excellent for cutting.

— 3 —
DRAGON WING BEGONIA

A cross between angel-wing begonia and wax begonia, the rugged Dragon Wing combines shiny green leaves with bright red or pink flowers. It forms a tidy mound 12 to 18 inches high and 10 to 12 inches wide. Baby Wing begonias grow to about the same size but feature smaller leaves and pink or white flowers. They perform like champs in both borders and containers. Give them sun in the morning and light shade in the hot afternoon.

— 4 —
EGYPTIAN STAR CLUSTERS

You may not know pentas (*Pentas lanceolata*) aka "Egyptian star clusters," but you should. This tropical African native is a butterfly favorite and blooms continuously during warm weather. Four-inch-wide clusters of red, pink, lavender, or white blossoms adorn deep green, lance-shaped leaves. Mounding plants grow 12 to 20 inches tall and do equally well in borders and containers. Give them full sun and moist soil.

— 5 —
LANTANA

Tell me you have tried lantana before. There is no tougher flower for the South. It thrives in heat, tolerates drought, intoxicates butterflies, and blooms from spring until fall. Old heirloom selections like 'Miss Huff' get to be huge plants 4 feet tall and 6 feet wide, but the newer ones you'll see in garden centers are short and spreading, growing about 2 feet tall and 4 feet wide. Blossoms can mix colors of red, orange, pink, or yellow, but some selections, like 'New Gold,' have blooms of a single color. Plant in borders and containers in full sun.

— 6 —
ZINNIAS

Common zinnias (*Zinnia elegans*) are the easiest annuals I know to grow from seed. They sprout and grow quickly in warm weather so it's not too late to sow. Just sprinkle the large seeds evenly over the soil, rake to just barely cover them with dirt, and water. That's it. Before long, you can have a solid, multicolored border stuffed with long-stemmed blossoms that are great for cutting. The more you cut, the more they'll bloom. Plant in full sun.

[RULE #4]

Butterflies are music on the wing.

Among the best plants for attracting them to your garden are butterfly bush, butterfly weed, zinnia, lantana, bee balm, marigold, salvia, Joe-Pye weed, purple coneflower, pentas, blazing star, firebush, Mexican sunflower, and glossy abelia. Don't forget host plants for butterfly larvae to eat, such as dill, fennel, parsley, and passion vine.

CAMELLIA to CREPE MYRTLE

CAMELLIA

*How I Suffer for My Craft and Make 10 People
Mad—A Tantalizing Tale of Betrayal*

Southern Living is a nice magazine produced by nice people about a nice place called the South. Everybody I work with is nice. No one yells, no one cusses, no one brings firearms or anthrax to work, no one posts naked pictures of themselves on the Internet (well, no one that you'd want to see), and no one runs puppy mills. We're nice.

Thus, it came as a big surprise when the lead story I wrote for the March 2010 issue generated a firestorm of criticism. The issue showcases Charleston, South Carolina, a city that epitomizes the beauty and gracious living for which the South is known. I proclaimed Charleston "the South's garden gateway," because so many of the iconic plants that define our landscapes did not come from North America but were brought here on ships from their native Asia through the bustling colonial port of Charleston. Among those plants were crepe myrtle, mimosa, sweet olive, Indica azalea, and gardenias. In fact, the first gardenias grown outdoors in the U.S. were planted in the Charleston garden of their namesake, Dr. Alexander Garden, in 1762.

Now, that's a nice story, isn't it? So why are people mad at me? Because I committed the mortal sin of trying to be objective. Man, I'll never do that again!

The source of the controversy is another iconic plant of the South, the camellia. Most sources credit its introduction to the South to French botanist André Michaux, who established the South's first botanical garden just north of Charleston in 1786. Records indicate that some of the earliest camellias planted in a private garden appeared at Middleton Place in the early 1800s and were gifts from André Michaux to Henry Middleton.

According to the folks at Middleton Place, Henry Middleton planted four camellias, one at each corner of his parterre garden. Each was a double red they called 'Reine des Fleurs' ("Queen of Flowers"). Only one of them survives today.

And that is why people (including some at nearby Magnolia Plantation, another beautiful must-see garden) call me a horticultural heretic. They say Michaux couldn't have given Middleton 'Reine des Fleurs' because 'Reine des Fleurs' wasn't named until 1845 and Michaux died in 1802.

I included that tidbit in my first draft of the Charleston story that I sent for checking to both Middleton and Magnolia. Shortly after, I received a phone call from Middleton, complaining about what I'd written. They said there were actually two 'Reine des Fleurs'—one given by Michaux and named by the Middletons and a totally different one officially named 'Reine des Fleurs' in

1845 by the people in charge of naming such things. So therefore, Middleton Place still claims to have Michaux's oldest surviving camellia.

To avoid devoting my entire story to the 'Reine des Fleurs' issue and thereby encourage readers to recycle the issue, I omitted the controversy altogether. That's when certain camellia-philes (who probably also collect beer cans, burned-out light bulbs, and giant balls of string) got furious. Here's a sampling from a camellia forum:

> "It saddens me that Southern Living has bowed to the 'Middleton Place Mafia'! Middleton Place has been caught in a LIE! Southern Living is perpetuating the LIE!"

> "When I write an article, I do my homework to make sure that what I am writing is true. Shame on Southern Living for propagating a myth that they cannot prove is true or false."

> "If you want to write stories without verifying sources or determining the accuracy of the facts, perhaps the National Inquirer (sic) would be more suited for you."

For the record, I have always dreamed of writing for the *National Inquirer*.

The Grump did not bow to the Mafia (although if Michael Corleone showed up at my front door, I think I would). I just refused to devote a great deal of space to a subject that interested maybe 10 readers.

Camellia-spat aside, if you're interested in the history of Southern plants, I encourage you to order a copy of *Gardens and Historic Plants of the Antebellum South* by James Cothran. You'll be surprised to learn how many of the "native" plants you grew up with actually entered the South from abroad through the ports of Charleston, Savannah, and New Orleans.

The Grump has learned his lesson. From this point on, the only Southern icon I will write about is myself.

[RULE #5]

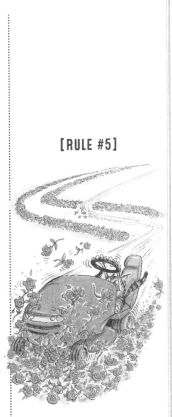

Never allow your cat to drive your lawn tractor.

He's too short to see over the steering wheel and usually runs over the flowers.

[RULE #6]

Never take a chain saw with you into a
tree unless you've made out a will.

—

CHAIN SAWS

understand why some folks own chain saws. They are crazy, violent agents
of Satan bent on causing pain and destruction. (You know who I'm talking
about.) But chain saws scare the pickles out of the Grump. Perhaps that's
because it's the only garden tool that can instantly remove an extremity when
you're not even trying.

Yet, if you have a yard and garden, there will be times when a chain saw
seems to be the only viable solution to a problem. Grumpy and his adoring
wife, Judy, recently rented a chain saw to remove some gigantic, loathsome
privet trees from her sister's yard. Privet deserves any death it gets. I just
hoped its demise wouldn't include mine.

We walked into our local equipment rental place to pick up our weapon of
mass destruction. The guy behind the counter pulled off the plastic protective
sheath from the blade. Surprise! The chain saw had no teeth. I'm not entirely
certain, but had we arrived at the job with a toothless chain saw, I think I
would have died waiting for the blade to gum its way through the trunks.

So, after installing a new set of flesh-ripping teeth on this demon, the guy
gave us the mandatory 15-second primer on how to operate it. "This here's the
throttle, this here's the choke, here's where you pour in the gas and oil, and
this is the number for the county coroner." Check.

He also showed me the chain saw's kick-back protector, a device that, if the snarling blade kicked back toward me after hitting a knot, would protect my head after cutting off Judy's. Safety first.

We headed on down to her sister's place in quest for the hated privets. Despite my terror in using it, I am happy to report that the saw made quick work of them and we both retained our arms and legs. That said, the experience left Grumpy with some important instructions to pass on to readers in case you want to remove a despised tree without involving the paramedics. First, always wear eye protection, such as plastic goggles, because that blade will hurl out slivers of wood in all directions. It's very hard to know where to cut after you've been blinded.

Second, wear earplugs, too. You won't believe how loud a chain saw is when you're holding one that's working. It's like wearing a metal trash can over your head and having people pound it with hammers on every side. Guns N' Roses could be playing right behind you and you'd never notice. Except for maybe the weed smoke.

Third, if the engine is cold, you'll need to pull out the choke before yanking on the cord to crank the machine. If you're lucky, the saw will start on your first try. Unfortunately, no one in recorded history has ever been this lucky. Successive generations of families have passed away at the cord, each one suffering heart failure after pulling for weeks or months. My advice—if the chain saw doesn't start within 10 pulls, push in the choke, put down the saw, and walk away for five minutes so that medics can insert an IV and otherwise attend to you. Then try it all again, provided you've put your affairs in order and left a will with your attorney.

Finally, I don't care if your electric knife is on the fritz and the Thanksgiving turkey weighs 60 pounds, do not let cousin Earl carve the bird with a chain saw! Nothing good will come of it.

ASK GRUMPY

Shady Advice

Q. We have a shady section of our yard where ivy will not grow, so the local nurseryman suggested houttuynia (chameleon plant). We liked its multicolored leaves and white flowers, so we planted two. Now they've taken over the entire yard. Every year, we pull out enough plants to fill several trash cans, but that doesn't slow them down. What can we do?
—Lynn

A. That nurseryman is an idiot. Chameleon plant is very invasive, spreading by roots, runners, and seeds. Once it's in the ground here in the South, it's almost impossible to eradicate. Spot treat it with herbicide according to label directions. If it has insinuated itself into all your other plants, mix up some herbicide and carefully paint it on the leaves with a paintbrush, avoiding foliage of your good plants.

CHASTE TREE

Chaste Tree Is Pure Delight

T he July 2009 issue of *Southern Living* features an incredibly entertaining and informative story written by me about three great trees for summer blooms. In case you were too cheap to buy it, let me discuss my favorite tree of the bunch—chaste tree (*Vitex agnus-castus*).

Native to southern Europe and central Asia, chaste tree quickly grows into a multi-trunked tree about 10 to 20 feet tall and wide with a broad, spreading habit. It gets its name from the erroneous medieval belief that a potion made from it could curb the libido. In reality, wearing a housedress with orthopedic shoes and multiple nose piercings is much more effective.

That doesn't mean that chaste tree doesn't have its pharmacological uses. An extract made from *Vitex* supposedly does a very good job of controlling PMS. Which means any of you guys out there who are routinely beaten every 28 days should plant one in the yard.

BLUE FOR YOU

But the best thing about chaste tree, in my uber-learned opinion, is the flowers. Chaste tree is one of the very few winter-hardy trees out there that sports true blue flowers (although they can also be pink, purple, or white). 'Abbeville Blue' bears large, spectacular panicles of deep-blue flowers in summer. Other selections I like include 'Montrose Purple' (purple blooms), 'Shoal Creek' (blue-violet), and 'Silver Spires' (white). If you buy an unnamed chaste tree from a nursery, buy it in bloom so you can see the color of the flowers and the general shape of the plant.

You'll find many ways to use chaste tree in the landscape: as a single specimen in the lawn, in a row along a property line or a driveway, limbed-up in a border with lower plants growing beneath it, as a small patio tree, and as a convenient place to hang wet laundry. Few trees are as easy to grow. It likes full sun and well-drained soil. Once established, it's very drought tolerant and has no serious pests. It also takes salt air and wind, so it's a good choice for the coast. Chaste tree is winter-hardy to USDA Zone 6; in Zone 5, it may be killed to the ground in winter but will sprout and bloom the following summer.

All of this does not make chaste tree the no-maintenance gift from heaven today's lazy gardeners so fervently seek. It's not the tidiest plant in the world and needs regular pruning to produce an attractive multi-trunked tree. Prune in winter. Clean out the entire center of the tree, removing all side branches from the main four to five trunks. Also remove messy, twiggy growth that tends to crowd the ends of the branches. As an option, cut entire plant to the ground in winter. It will sprout in spring and still bloom in summer, although later than chaste trees not pruned so severely. You can force a second bloom in summer by removing the first flush of blooms as soon as they fade.

⋛ BEE ALERT ⋚

Bumblebees love this tree above all others and will even spend the night sleeping on the flowers, like a partying frat boy passed out on a sofa. Keep this in mind if bees freak you out.

CHIPMUNKS

People generally abhor rodents, but I'll venture to guess you love chipmunks. Six to 12 inches long from nose to tip of fluffy tail, striped, puffy cheeks, and big, shiny eyes—why, they're so cute! Every child should experience chipmunks scampering across the ground, robbing bird-feeders, and providing necessary protein for pet cats. But sadly, many do not. And that is why Grumpy is extending this once-in-a-lifetime offer. It's Grumpy's Chipmunk Giveaway!

I am offering you prime breeding stock—males, females, ambiguous gender—of our all-too-common Eastern chipmunk (*Tamia striatus*) to get your nature park started. All you'll need is a plot of ground that contains soil, garden beds, rocks, or woods. Unlike their fellow rodents, squirrels, chipmunks don't nest in trees (Although they climb them quite easily—an amusing sight!) but they build extensive burrows in the ground, each with several entry holes. They dug so many burrows under Grumpy's row of camellias that his camellias began to sink! Now you know why he loves them so.

Chipmunks enjoy a varied diet. You'll want to provide a healthful and nutritious mix of acorns, peanuts, sunflower seeds, flower bulbs you just

[RULE #7]

Do not put up "Deer Crossing" or "Chipmunk Crossing" signs because deer and chipmunks cannot read.

planted, dried raisins and cranberries, truffles, shiitake mushrooms, Beluga caviar, escargot, insects, and worms. Nuts and seeds may be cached in the burrow for winter, but always serve caviar on a cracker. Your attention to detail will be most appreciated.

You'll notice this gratitude when chipmunks wake up in the morning and start singing. They'll sing and sing and sing! The song usually consists of a sharp, loud chirp that you'll mistake for a bird at first. But it will continue at a precise interval, pitch, and insufferable amplitude for nearly as long as it takes to get service from your hated cable provider. Females are especially vocal when they desire to breed—so much like people!—and project a staccato series of deafening chirps that make you want to take ice picks to your ears. A concussion grenade usually shuts her up, however.

How can you procure your starter pack of delightful Eastern chipmunks? Bring your cat to Grumpy's yard and stake out a burrow. Cats don't kill chipmunks right away—they like to play first—and that's your chance to seize these little, unharmed bundles of joy, plop them into a shoebox equipped with air holes, caviar, and crackers, and drive away. Hopefully, very far away.

Don't wait! If winter ever comes this year, chipmunks will shelter in their burrows munching a truffle or two until spring arrives and it's once again time to dig, chirp, and annoy.

Take advantage of this special opportunity to bring the joy of Chipmunks to your home! It's Grumpy's gift.

CHRISTMAS DECORATING

Putting up outdoor Christmas lights takes away too much time from my precious TV remote! So now I do it all in five minutes. You can too. Buy a cheap metal tomato cage that has three legs and hoops. Stand it with the biggest hoop on the bottom. Wire the legs together at the top. Take three 75-bulb strings of mini lights (LED lights if you want to impress) and wrap each one up, down, and around the cage so the plugs end up at the bottom. Voilà—Grumpy's five-minute Christmas tree! No teetering on ladders and ripping off gutters. After the holidays, unplug it, and store it in the garage until next year. How easy is that? Now give back my remote! We've been apart for too long and I probably missed something.

COLD

When my wife, Judy, tells me she was born and raised in Birmingham, I don't need to see her birth certificate to know that it's true. All I need to do is record the number of times she tells me that she's cold.

She's cold in the morning. She's cold at night. She's cold on Mondays, Wednesdays, and Fridays. She's cold at church. She's cold in the mall. And in winter, her feet are the coldest objects in our solar system outside of the British Royal Family.

Like Judy, many Southerners express discomfort at temperatures that people from other places consider positively balmy. If the famed 19th-century explorer Henry Stanley had been from the South, his first words upon meeting David Livingstone in the jungles of Tanzania would have been, "Dr. Livingstone, I presume you'll turn down the A.C. This rainforest is freezing."

I don't know the physical reasons for this. Maybe Southerners have no hemoglobin. Maybe they have only one artery in their body. Maybe they can't tell when they're dead. What I do know is that if global warming proves to be nothing but a theory, a lot of Southerners will be gravely disappointed.

Not me. I grew up in Maryland. I know what real cold is. Real cold is when you go to start your car in sub-zero January and the battery files a lawsuit. Real cold is when you jockey in the morning to be the last person in the bathroom. Those icicles are sharp.

I'll never forget the conference I attended some years ago on the Alabama Gulf Coast. It was May at Gulf Shores, and I engaged in an act so unspeakably weird as to render bystanders speechless. I went swimming.

As soon as I hit the 75-degree water, a collective gasp from the incredulous crowd sucked in sufficient air to form a low-pressure system. "Is he looney?" they all wondered. "Doesn't he have the sense to know you don't go swimming in May when it's cold?"

Judy doesn't swim in May. She doesn't swim in June either. In fact, she's not putting an ankle in until the water is warm enough to cook a three-minute egg.

It's no wonder Southerners cringe at the thought of leaving home and moving north. We're not talking about moving to Fargo. We're talking about people afraid of relocating to Tulsa. Tulsa is just too cold.

Sometime in the not-too-distant future, humankind will visit other worlds. Momentum at NASA favors an outpost on Mars, but Southerners should push for one on Venus instead. Mars, after all, is freezing most of the time, while the Venusian surface maintains a steady 736 degrees.

Judy says that's just about right.

CREPE MYRTLE

amous Birmingham neuropathologist and amateur worm farmer Dr.
Paymian Cash just confirmed what I've always known. Southerners have
a serious case of lagercephaly, also known as crepe-myrtle-on-the-brain.
Even though crepe myrtles adorn just about every yard, bloom for months on
end, and are incredibly simple to grow, Southerners obsess over what might go
wrong with them, why they don't look better, and what their neighbors will say
in the unlikely event they actually succeed in killing their trees.

Fortunately, as always, you have Grumpy, the world's foremost authority on
Things That Go Wrong With Crepe Myrtles. Grumpy doesn't mind staying up
into the wee hours every night clutching his bottle of Booker's bourbon while
addressing your concerns, because, hey, your worries are his.

So with that, let's get to this latest round of crepe myrtle questions.

ZOMBIE MYRTLE

Question: My crepe myrtle didn't leaf out this spring and is still bare. Do crepe
myrtles sometimes skip a year of growing and then come back to life?

Grumpy's Excellent Answer: Crepe myrtles skip a year of growing about as
often as you skip a week of breathing. Yours was probably killed to the ground
due to winter damage. If you see small green sprouts growing near the base,
your plant may grow back from the bottom, although the top is still dead and
always will be, no matter if it's featured on *The Walking Dead* or not.

ACID TEST

Question: Is crepe myrtle an acid-loving plant?

Grumpy's Excellent Answer: The only crepe myrtle I know of that requires acid is an old one called 'Pink Floyd.' It was the subject of several hit songs on the 1973 mega-platinum album "Dark Side of the Bloom." It's quite hard to find now, because it alternates between branching out and trying to get back to its roots. Fortunately, other crepe myrtles aren't fussy and accept acid, neutral, or alkaline soil.

NEW SUCKER EVERY MINUTE

Question: Suckers constantly grow from the base of my two big crepe myrtles. Is there anything I can do to prevent this annoying growth?

Grumpy's Excellent Answer: One way would be to submerge your yard under 20 feet of water, but your neighbors would be peeved. Instead, closely inspect the base of each shoot where it connects to the trunk. You will see a little swollen knob. Cut off this knob flush with the trunk. This will reduce or prevent regrowth. If the suckers are coming from the roots, however, that's probably a result of cutting the roots at some point, and there's nothing much you can do to stop it.

WHAT'S THE WHITE STUFF?

Question: What can I do to prevent my crepe myrtles from getting this white stuff all over the leaves each summer?

Grumpy's Excellent Answer: Assuming your crepe myrtles aren't growing beneath a flock of pigeons, they probably have a fungus called powdery mildew. It covers and distorts the leaves and can keep flower buds from opening. Hybrids such as 'Natchez,' 'Miami,' 'Dynamite,' 'Zuni,' and 'Pink Velour' resist mildew, but many of the older types don't. You can't take off the existing mildew, but you can keep mildew from spreading by spraying healthy foliage according to label directions with horticultural oil or neem oil.

FRAZZLED NOT DAZZLED

Question: My neighbor gave me 6 miniature crepe myrtles named "Dazzle" three years ago.

ASK GRUMPY

Spelling Bee

Q. Why do you spell it "crepe myrtle?" Every book I've ever read spells it "crape myrtle."

A. That's because every book you've read is wrong. Fortunately, *Southern Living* has been a shining beacon of enlightenment bringing knowledge and wisdom to the breadth of humanity for the last 50 years. No need to thank us. We're just that kind of folks.

I've planted them in various locations, given them fertilizer and tons of coffee grounds, but they're still only 6 inches tall. What do you suggest?

Grumpy's Excellent Answer: Look on the bright side. Your crepe myrtles may be puny, but I'll bet they're very alert! Dazzle is the name for a series of miniature crepe myrtles of various colors that came out a few years ago. They form tidy mounds 3 to 4 feet tall and wide. 'Cherry Dazzle' with cherry-red flowers is Grumpy's favorite. The recipe for success here is fertile, well-drained soil; full sun; and regular watering when they're getting established. Considering their slow growth, you might want to move them to a more favorable location this fall.

ASK GRUMPY

Flowering Time

Q. All of the neighbor's crepe myrtles are blooming, but my red one still hasn't a single flower. Will it ever bloom?

—Linda

A. People grow lots of different kinds of crepe myrtles. Some bloom early and some later. So be patient! Provided it is planted in full sun, it will bloom. Crepes that have been "murdered"—cut back to hideous stumps in spring by an ignoramus with a chain saw—actually bloom earlier, as this crime sends the plants into a fast-growth mode. This is no excuse, however. Do not commit crepe murder! If you do, we will find you and humiliate you in front of your family, friends, and neighbors.

FLAKING BARK

Question: The bark on our crepe myrtles is flaking off in big pieces. Are they going to die?

Grumpy's Excellent Answer: Well, of course—eventually everything dies. But you needn't worry just yet. Crepe myrtle naturally sheds last year's outer bark in summer to reveal beautiful new bark underneath, like the chestnut-brown bark of 'Miami' and 'Natchez.' Such bark is especially showy in winter and helps make crepe myrtle a multi-season champ.

TRANSPLANTING TIME

Question: When is the right time to transplant a crepe myrtle?

Grumpy's Excellent Answer: Definitely not when it's around 100 degrees. The best time is when the tree is dormant and has dropped its leaves. This means fall, winter (for some), and early spring.

NOT TONIGHT, DEER

Question: My sister-in-law has trouble with deer eating all of her plants. Will they eat crepe myrtles?

Grumpy's Excellent Answer: Not unless the only other available food comes floating down the Ganges River.

[RULES #8, #9 & #10]

Prevent crepe murder at all costs.

You should prune your crepe myrtle like you prune your dogwood—in other words, just about never. The older it gets, the less pruning it will need.

You can also prevent crepe murder by choosing selections that need little or no pruning.

Grumpy heartily recommends 'Acoma' (white, 6 to 10 feet), 'Catawba' (deep purple, 12 to 15 feet), 'Near East' (light pink, 10 to 15 feet), 'Pink Velour' (neon pink, 10 to 12 feet), 'Siren Red' (dark red, 8 to 10 feet), 'Velma's Royal Delight' (bright purple, 4 to 6 feet), and 'Zuni' (medium lavender, 6 to 10 feet).

Just don't put them anywhere near your pool.

Unless, that is, you enjoy fishing crepe myrtle flowers from the water every 45 seconds. Other messy trees to avoid include river birch, mulberry, hackberry, sweet gum, chinaberry, mimosa, and camphor tree. Good trees for the perimeter of a pool include palm, live oak, banana, juniper, holly, and Japanese maple.

—

HOW TO MAKE

A CREPE MYRTLE BLOOM TWICE

After the first summer flowers fall, a crepe myrtle will form clusters of round, green seedpods. Promptly remove these clusters before the pods turn brown by cutting just below them on a branch. The crepe myrtle will respond by sending out a new crop of flowers for late summer and fall.

‹‹‹‹‹

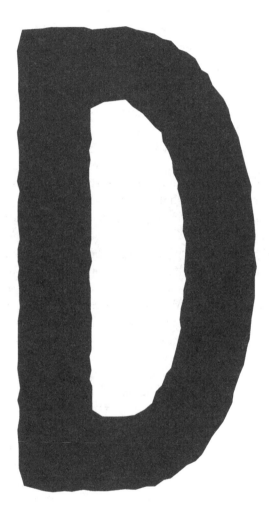

DAD'S GARDEN ᴛᴏ DORM ROOM PLANTS

DAD'S GARDEN

Every year, America takes a special day, Memorial Day, to honor the fallen heroes who made this country great. In that vein, Grumpy would like to take this opportunity to remember the biggest hero in his life.

The man who set me on my path is my dad—Edward J. Bender Sr. If he were with us today, he'd be 100. Although he was never grumpy, it is safe to say that without his influence, compassion, and indefatigable enthusiasm, the Grumpy Gardener would never have happened.

Dad was a gardener. He loved working with plants—all kinds of plants. One of my earliest memories was picking dwarf 'Golden Bantam' corn from a teeny vegetable plot in our backyard about the size of a card table. We harvested about eight ears a year. We had to rush them to the boiling water to keep them from turning to starch, but there was something about growing corn in the backyard that was just so cool.

Later on, the county started providing public land for "victory gardens." For $10 or so, a family could rent a decent-sized plot to grow its own vegetable garden. There were just two catches. First, there was no water, so we had to take about 20 one-gallon milk jugs filled with water to the garden every time we went. When they ran out, we drove to a nearby pond and refilled them. Second, the moment plants started coming up, rabbits would show up for their nightly meal. So we needed a fence. Dad built a fence about 3 feet high with wooden posts and wire. It even had a latched gate. We'd put it up in spring and then in fall, take it down, roll it up, put it in the trunk of our Rambler station wagon (Truly one of the worst cars ever made, but whatcha gonna do?), and take it home.

We grew all the requisite veggies—corn, peppers, squash, Swiss chard, carrots, beets, tomatoes, cabbage, broccoli, onions, beans, and kale. We also grew one really strange veggie that made everyone look at us like we were from Mars—'Clemson Spineless' okra. No one in Baltimore County, Maryland, had ever seen it. But my mother was from Southern Pines, North Carolina, and she fixed truly fine fried okra. I never could get enough.

So much work went into that garden. Every fall, Dad would bag up all the leaves that fell in our yard and spread them on the vegetable garden to improve the clay soil. Every winter, Dad drew up a new planting plan. When the time came, he ordered seeds. Everything was grown from seeds. (Who does that anymore?) Oh, he also insisted that a vegetable garden must have flowers, so he'd ring the garden with marigolds, just to make sure the other families recognized who the real gardeners were.

His passion for gardening didn't stop with vegetables. He loved trees, shrubs, and flowers too. Early in my teen years, a new church was built nearby our house that we would go to on Sundays. Dad became the church's unofficial gardener. We transplanted dozens of trees from the woods to decorate the grounds—dogwoods, beeches, maples, black gums, sweet gums, and tulip poplars. When Dad retired, he added a rose garden and extensive flower gardens. He tended them every day. I can't think of a better way to retire.

In my book *Passalong Plants*, I chronicle the stories of wonderful, old-fashioned plants that connect generations of family and friends by being passed along from gardener to gardener. Whenever you see a plant you received, you remember when you got it and the person who gave it to you. I got a special plant from my dad.

It's an old-fashioned mum that's been in Dad's family for generations. It's a tall, lanky, almost vining mum that forms ever-expanding clumps. The small, deep-red flowers with yellow centers open in late fall. Since nobody knows the true name, I named this mum 'Antares' in honor of the giant red star in the constellation Scorpio. Every time it blooms, I remember the person who set me on the path I still walk today.

Here's looking at you, Dad.

HOW TO PICK
A DAFFODIL

Don't cut the stem, says Brent Heath of Brent and Becky's Bulbs in Gloucester, Virginia. The bloom will last longer in water if you use your thumb and finger to snap off the stem at the base so it has a white bottom.

-‹‹‹‹‹-

DAHLIAS

When Kathy Whitfield took her mother to the mall in the fall of 1997, she had no idea that outing would change her life. The pair stumbled upon a sea of blooms in myriad shapes, sizes, and colors set up by the local dahlia society for its annual show. "I didn't know what a dahlia was," Kathy admits. "The flowers were so perfect—they didn't look real." People behind a nearby table invited visitors to join the dahlia society. She recalls, "My mother said, 'You go join.' And in the South, you do what your mama says."

A few months later, a letter arrived at the Whitfields' mailbox in Hoover, Alabama. Kathy retrieved it and told her husband, "Ed, I think I've joined something." Ed looked at the letter and announced, "I know what dahlias are! My grandmother grew them." The die was cast. Today, the Whitfields grow 550 dahlias of more than 75 kinds in their backyard.

Dahlias are tender perennials that grow from tuberous roots. You should dig up and store them over winter in the Upper and Middle South (USDA Zones 6 and 7), but leave in the ground year-round south of there. Dahlia fanciers divide them into classes based on flower form. Blooms come in all colors except true blue, range from 2 to 12 inches wide and 1 to 7 feet tall, and are great for cutting.

Anyone who grows more than 500 dahlias every year has my respect. I asked Kathy for her best tricks to help you get started on your first 100.

BEAT THE HEAT

Dahlias dislike long, hot summers, making them challenging to grow in the Lower South (Zone 8), where Kathy lives, and not recommended for the Coastal and Tropical South (Zones 9 and 10). They wilt in hot sun and often stop blooming when the mercury tops 90 degrees. Big-flowered kinds are the most heat sensitive. Kathy shields dahlias in summer beneath 50-percent polyethylene shade cloth (available at gemplers.com), which blocks half of the sunlight. She also sets up beach umbrellas to shade some plants at midday. Don't want to fool with adding shade cloth and umbrellas? Grow them in light afternoon shade.

PREPARE THE SOIL

Dahlias prefer moist, well-drained soil with lots of organic matter. Ed and Kathy grind up and compost fallen leaves that they add to the soil with soil conditioner and mushroom compost. Plants grown in good soil don't need much fertilizer.

PLANT IN SPRING

April and May are good months. Plant the roots about 1 foot deep, spacing tall selections (over 4 feet tall) 4 to 5 feet apart and shorter ones 1 to 2 feet apart. Kathy sprinkles a teaspoon of Epsom salts and a teaspoon of Osmocote fertilizer in each hole.

WATER WISELY

Don't water dormant roots after planting until sprouts show above ground or the roots will probably rot. After that, water only when plants look wilted in early morning before the sun hits them.

SUPPORT YOUR PLANTS

All but very short dahlias need to be tied to a 6-foot rebar stake driven into the ground beside them.

MAKE THE CUT

Dahlias with full, tight blooms (such as formal decorative ball and pompon types) make excellent, long-lasting cut flowers. "For Sunday church displays, we'll cut them on Saturday morning and make the arrangements, and they'll still look good for Wednesday night," says Kathy.

ORDER EARLY

Buy dormant roots in February and March for best selection. Two great mail-order sources are dahlias.com and hilltopdahlias.com.

DAISIES

On the Chopping Block

Q: Will deadheading my 'Becky' Shasta daisies prolong blooming?

—Jennifer

A: In gardening terms, "deadheading" doesn't mean tripping to Jerry Garcia. It means promptly cutting off old flowers to prevent seed production and encourage plants to make new flowers. It also keeps plants that drop lots of seeds from becoming invasive. 'Becky,' a tall heirloom form of Shasta daisy, benefits from this, as do many perennials, annuals, and summer-flowering shrubs. So clip away! Faded flowers may be dead, but future daisies will be grateful.

DANDELIONS

f the sight of bright yellow dandelions dotting your otherwise perfect lawn drives you batty, blame it on the Pilgrims. They reportedly brought the plant to America from its homeland in northern Europe in the 1600s. What else would you expect from guys wearing belt buckles on their hats?

Of course, the Pilgrims had good reason for doing so. The common dandelion (*Taraxacum officinale*) is among the more nutritious and useful of herbs, with a long history of culinary and medicinal use. Its leaves, whether boiled or eaten fresh (yum!), are high in potassium, calcium, iron, and Vitamins A, C, B1, and B12. The dried and roasted roots make an acceptable coffee substitute for people who don't like coffee, and the fermented flowers produce dandelion wine and beer. Dandelion tonics are a folk medicine remedy for liver problems. The Old Farmer's Almanac says they also act as a powerful diuretic—just the thing you want to imbibe before a transatlantic flight. Beekeepers value dandelions as a rich source of pollen and nectar.

This deep-rooted perennial forms a rosette of sharp-toothed leaves 6 to 12 inches long. Their resemblance to lions' teeth gives the plant its common name—"dandelion," a corruption of the French *dent de lion* ("lion's tooth"). Blossoms appear atop hollow stems 4 to 15 inches high. They're followed by the puffball seedheads that children like to blow on, releasing seeds to fly hither and yon.

Dandelions are mortal enemies of lawn lovers, who mercilessly execute them with broadleaf weed killers, even though the flowers are quite pretty. But more and more health-seeking folks grow the culinary types (selected for larger, thicker leaves) found in specialty seed catalogs. Culinary selections such as 'Pissenlit' (I told you they were diuretic), 'Catalogna,' and 'Ameliore' give the best yields and enjoy full sun and fertile, well-drained soil. Pick only young leaves before flowers appear; old leaves, like old girlfriends, can be bitter.

ASK GRUMPY

Daylily Drama

Q. We're having a very rainy summer, and rust-colored spots and streaks have appeared on the leaves of my daylilies. They're an old, double-orange variety given to me by a neighbor. Do I need to eradicate them and start over with a different kind?
—Kathy

A. Don't eradicate them, but do take action. Cut all foliage off at the ground and throw it out with the trash. When the new leaves get about a foot high, spray them according to label directions with either Immunox or Natria Disease Control. Remove and throw out all withered foliage every winter. To avoid future disease, don't wet healthy foliage when you water. FYI—your daylily sounds like an old pass-along plant called "Kwanso." It spreads quickly. You can't kill it.

DEATH BY DEER

13 Garden Plants Deer Will Utterly Destroy

'm gonna save you some money. I'm gonna save you some time. I'm gonna save you a LOT of heartache, anger, acid reflux, and embarrassing eye twitches. Because if you live where deer cruise the neighborhood at night, there are certain plants you should NEVER stick in the ground lest you find them the next morning on a pleasant little journey down Bambi's digestive tract. Let's start with the Big Three.

THE BIG THREE

Hostas, daylilies, and roses. To a deer, these are fresh-caught Maine lobster served with melted Irish butter. They will scarf down every one they see, even when not offered a suitable wine pairing. You might think thorny roses would be undesirable, but you don't know Bambi. To him, a little physical pain is more than worth the emotional trauma he's going to cause you. Don't even think of planting these three plants in deer country unless your garden is surrounded by an electric fence the size of the one in *Jurassic Park*. Hope there's not a power outage.

10 MORE DINNERTIME FAVORITES

American arborvitae (*Thuja occidentalis*). Rows of these pyramidal, needleleaf evergreens are often planted in the burbs to screen out ugly neighbors. Deer, however, think all humans should be friends and that can't happen with arborvitaes in the way. Good dining makes good neighbors!

Blueberry (*Vaccinium sp.*). Did you know that blueberries are among the most potent sources of health-giving antioxidants? Deer certainly do, which is why they will gobble down every one, along with the foliage too. How kind of you to plant them.

Euonymus (*Euonymus sp.*). Grumpy ain't gonna shed any tears over this one. He hates most species of euonymus, particularly the gruesomely garish golden euonymus (*E. japonicus 'Aureomarginatus'*). If the deer don't get them, scales and mildew will. Good riddance.

Indian hawthorn (*Rhaphiolepis indica*). Around the Southern coast and in places with alkaline soil, this broadleaf evergreen is enjoyed as a substitute for acid-loving azaleas. Deer feel the same way. Yum.

Japanese aucuba (*Aucuba japonica*). This is one of the better broadleaf evergreen shrubs for shade, especially the popular gold dust plant (*A. japonica 'Variegata'*) with bright yellow spots on deep green leaves. Once a deer spots it, though, it's "sayonara."

Japanese pittosporum (*Pittosporum tobira*). It grows in many of the same places in the South as Indian hawthorn does. Until deer find it, of course, and then your garden looks so much more open and uncrowded than before. Fist bump!

Japanese yew (*Taxus cuspidata*). Among the most common evergreen shrubs for foundation planting and hedges in cold-winter areas, Japanese yew bears soft, red fruits that people find quite toxic. Deer, of course, do not. They relish the leaves as well. Here's looking at yew, kid.

Pansies and **violas** (*Viola sp.*). This one is a no-brainer. If people can put pansy and viola flowers on salads and eat them, deer surely can. FYI, their favorite dressings are Ranch and Thousand Island.

Rhododendrons and **azaleas** (*Rhododendron sp.*). What's up with this? Are deer determined to remove all of America's favorite plants from the landscape? Yeah, pretty much.

Tulips (*Tulipa sp.*). OK, since I just told you to forget about planting pansies and violas for spring color, you think you'll plant sweeps of tulips instead. Wait until the herd sweeps through your yard! Plant daffodils instead. Deer won't touch them.

DOGWOODS

Where Have All the Dogwoods Gone?

f you live in the Southeast, you probably remember all the "dogwood trails" that people followed when our native flowering dogwoods bloomed each spring. Thirty years ago, dogwood was the #1 flowering tree. Sadly, no longer. The trails have steadily eroded until we see only remnants now. Where have all the dogwoods gone?

Answer: To that old compost pile in the sky. Dogwoods aren't terribly long-lived as trees go. No dogwoods living today saw the Greeks build the Parthenon. But that's not why you see only an occasional dogwood nowadays. It's because when a dogwood died, folks replaced it with a tree they thought was easier. The crepe myrtle.

Think about it. Today, in many neighborhoods, you can scarcely pass by a single Southern house that doesn't have a crepe myrtle. And it's easy to understand why. They bloom for a long time, offer many different colors, boast handsome bark if you don't murder them with bad pruning, and tolerate drought and most soils. Plain and simple—they're easier to grow than dogwoods.

Other factors may also be at work here. Dogwood anthracnose, a disease caused by the fungus *Discula destructiva* (what a great name), has laid waste to many thousands of stressed dogwoods over the last decades. What is causing the initial stress? I suspect the global warming that has noticeably lengthened our hellish Alabama summers and shortened our already mild winters. Twenty-five years ago, blooming dogwoods filled the woods behind my house in spring. Today, most of those trees are gone.

DON'T GIVE UP ON DOGWOOD

But that doesn't mean you shouldn't try dogwoods where you live. In Grumpy's opinion, flowering dogwood (*Cornus florida*) remains the best small tree for multi-season interest. Not just in the Southeast, either—for the Northeast and Midwest too. Showy blossoms of white, pink, or red appear in spring before the leaves. A spectacular red-flowering selection called 'Cherokee Brave' grows in my yard today.

Dogwood is also one of the first trees to change color in fall. The leaves may turn scarlet, but crimson or burgundy-red is more the norm. After the leaves drop, bright red fruits are revealed that persist all fall and winter—until they're gobbled by robins, cedar waxwings, and mockingbirds.

WHAT A DOGWOOD NEEDS

Contrary to popular belief, flowering dogwood grows just fine in full to partial sun. It'll grow well in shade too, but it won't bloom. The trick to growing it in full sun is giving loose, acid, fertile, moist soil—lots of organic matter, no rocks or clay—and extra water during hot, dry stretches. Soak the roots with a hose; don't rely on lawn sprinklers. If you let the tree wilt, the leaves will scorch badly (brown and curl on the edges) and the tree may not set flowerbuds. Also, spread a generous layer of mulch under the tree (but don't pile it up against the trunk) to cool the roots and keep the soil moist.

DORM ROOM PLANTS

ouseplants and college students just don't mix, especially if the student is male. There are so many other pressing concerns they must attend to—throwing a kegger, asking Mom for money, and figuring out what brooms are for. If you want their rooms to appear more habitable by adding houseplants, you need to choose ones they can't kill from utter neglect or watering them with PBR. Here are six suggestions.

—1—
CAST-IRON PLANT

Cast-iron plant (*Aspidistra elatior*) was made for brown-thumb gardeners. Sturdy, long-lived, and nearly bulletproof, this evergreen perennial tolerates low light and nearly total neglect. Place it about 4 to 5 feet from a south-facing window. Let the soil surface go dry between waterings.

—2—
RUBBER PLANT

Anyone who has ever grown or seen a houseplant in their lives knows good old rubber plant (*Ficus decora*). It gets its name from the milky, latex sap that flows whenever you cut off a stem or leaf. Unlike some kinds of finicky Ficus (for example, weeping fig), rubber plant accepts a wide range of growing conditions without dropping leaves. It accepts low light (but not direct sun) and needs watering only when completely dry. One choice selection, 'Abidjan,' features glossy, dark-green to maroon leaves with red midribs.

—3—
THE ONE AND ONLY SNAKE PLANT

Snake plant (*Sansevieria trifasciata*) is legendary. If you weren't aware that all plants need sunlight and water sometime during their lives, you could still keep this one going for a year. A friend told me he moved out of his dorm room one semester, went home for six months, and when he returned the snake plant he'd left behind looked happy as a clam.

There are lots of snake plants, but the one called 'Laurentii' is by far the most popular. It features spear-shaped leaves that are dark green with gold edges and silver frost. It grows up to 4 feet tall. It asks for little more than dim light (it'll look better with bright light), good drainage, and watering every couple of months. If your student kills this, I fear nuclear physics is not a viable career choice.

— 4 —
VARIEGATED PEPPEROMIA

My son, Brian, made a surprisingly good choice when he wandered through houseplant heaven at Home Depot and picked out a variegated pepperomia because he liked the foliage colors. Had he known it would be hard to kill, he undoubtedly would have chosen something else. Pepperomia is good for dorm rooms because its needs are few—bright, indirect light (no direct sun), good drainage, and watering once a week. It also likes confined roots, so you don't have to repot it between freshman and senior years (like he ever would). Just as important, its name sounds a lot like "pepperoni"—something all college students seek out in mass quantities.

— 5 —
ZZ PLANT

No, this one doesn't get its name from my favorite Texas rock band of all time, ZZ Top. ZZ is the short form of its bizarre botanical name, *Zamioculcas zamiifolia*.

ZZ is one plant that could challenge snake plant to a cage match in Ultimate Survival. It sends up 3-foot stems adorned with succulent-looking leaves so glossy and deep green they look plastic. Surviving in very low light (no direct sun), it needs watering maybe once a month (but let the soil dry out completely before you do). ZZ is so easy it's like a gut course for a football player.

— 6 —
PLASTIC FLOWERS

No-care plastic flowers last forever, just like student loan debt. Plus, many are made from recycled plastic soda bottles, demonstrating your child's environmental awareness. Fill the room with plastic flowers! No water, no fertilizer, no taste!

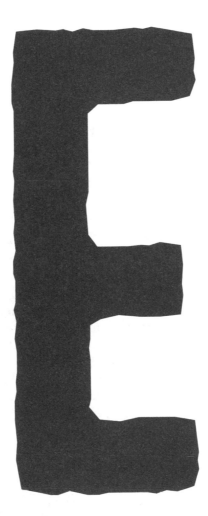

ELECTRIC BUG ZAPPERS to EPSOM SALTS

ELECTRIC BUG ZAPPERS

A crackling flame lit up Harvey's chortling face from ear to beer. "Woooo, Vern, did you see that one?" he called to his buddy as he sucked down another Bud Light. "Man, looked just like a dang grease fire. Think we just fried a bat!"

Scenes like this play out in backyards across America every summer as manly men filled with testosterone and fueled by alcohol prosecute civilization's eternal war against annoying insects. Their weapon of choice—a bug zapper that combines the eerie glow of a black light with an electrified metal grid to produce the snap! crackle! pop! of electrocuted insects that makes every minute sitting out in the black of night more exciting than watching a meteor shower.

"Zzzzzzzzzzzt!" snaps the bug zapper.

"Dang!" exclaims Harvey, taking another swig. "That bad boy was bigger than a VW!"

Do bug zappers actually work? That depends on what you're counting on them to do. If you get a kick from igniting hundreds of moths, beetles, and other insects attracted to lights at night, yeah, they work. But fry flies? Nope. More importantly, they don't attract the one insect that the vast majority of electric bug zappers are sold to attract—the mosquito.

How come? Well, mosquitoes don't find people by sight. If they could, how could they locate you at night? Lights don't attract them either. Ever seen mosquitoes buzzing around a street light? No, they find you by smell. Humans emit a host of chemical molecules that mosquitoes hone in on and trace back to you. The most powerful of these is the carbon dioxide that you blow out into the yard every time you exhale. This is why dead people never complain about mosquito bites. Mosquitoes can't find them.

Admitting this fact, some bug zappers combine the black light and electrified grid with a chemical

ASK GRUMPY

Worm Your Compost

Q. I have an elevated barrel composter that you spin to mix the contents. I'm worried that without ground contact, there won't be any earthworms inside. Do I need earthworms for composting?

—Liza

A. Excellent question! If the compost is properly mixed, moisturized, and oxygenated, billions of microbes will do the composting. If they're working really fast, the compost will get too hot for earthworms. If not, add a shovelful of good topsoil from your garden. It will probably contain earthworm eggs. Then add some finished compost to each new batch.

attractant, such as octenol. Unfortunately, octenol is a much less effective attractant than plain, old CO_2.

If a bug zapper doesn't kill biting insects like mosquitoes and flies, does it provide anything more than entertainment for rednecks as it immolates yet another moth? Nyet. In fact, it does more harm than good by indiscriminately killing all winged insects that touch it. Many are beneficial insects that feed on or parasitize harmful ones. Some are important plant pollinators, while others end up as dinner for wildlife.

So if the evening's a little slow, nothing's on cable, and you and Vern just need an excuse to crack open a cold one, by all means, ignore common sense and the environment and turn on that bug zapper. But you'd better not expose any bare skin come morning. Because Aedes mosquitoes—the ones that transmit dengue fever, West Nile virus, eastern equine encephalitis, and Zika virus—are most active during the day.

ELEPHANT'S EAR

Are you one of those demure people who always hide in the back and hope not to be noticed? Then stop it. Right now. To get anywhere in life, you need to attract attention. You can start with your garden. Plant elephant's ear. There is nothing subtle or shy about it.

There are two groups of plants people refer to as elephant's ear. The first, *Alocasia sp.*, holds its huge spear-shaped leaves upright. For that reason, it has earned the shockingly obvious common name "upright elephant's ear." It's not quite as cold-hardy (at best to USDA Zone 8A) and therefore not as widely grown as the other group, *Colocasia sp.*, whose humongous, heart-shaped to spear-shaped leaves hang down. Most of these are winter-hardy to Zone 7A, and they are the ones this post is about. For clarity, I'll call them hangy-down elephant's ears.

Most hangy-down elephant's ears are derived from an Asian species called *Colocasia esculenta*, also known as taro. It's one of the world's oldest cultivated plants and grown in many tropical countries for its edible root. Hawaiians call it "kalo" and grind up the root to make a starchy, goopy food called "poi" that's served with practically every meal.

Mmmmm...doesn't that sound good? I've tried poi and it tastes like moist air. You need to combine it with something that has an actual flavor. Maybe a slaw dog.

In the garden, taro looks like the old, familiar green elephant's ear whose huge roots you buy at big box stores in spring. But in recent years, plant breeders have introduced many exciting new forms that have gardeners tittering with poi…oh wait, I meant joy. Now we have purple leaves, nearly black leaves, spotted leaves, banded leaves, yellow leaves, red-stemmed leaves, puckered leaves, and leaves so shiny they look like the skin of an oiled-up body builder you wouldn't let sit on your sofa. Depending on the type, plants grow from 3 feet tall up to 7 feet.

HOW TO GROW

To grow hangy-down elephant's ears that will thrill, chill, and fulfill you, give them lots of four things—heat, sun, water, and nitrogen fertilizer. Grumpy finds it easier to supply all four when they're grown in containers instead of the ground, but that's up to you. Plant the tubers about 6 inches deep.

As mentioned before, don't expect these plants to survive winters where the ground freezes or temps drop below 10 degrees. Heavy mulching in late winter can provide an extra zone of hardiness, maybe up to USDA Zone 6. So how can you save a showstopper plant you've paid big bucks for? Grow it in a container you can take inside for winter to a cool basement or garage that doesn't freeze. Keep the soil slightly moist to preserve the roots. Take it back outside the next spring when you feel a good sweat coming on. Serve up some poi and enjoy!

EMPRESS TREE

Want to get rich quick without buying lottery tickets or waiting on Publishers Clearing House? Do I have the tree for you! Not only does it sport showy, vanilla-scented, lavender-blue flowers, but also it grows faster than mildew in a shower, and its wood is so valuable that people steal huge trees in the dead of night! So if you're tired of slumming it in a cramped 7,000-square-foot house—too embarrassed to have people over—plant a farm of empress trees and you'll soon be hot tubbing with Bill and Melinda!

Many years ago as an unemployed college graduate, I had this very same idea. I was a history major, and while most intelligent Americans were frantic to hear me recount the thrilling epic of the Taft-Harding Pimento Cheese Act, they wouldn't pay me for it. It was then, while reading the back page of that world renowned scholarly journal *Parade* magazine, that I discovered the "miracle tree" that would bring me the riches of Solomon.

Unfortunately, *Parade* totally missed the point. They extolled empress tree as a heavenly shade tree that would grow 10 feet a year and flaunt giant, exotic leaves. You could almost see it grow before your eyes, provided you had a really, really slow afternoon (like recent history grads often do). But they said nothing about how stinking rich you could become if you cut it down and sold its valuable wood.

Named for Anna Pavlovna, daughter of Czar Paul I, empress tree (*Paulownia tomentosa*) is native to China, where its wood has been used more than 1,000 years for making furniture, musical instruments, carvings, pots, bowls, and spoons. The Japanese prize it highly for making sandals. The reasons are that the wood is blond in color, very easy to work with, nearly as light as balsa but twice as strong, has a silky feel, and resists insects and decay. Nice trees with straight trunks can fetch thousands of dollars, which is why they're subject to rustling. Many landowners with empress trees on their property have gone to bed with good will toward all only to discover stumps in the morning.

Let us observe a moment of silence.

I didn't have what it takes to be a tree rustler (a chain saw and a pickup truck), but I did have a friend with some spare land. So I ordered 24 seedlings from a very disreputable mail-order nursery in Illinois (I won't mention the name. Let's just say it rhymes with "rowan.") They were seedlings all right—tiny peat pots holding 3-day-old seedlings that still had only their tiny seed leaves. Most were already dead. When I complained, they suggested I give them a year to recover from transplanting shock. I replied that I would give them 30 days to refund my money or prosecute them for mail-fraud. They finally relented.

There went my shot at becoming American royalty. I settled for being the Grump. But since you're reading this, I guess that's not so bad.

Empress tree is incredibly easy to grow. However, like box elder, mulberry, and tree-of-heaven, it belongs to the garbage can class of trees. Not only does it seed all over creation, but also it thrives in absolutely terrible soil where few other trees will. You'll often see it growing on old mining sites, next to railroad tracks, out of cracks in the pavement, or on rocky cliffs. If you cut empress tree to the ground in spring, it truly will grow 10 feet in a year and sprout gigantic leaves up to 2 feet long. Lack of

ASK GRUMPY

Up in Smoke

Q: I cut down an oak and a pine tree in my yard. Is it okay to use both for firewood?

—Carl

A: Well, hardwoods like oak, hickory, and ash are preferable to softwoods like pine. The main reason is that the resin in softwoods can coat your chimney with flammable creosote and lead to a chimney fire. So if you burn softwoods, clean your chimney once a year.

cold-hardiness is one limitation, though. Flowerbuds are usually killed north of USDA Zone 6. An empress tree without her crown jewels is very disappointing.

Despite what *Parade* said about it, I wouldn't recommend empress tree as a shade tree for the average yard. It grows quite large (up to 80 feet tall if a bulldozer doesn't intervene), drops a lot of litter, and has huge leaves that produce shade too dense to grow grass beneath. The best use of empress trees I've ever seen was the ones that once formed a massive allée at world-famous Longwood Gardens in Kennett Square, Pennsylvania. Sadly, that allée no longer exists. I wonder if some rustler got rich?

EPSOM SALTS

Of all the old wives' tales swirling around the gardensphere, the magical ability of Epsom salts to goose your plants into health and vigor ranks as #1. Plant not blooming? Give it Epsom salts. Plant not growing? Epsom salts. Plant singing off-key? Epsom salts.

The legendary benefits of Epsom salts aren't restricted to plants. People cash in too. Fans of Epsom salts claim they speed the healing of wounds, soothe sore muscles, help you sleep, soften your skin, and most importantly, cure constipation. (Eating Mexican food from a street vendor in Guadalajara has the same result, of course.)

Named for the town of Epsom, England, where they were discovered in a spring in the 17th century, Epsom salts are a chemical compound called hydrated magnesium sulfate. Magnesium sulfate supplies two essential plant nutrients—magnesium and sulfur. Thus, it stands to reason that supplied in the right amounts, they'd be good for plants.

People commonly use Epsom salts to feed plants that crave magnesium, including tomatoes, peppers, and rose bushes. They claim that Epsom salts mixed with water and poured around the bases of plants or sprayed directly on the foliage result in more and bigger flowers and fruit.

The thing is, unless you do a soil test, you'll never know if your soil lacks magnesium and sulfur. Dolomitic lime contains magnesium, so if you've been liming your soil, chances are it has plenty already. Plus, magnesium and sulfur are only two of the many vital nutrients plants need. They also require nitrogen, phosphorus, potassium, iron, calcium, manganese, zinc, and other micronutrients. You don't get those from Epsom salts.

Grumpy's advice is use Epsom salts from time to time if you think your plants could use a kick in the pants, but don't solely rely on them. Also use an organic, slow-release, complete fertilizer according to label directions.

And build good soil that stores nutrients by adding lots of organic matter like composted cow manure and chopped leaves.

What's the correct dose of Epsom salts to apply? For foliar feeding, it's 1 tablespoon per gallon of water. For soil drenching, add ½ cup per gallon of water. To cure constipation, I have no idea. See what works best for you!

Dr. Strangelawn

Q. I've already fertilized my fescue lawn with 6-24-24 lawn food but thought I'd supplement with a concoction that I can apply with my hose-end sprayer of ammonia, detergent, corn syrup, and Epsom salts. What about adding beer for microbes?

—Jon

A. In Grumpy's opinion, the miraculous liquid known as beer should never be consumed by a lawn, only by the lawn's owner. Jon, you sound like a mad scientist. I don't see any advantage in supplementing the commercial fertilizer with all that stuff. Epsom salts contain magnesium and sulfur, which quality lawn fertilizers already have. So don't feed again until next spring. Then switch to a fertilizer that is relatively high in nitrogen (the first number), has no phosphorus (the second number), and has moderate potassium (yep, the last number). Apply at the rate and frequency specified on the bag for your type of grass.

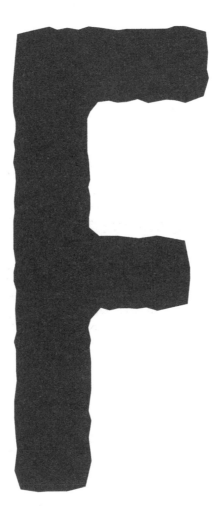

FAKE CHRISTMAS TREES to FUNGUS

FAKE CHRISTMAS TREES

Certain things you will never see on the pages of *Southern Living*: Abraham Lincoln in a hot tub, a toilet (even a low-flush one), a Mongolian recipe with ingredients you can't buy at your local Publix, or pretty Southern girls with tattoos.

Oh, and one more thing. You will never see an artificial Christmas tree.

I can understand the reluctance to feature the first four. Lincoln, after all, has been dead for years. But what's the big deal about artificial Christmas trees? Wouldn't millions of people who can't have real trees because of allergies appreciate a story filled with tips on how to choose and decorate an artificial tree so it looks like a real one?

Nope.

Shame, I say, to the editor. Why do you think the Grumpy Gardener enjoys such an ardent legion of fans?

You see, Grumpy isn't a slave to convention. He searches far and wide to solve the problems of his readers and open their eyes to better ways. And when it comes to featuring artificial Christmas trees, dang, y'all! You're just dumping mud on a season of joy.

This seems like heresy, especially coming from somebody who's spent 34 years writing for the bastion of all things traditional. But putting up a real Christmas tree is like giving yourself a root canal. Some people set up a different Christmas tree in every room of their house. I appreciate such spirit and thoughtfulness, but taking a bath in a tub filled with needles is uncomfortable and leaves you sticky all over and smelling like spruce.

Of course, people with children feel compelled to buy a real Christmas tree because to refuse is akin to handing their souls to Satan. So they take the kid to the Christmas tree lot and make a fatal mistake. They say to the kid, "Go ahead. You choose our Christmas tree." Stupid, stupid, stupid! There are but two possible outcomes. The kid will choose either a horribly ugly tree that's naked on one side OR a tree the size of a giant sequoia that requires a crane to install.

But you promised!

Now the tree is home. It's just the Saturday after Thanksgiving, though—too early to decorate and miss all that football—so you must cut off the bottom inch of trunk to allow it to absorb water when you stand it outside in a bucket. But dang, y'all! You don't have a saw. You must then spend the next two days performing the amputation using a plastic knife you brought back with the take-out BBQ.

Whoa, howdy, it's now that wonderful day when you bring the tree indoors! Go ahead, try to stand it up in the spot you picked out. What could go wrong? One, you have 8-foot ceilings and the sequoia towers 10 feet-plus. Two, with a trunk so thick it could hide a steer, the tree won't fit in your stand. Three, the nearest electrical outlet for the lights resides in the opposite wall. But don't worry about that—you forgot to buy extension cords anyway. Needles start dropping before your eyes. It doesn't matter that you've spread a skirt beneath the tree. Ninety percent of them will burrow into your carpets. Extracting them is like combing a sheep dog for fleas. For every one you find, 50 escape to bite you.

No more holiday terrors for Grumpy. This year, we bought a nice artificial tree. It doesn't need water. It doesn't need a crane. It's prelit with both multicolor and white mini-lights. The needles look like a real spruce's, but they never drop. The tree takes mere minutes to set up and put away. You can place fir "aroma sticks" around the base to produce that treasured Christmas tree smell. It's a jolly holiday once more.

FIRE ANTS

Fire in the Hole

Q. I'm getting all sorts of advice about killing fire ants—from pouring boiling water on the mound to covering it with ashes from the grill to putting grits on the mound because the ants eat them and "blow up." What do you think of these home remedies?

—Brenda

A. Aaarrghh! Home remedies like these don't work, because while they kill visible worker ants and make you feel all warm and fuzzy inside, they don't kill the queen. And if her head doesn't roll, she'll just lay more eggs that turn into ants that build more mounds. Instead, use a lawn spreader to put down one of those granular fire ant killers according to label directions. The bag may claim that a single application per year is enough, but here in the South, our growing season is so long that Grumpy has to do it twice.

FIND PEACE IN THE GARDEN

Welcome to the Grumpy Gardener, quite possibly the only gardening book that truly cares about the real you. Grumpy knows many of you are angry, upset, sleepless, fearful, and stressed out for different reasons. Let me offer one simple suggestion guaranteed to make you feel better. Turn off the TV, click off Facebook, walk outside, and experience the magic of nature.

As I write this, I'm sitting on our screened porch in the backyard. It's my favorite room in the house. It's one story above the ground and looks out on the woods. From it, I feel the cool, silky breeze of fall. I hear chickadees chattering, the cardinal's chirp, and the skittering of chipmunks hunting acorns among the oak leaves. Although our record drought (56 consecutive rainless days and counting) has dulled the luster of autumn foliage this year, the coral bark maples still shine their characteristic soft, pink-tinged yellow, the black gum wears a scarlet cloak, and the season's first sasanqua bloom has opened. Nature engulfs me and quiets my mind.

Today, the most common response to anxiety is to take a pill. It's so easy. But it's just as easy to walk outside either alone or with others and let nature be the pill. Studies show that regularly immersing yourself in the natural world is the best tonic in your medicine cabinet. It reduces blood pressure and lowers the level of stress hormones in your body. When I'm in the garden or walking in the woods, the burdens of the world lift from my shoulders. It feels good. Really good.

We live on the most amazing and beautiful planet in the galaxy—the only one we know of at this moment capable of sustaining human life. And with that gift, we get everything else—the daffodils, the dolphins, the kangaroos, the penguins, the blue skies, the sunsets, the oceans, the jungles, the mountains, the prairies, the running of the salmon, and the migration of the monarchs. We pay for none of it. We are rich beyond belief.

Today or tomorrow or next week if you can, do yourself a tremendous favor. Get outside. See, hear, touch, smell, and (if safe!) taste the bounty of the "blue marble." Rake some leaves. Pick a flower. Plant a bulb. Go on a hike. Listen to the tap of a distant woodpecker.

But do not be grumpy. That's my job.

Avoid wetting the foliage when you water.

Wet foliage encourages disease. Exceptions are plants that like damp conditions, such as ferns and moss. And don't use lawn sprinklers to water your garden beds. The right amount of water for grass is seldom the same as that for flowers, trees, and shrubs. Water these with a hose.

FUNGUS

There's a Fungus Among Us

A re you in awe of the big white mushrooms that sprout overnight in your lawn after a heavy rain? Wondering what you can do to kill them?

Mushrooms, no matter their size or color, are but a very small and visible part of an underground fungus that survives by breaking down organic matter in the soil. In many cases, this organic matter is dead roots or buried wood. In a sense, mushrooms are the fruit of the fungus. They rise from the ground to spread spores so that the fungus can reproduce. The body of the fungus, called the mycelium, sometimes covers the ground with a whitish film, but usually remains invisible underground. It can be huge too. The mycelium of a single Armillaria fungus discovered in Oregon covers about 2½ square miles, making it the largest living thing on Earth. Godzilla is a distant second.

Fungi thrive in moist conditions, so that's why mushrooms appear after a heavy rain. There is no fungicide you can put on the lawn that will kill the mycelium below. When the mycelium has completely consumed the organic matter in the soil, there will be no more mushrooms.

GARDENIA TO GRUBS

GARDENIA NEEDS SOME WHITENING STRIPS

will never forget the time my older brother was describing the color of swans to my young son.

"They're white, just like my teeth," said my brother.

"Your teeth are yellow," countered my son.

Well, there just isn't any way to recover from that.

Yellow teeth remind me of the biggest failure of gardenia. It's almost impossible to photograph one in full bloom where all the flowers look nice, bright, and white. Older flowers turn yellow as new white ones unfurl. It's like gazing at an ear of yellow-and-white corn. Could someone not invent some gardenia whitening strips?

Don't get me wrong. I love gardenia (*Gardenia jasminoides*), also known as Cape jasmine. No plant better expresses the grace and beauty of the South.

How the plant acquired both its common and botanical names is an interesting story to those who find such things interesting. According to James Cothran's *Gardens and Historic Plants of the Antebellum South* (a totally excellent reference the Grump highly recommends), "Cape" refers to Africa's Cape of Good Hope, where the shrub was thought to have originated. In fact, it hails from China. "Jasmine" is a misnomer too. After gardenia found its way to England in 1754, Phillip Miller, author of the *Gardener's Dictionary*, mistakenly classified it as a jasmine. Twit. Just because it smells good, I guess.

In 1758, John Ellis, an English merchant and naturalist, visited Richard Warner's garden near London to see an exciting new plant with fragrant, double, white flowers brought from Africa by a sea captain. Ellis sent a specimen to his friend Carolus Linnaeus, the renowned Swedish botanist and creator of horticulture's system of binomial nomenclature. This system assigns every plant a genus name and species name. For example, dawn redwood is *Metasequoia glyptostroboides*. There is a similar system for animals. For example, the scientific name for the Grumpy Gardener is *Hunkiness maximus*.

Linnaeus planned to name the shrub Warneria, but Ellis would have none of it. He'd been obtaining American native plants from Dr. Alexander Garden, a well-known physician in Charleston, South Carolina. Ellis insisted the new shrub be named Gardenia. Linnaeus relented.

The first gardenias to make it to America appeared in Dr. Garden's garden in 1762. Unfortunately, none of the plants survived for long. Maybe Dr. Garden treated them with leeches. Maybe they didn't have medical insurance. More gardenias soon arrived, however. The first gardenias offered for sale that we know of were listed in John Bartram's *Catalogue of Trees, Shrubs, and Herbaceous Plants* in 1807. (Hmm...wonder if Bradford pear and golden euonymus were included?) Once people smelled the flowers, gardenias were a smash hit.

I cannot think of a single plant more sensuously fragrant than gardenia. The fragrance is heavy, intoxicating, almost overpowering at times. One bloom can perfume a room.

Being old school, I prefer the large, double-flowered varieties whose flowers make perfect corsages, like 'First Love,' 'August Beauty,' 'Miami Supreme,' and 'Mystery.' For some reason, single-flowered types like 'Kleim's Hardy' have gained favor in recent years for their open, star-shaped blooms. Frankly, I think they look weird.

Nope, for my money, I'll take the old-fashioned doubles every time. Until they turn yellow.

GARDENIA Q&A

Q. When I moved into my house, I inherited six very large gardenias. I would like to cut them back, as they're blocking the windows. When is the right time? Do they bloom on new growth or old?

—Jennifer

A. Gardenias set their flowerbuds in late spring after the new growth starts. Go ahead and prune yours back in fall. Remember that after you do this, people will be able to see in, so behave yourself.

Q. The leaves of my poor gardenias are turning black! I tried rubbing it off, but a lot remains. What should I do?

—Sheri

A. Your gardenias are under attack from sucking insects. These bugs secrete a sticky honeydew that feeds black mold. Get rid of the bugs and you'll get rid of the mold. To do this, either spray your plants with horticultural oil or apply Bayer Advanced Tree & Shrub Protect & Feed.

[RULE #12]

The purpose of a kinked garden hose is to make you stop, look at the world around you, and waste precious time.

—

It's a mistake to copy what your neighbor is doing in his garden.

He likely has no idea. In fact, he's probably waiting for you to make the first move. If that's the case, have some fun with him by tying a cow to your birdbath.

GIFTS TO GET EVEN

Let's face it—when it comes to gifts, men are clueless. We, being problem solvers, think women want something practical you can use. Hence, we give you laundry baskets, vacuum cleaners, brooms, BBQ tools that only we'll use, paper shredders that only we'll use, keg chillers that only we'll use, and new ironing boards that only you'll use.

Don't get mad, ladies. Get even. If your husband or boyfriend likes to garden (or even if he doesn't), here are 10 gifts to present him with on Christmas Day to show him the error of his ways.

1 A dump truck load of cow manure blocking the driveway—and a shovel. Giggle as he suffers a stroke while dashing outside during every timeout of the big football game to shovel the (crude barnyard term for manure) into the backyard vegetable garden and misses the key game-winning play anyway!

2 Two thousand tulip bulbs, a bulb planter, and a planting plan. Note: For this to be truly effective, the forecast high temperature for the next week should be in the single digits and the ground should be harder than year-old fruitcake.

3 A free flower-arranging lesson. Most men get violently ill at the thought of arranging flowers. Those who don't will probably love the next gift.

4 A cachepot. What guy wants a cachepot? First of all, we can't pronounce it. Second, you won't let us use it for storing loose change, fishing lures, interesting rocks we found while walking the dog, or bottle caps from beers we want to remember or maybe trade with others.

5 Water picks. Men know these are used for cleaning teeth. But we just can't figure out how they work. Do you fill them with toothpaste and somehow squeeze it out? Please let us know.

6 Winter daphne (*Daphne odora*) in bloom. Oh, this is diabolical! It smells soooo good, it looks soooo pretty, but no matter where you plant it or how you care for it, it's going to die suddenly before your eyes.

7 A yard man to help around the house when your guy is out of town. The yard man must bear a striking resemblance to Blake Shelton, work only with his shirt off, and be available to help you with "special projects" as the need arises.

8 A Norfolk Island pine Christmas tree. Really, doesn't every home need a tree that ultimately grows 90 feet tall, so you have to cut a hole in the roof to let it out? You may think you can donate it to the botanical gardens, but they know you're coming and they're not opening the door.

9 A chain saw that absolutely will not crank no matter how many times he yanks the cord or adjusts the choke. When he inevitably chokes himself with the cord, you've gotten your revenge.

10 A dibble. Don't tell him what it's for. Just watch what he does with it.

GINKGO TREE

Bad, Bad Boy

Q. Five years ago, I planted a fruitless, male 'Autumn Gold' ginkgo tree. I was thrilled with my choice until this weekend, when I discovered it had stinky, rotten ginkgo fruit on one branch. Was I deceived? Will my neighbors start to hate me? Should I give my tree a sex-change operation? Please, help me, Grumpy!
—Penny

A. Surprise! Surprise! Do you remember the scene from *Jurassic Park* where they discover that their all-female group of dinosaurs is managing to reproduce? As Jeff Goldblum's character observes, "Life finds a way." In this case, it seems your male tree despairs of ever finding a female tree to pollinate in order to produce that malodorous, seed-bearing fruit. So it's grown a female branch to get the job done. Identify the offending branch, and cut it out. Your ginkgo will be celibate and sad once more.

GOLDENROD

Stupid myths abound. Some people believe Kellyanne Conway is the daughter of Elon Musk. Others say J. Edgar Hoover secretly wore women's clothing. Still others insist that goldenrod causes hay fever.

The first two myths are somewhat understandable, but not the last. Goldenrod does NOT cause hay fever. Its pollen is too heavy to float through the air. To get hay fever, you'd have to stick a goldenrod bloom right up your nose, which means you lack any sort of basic judgment at all.

Meteorologists can consult their charts and tell you exactly what minute on a particular day in September when autumn starts. But Grumpy doesn't need a chart. All he has to do is wait for goldenrod to bloom. When roadside fields turn into golden gardens, autumn has arrived.

Dozens of species are native. They're easy to grow, pest-free, drought-tolerant, and adapted to most soils. Not to mention their sprays of golden flowers, prized by butterflies, combine sensationally with purple asters, red salvias, purple ironweed, wild ageratum, and orange dahlias.

The Brits love goldenrod. It's hard to find a garden in the U.K. without goldenrod in it. Many Americans, though, regard it as a weed—and to be fair, some species are weedy, such as Canada goldenrod (*Solidago canadensis*), which spreads aggressively by runners.

However, many goldenrods are well-behaved and stay put in the garden. My favorite is a selection of rough-leaved goldenrod (*S. rugosa*), aptly named 'Fireworks.' Forming a compact, many-branched clump about 3 feet tall and wide, its sprays of tiny yellow flowers explode into bloom.

Showy goldenrod (*S. speciosa*) earns its name too. It grows stiffly upright to about 4 feet tall with arrowhead-shaped panicles. The individual flowers are big for goldenrod and look a little like yellow asters to me. This species is good for cutting.

Sweet goldenrod (*S. odora*) is another winner. It's also called anise-scented goldenrod, because its leaves emit an anise scent if you crush them. This one grows tall and upright, 4 to 6 feet high, with flat-topped flower heads. It thrives in poor, dry soils.

Goldenrods have two basic needs. One—lots of sun. Two—someone smart enough to plant them.

I bet Elon Musk likes goldenrods.

GRASS FOR SWINGERS

I f you live in the 'burbs, chances are that at one time or another, you've been tempted to plant pampas grass. Count yourself lucky if you refrained. Because almost every place you could have put it would have looked downright awful.

This is predictable for a couple of reasons. First, pampas grass (*Cortaderia selloana*) is native to the pampas region of Argentina, where the landscape looks like a vast desert. Keep your eyes peeled for llamas! If you hit one, it could totally wreck your dune buggy.

Second, pampas grass gets huge. Established clumps can reach 10 to 12 feet tall and wide. Plant it in the midst of a flower border and it will swallow everything around it. Plant it in the middle of the yard and it looks like you stuck a basketball goal out there.

Given the fact that the Merriam-Webster Dictionary defines the word "tacky" as "bearing a close resemblance to pampas grass in residential settings," why do people keep planting it? That's easy—the outrageously gaudy floral plumes up to 3 feet long that tower above the cascade of foliage in summer. It's the perfect plant for hiding the propane tank or screening the next-door neighbors who park two vehicles for every family member and only one of the lot actually runs.

Thus, you can see why people who have pampas grass are peeved when it doesn't bloom. There are a number of possible causes for this tragedy.

1 Pampas grass loves hot summers and mild winters. North of USDA Zone 7, it won't bloom and may not even live. So sad.

2 Pampas grass likes lots of sun. It won't bloom in shade.

3 Young plants often take a few years to start blooming. So if you buy a plant that isn't blooming, be prepared to wait.

[RULE #14]

No kind of grass will grow in full shade— not even the illegal kind.

So either mulch the area or plant a shade-loving ground cover, like Japanese pachysandra, mondo grass, evergreen ferns, or moss.

4 Huge, old clumps need periodic dividing to rejuvenate them. Winter is the time to do this. Wear gloves as the leaves are sharp and can cut your hands to ribbons. Cut the old foliage to the ground before digging and dividing. A power hedge trimmer makes quick work of this. If the clump is all alone by itself with no combustibles around, set it ablaze. This won't hurt it, and it sure is fun.

5 In the future, buy named selections such as 'Ivory Feathers,' 'Andes Silver,' and 'Sunningdale Silver' that bloom reliably.

IS THERE ANY PLACE BESIDES ARGENTINA WHERE PAMPAS GRASS LOOKS GOOD?

Actually, yes. If you want a tall hedge that you won't have to shear, a row of pampas grass does the job nicely. And like other ornamental grasses, it looks quite at home next to a large body of water. Here in the South, people frequently plant it at the beach with Grumpy's blessing. It grows in sand, tolerates drought, and bends gracefully in the salt breeze.

You may also want to plant pampas grass to enrich your social life. Apparently, a big clump of it in front of your house advertises that the owners are swingers. Now we know why so many people plant pampas grass. They're looking to make new friends who love dancing to Benny Goodman.

ASK GRUMPY

Rock Those Rollers

Q. We've been growing half-runner green beans for 60-plus years. This year, there is a pest that rolls up the ends of the leaves. When we look closely, we see a worm inside. What will get rid of it without hurting the beans?
—Marie

A. Sixty-plus years? Forget pomegranate juice and spinach shakes— eat more beans, people! The caterpillars rolling up the leaves are called "leaf rollers." (I know...crazy, right?) To get rid of them, pick off and squash all rolled leaves. Then spray your plants with a natural pesticide called spinosad.

HOW TO RIPEN
GREEN TOMATOES

Line the bottom of a cardboard box with newspaper. Place a single layer of tomatoes (make sure none of them touch) on the bottom, with a single apple or banana. Cover the tomatoes with another layer of newspaper. Ethylene gas released by the ripening fruit will ripen the tomatoes more quickly.

[RULE #15]

Neem oil is a safe, natural control for many insects, mites, and diseases.

You can get it at most garden centers. NATRIA Disease Control is a safe biofungicide that smells a little funky but does a great job on black spot, mildew, and other leaf diseases.

GRUBS BE GONE AND BEETLES BE BANNED

The Japanese beetle is unmistakable with its green thorax, green head, and copper wings. It often dines (and mates) alongside hundreds of its fellow warriors.

FAVORITE TARGETS

It's probably quicker to name the plants it doesn't eat than the ones it does. Anything in the rose family (roses, apple, crabapple, plum, etc.) and mallow family (hibiscus, hollyhock, rose-of-Sharon, cotton, etc.) are toast, but it also consumes pines, crepe myrtle, annuals, perennials, and veggies.

DAMAGE

Devoured flowers and skeletonized foliage result. (Everything is consumed but leaf veins.) Larvae (white grubs) in ground eat lawn roots, killing grass.

FIGHT BACK

Spray target plants according to label directions with neem oil. Don't spray flowers, though, as neem is toxic to bees. Sevin (carbaryl) is also very effective, if you don't mind "chemicals." Treat infested sod with a granular grub control applied with a spreader. Don't bother with Japanese beetle traps. They only attract more beetles to your yard.

HOLIDAY PLANTS *to* HYDRANGEAS

HOLIDAY PLANTS

Grumpy says this is the most wonderful Christmas of all! So instead of loading you down with expensive jewelry, silverware, sports cars, and Napoleon brandy, your family gave you what you really wanted—blooming holiday plants. Here's what you need to know to avoid killing these cherished gifts by the weekend.

—1—
AMARYLLIS

Given the phallic shape of this bulb's flower stalk before the bud opens, it's only natural that whoever you give this to might question your intentions. But then the flowers open and they're absolutely gorgeous and people get their minds out of the gutter.

What to do now. If you're lucky, you received an amaryllis bulb that's produced two flower stalks, doubling your pleasure. A succession of opening blooms should keep the plant looking good for a couple of weeks. After the last bloom fades, cut off the stalk, but be careful where you do this, because the cut stalk will gush water.

What to do later. After you cut off the old stalks, thick, straplike leaves will start growing. These will produce food for the bulbs to make next year's flowers. Place the pot in a bright window, and keep the soil moist but not soggy. Again, provide good drainage. After your last spring frost, you have a couple of options. If you live in the Lower, Coastal, or Tropical South (USDA Zones 8-10), you can plant your bulb in the garden. It will start blooming the next spring (not at Christmas).

In colder climes, take it outside to a sunny spot after the last frost. It can stay in the same pot for years. I water mine when the soil gets dry and fertilize monthly spring through summer with Miracle-Gro. In October, I quit watering altogether to get the plant to enter a dormant phase. The leaves slowly shrivel and yellow, and I cut them off. I take the bulb and pot indoors to a cool, dry garage for a couple of months. Then I water it once and wait for new growth to pop out of the top of the bulb. When I see a new flowerbud emerge, I move the plant into bright light upstairs, water again, and await the show.

—2—
CHRISTMAS CACTUS

Unlike poinsettia, this is a plant you can keep for years and years and have it bloom beautifully every time. Grumpy has had his three plants for 6 to 7 years now. Two magenta ones actually begin blooming around Thanksgiving, while my salmon-pink one starts a little later.

What to do now. Give Christmas cactus about the exact same care as poinsettias indoors. Keep the soil evenly moist while it is in bud or blooming, but never let the plant sit in a saucer of water.

What to do later. If you have a room with bright natural light, you can keep your plant growing year-round indoors. Or you can do what Grumpy does. After the last spring frost, I move my Christmas cactus onto my screened porch outside. The bright, indirect light is perfect as hot, direct summer sun burns Christmas cactus. I water each plant thoroughly once a week, making sure each pot drains well. The soil should go slightly dry between waterings. I fertilize them once a month spring through summer with Miracle-Gro. As fall progresses, the shortening days spur the plants to form flowerbuds. I bring them inside when nightly lows start dropping into the upper 30s.

⟶ 3 ⟵
KALANCHOE

First, let's get the correct pronunciation question out of the way. Some people say, "Kuh-LANK-koe." Some say, "Kuh-LANCH-oe." And some say, "Kal-en-KO-ee." Grumpy doesn't care how you say it, just that you know what to do with it. Like Christmas cactus, this is a plant you can keep for years and get to rebloom in winter with no problem.

What to do now. Kalanchoe likes the brightest light it can get indoors, including direct sun. It's a succulent that doesn't need much water in winter. Water it once so that water runs out of the pot (again, good drainage is mandatory), then don't water again until it starts to wilt slightly. Flowering can last for months, extending into the spring.

What to do later. Unless you have a room that gets direct sun, I recommend taking your kalanchoe outdoors soon after your last spring frost. I keep mine on the deck, where it gets dappled sun all day. I water it only when it's dry, being careful not

[RULE #16]

Hiding a nice house behind a hedge of shrubs is like putting plaid flannel pajamas on Taylor Swift.

If a house is pretty, show it off.

to overwater. I fertilize it with Miracle-Gro once a month spring through summer. Older stems eventually become woody with sparse, light-green leaves. Clip them off at the base to spur new, healthy growth. Like poinsettia and Christmas cactus, kalanchoe sets flowerbuds as nights lengthen in fall. However, don't expose it to artificial light at night or it won't set buds. Bring it inside for the winter before the onset of freezing weather.

— 4 —
PAPERWHITE NARCISSUS

Forcing the bulbs into holiday bloom indoors is one of the better goof-proof, feel-good holiday activities. Even my wife likes to do this. All you have to do is nestle the bulbs into a saucer or shallow container filled with an inch of gravel and then add water up to the bottoms of the bulbs.

What to do now. There isn't much. However, you'll find that if you give your paperwhites bright light and temps below 65 degrees, they won't grow so tall that they come crashing down in the middle of the night. Your paperwhites will last longer and look better if you can keep them outdoors in the cool air for most of the day, as long as it doesn't freeze.

What to do later. Well, if you live in the Lower, Coastal, or Tropical South (USDA Zones 8-10), you can plant them in the garden after the last frost. They're not winter-hardy north of there. Elsewhere, chuck 'em. They're cheap, so buy new ones next fall.

— 5 —
POINSETTIA

Before I get into care issues, let Grumpy just quash one stupid myth about poinsettias that keeps some people from enjoying them. They do not spontaneously combust. Never happens. They are also not poisonous. If you want to poison yourself, eat an azalea. But a poinsettia, while not tasty, is not toxic.

ASK GRUMPY

Honeymoon's Over

Q. We're newlyweds and just moved into our first house, but the yard and garden are atrocious! What are some quick and inexpensive additions that will make us the talk of the neighborhood come springtime?

—Corinne

A. Two words: pink flamingos. Set out about a dozen in dramatic poses and you'll be discussed at length. Seriously, the best advice I can give is to clean up any intolerable mess but leave most things alone. Bulbs and perennials are still dormant and out of sight. That bush you find hideous today may burst into glorious bloom in a month. Once spring comes, you'll see what you have and can decide what to keep or move. Then hire a local garden designer. In the meantime, pick up a copy of *The New Southern Living Garden Book*. It'll give you lots of great ideas.

What to do now. Poinsettia breeders have greatly improved the plants over the decades, making them much more adaptable to lower light levels indoors. So instead of defoliating to the point of nekkidness a week after Christmas, they can actually look good indoors for a couple of months.

Give your poinsettia bright, indirect light (direct sunlight is not required) and temps around 65 to 70 degrees. Keep the soil moist, but not soggy. Good drainage is essential, lest the plant quickly transform into a lump of mush. Remove any foil from around the pot, or at least poke drainage holes in it. Never let a poinsettia sit in water that's accumulated in a saucer. Empty the saucer.

What to do later. If you live in south Florida, extreme south Texas, or other places it doesn't frost, you can plant your poinsettia outside and it will grow into a small tree that will bloom every year in winter. If you don't, chuck the plant as soon as it starts looking peaked. Greenhouse poinsettias are the product of very specific growing techniques. In your home, you'll never be able to get it to look as pretty again as when you bought it.

HOSTAS

hat the world needs now is love, sweet love. It certainly doesn't need any more hostas.

Don't misunderstand. I love hostas. Pretty much everyone with a shady spot in the garden who can grow hostas loves hostas. Yet there are just too many different kinds. Dozens of new ones are introduced every year and people want them all. Hosta support groups are springing up like mushrooms for addicts who collect hostas. Members sit in circles, and each person introduces himself or herself by saying, "Hi, my name is (insert name) and I'm hot for hostas." The group responds, "Hi, (insert name). We're hosta hotties too."

In truth, there is a lot to love about hostas. Their genes combine and recombine to produce a mind-spinning array of sizes, shapes, and colors. Plants range in size from 3 to 4 inches to 5 feet tall. Leaves may be heart-shaped, lance-shaped, oval, or nearly round with smooth or wavy edges. Leaf surfaces may be smooth, quilted, puckered, or deeply veined in colors of light to dark green, chartreuse, yellow, golden, and blue. Many are variegated with white, cream, or yellow. White, lavender, blue, or purple flowers stand atop the foliage in summer. Some flowers are fragrant.

But the big kicker is that while some hostas tolerate sun, all love the shade. People with shady yards and desperate for summer color find that in spades with hostas. Once they plant one, they must have three. Once they have three, they must have eight. Once they have eight, they must have eighteen.

Hostaphiles are often emaciated, because they spend so much time with their beloveds they forget to eat.

Though Grumpy has escaped hostaphilia, he does admit to growing a half-dozen or so in his garden. North-central Alabama does not provide the ideal climate, though. Having visited gardens in the Midwest and Northeast with huge and magnificent hostas, I conclude that most of these plants prefer longer and colder winters than we have here. They're still worthy plants, however, especially when combined with other shade-tolerant perennials offering contrasting growth habits and leaf textures, such as carex, astilbe, and pulmonaria.

Please do not plant them in straight lines in your garden with little white name tags sticking up like headstones! Creating Hosta Memorial Cemetery tells the world you are in drastic need of an intervention.

Fortunately, two creatures are likely to stage one. Deer and voles find hostas irresistible, and there is little you can do once either has discovered your plants. The best defense for the latter is to pull away all mulch and plant litter from around your plants. Voles hide in this stuff to munch away unseen by predators. As for deer, if you have lots of them, these four little words will describe the inevitable result.

Hosta la vista, baby.

ASK GRUMPY

Divide and Conquer

Q. When is a good time to divide hosta?

—June

A. Early spring is a good time, right as little clusters of hosta shoots pop up out of the ground. Lift the hosta clump from the garden and use a knife or sharp trowel to cut the clump between the shoots, making sure each shoot has roots. Then, replant.

[RULE #17]

Shade, like dying plants, is not so much a problem as an opportunity.

For color in shade, try these perennials: hosta, heuchera, Lenten rose, hardy begonia, variegated Solomon's seal, Japanese anemone, toad lily, lungwort, and ferns.

———

HYDRANGEAS

My mother-in-law hated blue hydrangeas and called them tacky trailer park plants. She poured hot grease from her kitchen on the roots, trying to kill them, but it never worked. Those blue blooms just kept coming, clashing with her glorious golden euonymus and red plastic poinsettias.

If only she'd known the trick I'm going to tell you, she could have turned her hydrangeas pink—a color that goes so much better with red plastic poinsettias. She didn't need to adjust her attitude; she merely needed to adjust her soil.

You see, for most French hydrangeas (*Hydrangea macrophylla*), the flower color indicates the pH of the soil. In strongly acid soil (pH below 6), flowers turn blue. In alkaline soil (pH above 7), flowers turn pink or even red. In slightly acid or neutral soil (pH 6 to 7), blooms may be purple or a mix of blue and pink on a single shrub. Keep in mind that selections vary in their sensitivity to pH. For example, 'Ami Pasquier' stays crimson in all but the most acid soil and 'Purple Tiers' remains purple.

What about white hydrangeas? Sorry, they don't play along. They stay white regardless of the soil pH.

Okay, here's the trick I promised you. To make soil more acid, sprinkle ½ cup garden sulfur over the soil beneath the hydrangea, and water it in. To make it more alkaline, do the same with ground lime. Endless Summer Color Me Pink and Color Me Blue products supply pelletized lime and sulfur respectively. Depending on the size of your plant and your soil conditions, you may need to apply it several times. Be patient; results may take months.

French hydrangea blooms are so gorgeous in the garden that it's only natural to want to cut them to display on your porch or bring inside. But it can make you go nuts when the blooms wilt an hour after they go in water. How can you stop this?

Here's a nifty idea from Elizabeth Dean of Wilkerson Mill Gardens (hydrangea.com), a fine mail-order source for hydrangeas. Plunge the cut stems in cool water immediately after cutting. Pour about 1 inch of boiling water into a container, and let it cool for a minute or two. Cut the stems to the lengths you want for your arrangement. Hold the bottom 1 inch of the stems in the hot water for about 30 seconds. Then transfer the stems to cool water. Done!

[RULE #18]

Find a new way to enjoy hydrangeas all winter long.

Spray-paint the old, brown flowers blue or pink. But not orange. That's tacky.

HYDRANGEA Q&A

Q. My hydrangeas will not leaf out on the old wood. All new growth comes from the bottom. Is this because we had a warm spell in early spring followed by a sudden freeze?

—Janet

A. Exactamente! The unseasonably warm weather woke up the hydrangeas too early, and then the later freeze killed your plants to the ground. There's no lasting damage, though your plants may not bloom this year. Cut off the dead branches, and let new growth come up.

Q. I have a 'Limelight' hydrangea that was loaded with blooms so big that they bent the branches. Should I cut off the spent blooms now? How much can I cut it back?

—Jo-Ann

A. 'Limelight' blooms on new growth, so now is actually a good time to remove the spent blooms and shorten or remove branches. Cutting it back aggressively means fewer but bigger blooms that are even more likely to bend the branches. Shortening branches by less than a quarter will give you an abundance of blooms and sturdier stems.

THE EASIEST HYDRANGEA OF ALL

The blue,,purple, and pink French hydrangeas (*Hydrangea macrophylla*) still rule the hydrangea world, but a challenger is coming up fast. New colors and forms, a long blooming season, and an iron constitution makes panicle hydrangea (*Hydrangea paniculata*) a formidable opponent. You should plant one or two today.

No other hydrangea can match its tolerance of heat, cold, and drought. You can grow it from Canada all the way down to the Gulf Coast (USDA Zones 3-9). It thrives in full, blazing sun and pests don't bother it. All it requires is good drainage. Because it blooms later than most other species (summer into fall), it fills the gap in hydrangea color.

The most familiar form used to be "Pee Gee" (*H. paniculata 'Grandiflora'*), sometimes called "the crepe myrtle of the North" for its summer bloom and cold-hardiness. It's often trained into a small tree up to 20 feet tall. Rounded clusters of white flowers slowly age to pink. Recently, it's been shoved aside by 'Limelight,' a sensational shrub that grows 8 to 10 feet tall and wide with large clusters of white blooms tinged green at the top. A compact version, 'Little Lime,' grows 3 to 5 feet tall and wide. After 'Limelight' sold like gangbusters, breeders worked to create new selections whose flowers changed from white to pink to red as they age. Some, like 'Zinfin Doll', 'Vanilla Strawberry,' and 'Pinky Winky,' offer flowers that change color from the bottom-up, giving a two-toned effect.

Flower clusters of others, such as 'Fire Light' and 'Diamond Rouge,' turn from white to pink to finally red at the same time.

Or, at least, they're supposed to. Having grown some of these in my Zone 8A garden and observed others around the country, it's my belief that the farther north you live, the more intense and likely the pink and red colors are. Up north, these hydrangeas bloom later and the nights cool off sooner. Those cool nights trigger the color change. If they don't arrive until late September and the weather is dry, flowers often turn tan instead. They're still attractive, especially combined with yellow fall foliage.

Unlike oakleaf hydrangea (*H. quercifolia*) and once-blooming French hydrangeas, panicle hydrangea blooms on new growth. So you won't lose a year's flowers to cold winters or pruning at the wrong time. The best time to prune is late winter (removing last year's dried blooms is optional). Most of the new selections grow 4 to 6 feet tall and wide. Feel free to shorten plants that grow too tall.

IMPATIENS TO IVY

Forecasting the day of your last spring frost is easy.

It always comes right after you set out your impatiens.

—

IMPATIENS

A ll right, before we start talking about one of the greatest garden flowers of all time, Grumpy is going to get something off his chest. And it's not Fruit of the Loom.

It has to do with the name, "impatiens." This name serves as both the singular and plural. To wit—you can have six impatiens, four impatiens, two impatiens, or one impatiens. You cannot, however, have an "impatien." That's because the botanical name is *Impatiens walleriana*. Got that? Let's move on.

Moreover, it is not acceptable no matter what level your lack of schooling to call this plant "impatience," just because it sounds the same. There is nothing inherently eager or anxious about impatiens, although it does hurl its seeds some distance away instead of merely dropping them. We shall not speak of this again.

Before there were purple loropetalum, 'Endless Summer' hydrangea, and 'Knockout' rose, there was impatiens—a new garden plant that met a widespread need and changed what homeowners grew. Shade afflicted many gardens and very few flowers bloomed well in shade. Then sometime in the 1970s (My memory is a little fuzzy on this—but nothing else!), a new annual native to Africa showed up in garden centers here. It came in just about every color but blue and yellow and bloomed nonstop from spring until frost. Best of all, it liked the shade. America, meet the impatiens!

Well, it didn't take long for gardeners to make impatiens the top-selling annual flower in the country. It proved an excellent bedding plant and a superior candidate for hanging baskets, window boxes, and other containers. It was the mainstay of my mother's garden and most other gardens in the neighborhood. If you watered it every day, you could even grow it in sun. Howdy-doody!

In gardening, though, it's a bad idea to become too popular. This is because the greater the number of a particular plant in close proximity, the easier it is for a pest to show up and propagate quickly. In 2011, a devastating fungal disease called impatiens downy mildew appeared and spread throughout wholesale and retail nurseries across the United States. Early symptoms included yellowing and downward curving of infected leaves, soon followed by white fungal growth on the leaf undersides. Infected plants practically died overnight. People using overhead sprinklers to water saw entire sweeps melt away before their eyes, because sprinklers quickly distributed the disease spores. There is still no chemical treatment.

America's favorite bedding plant faced annihilation. Shade flowers would have to be plastic once more. Fortunately, a savior arrived in the form of a related species, New Guinea impatiens (*Impatiens hawkeri*), so-called because it's native to New Guinea. When it first appeared here, it was a novelty. It didn't bloom as profusely as regular impatiens, but it took more sun and its foliage varied from dark green to bronze to variegated with yellow. Most importantly, it was immune to impatiens downy mildew.

Breeders raced to cross the two species, hoping to produce a disease-resistant plant that also combined the best ornamental characteristics of both. They succeeded. The new hybrids offer larger flowers in a wide range of colors, as well as colorful foliage.

Older, disease-susceptible impatiens are still sold, so if you're not into waking up to a dead garden, make sure the plants you buy are the new ones. Just remember—you can buy 10 impatiens or 100 impatiens. But you cannot buy an impatien. That dude doesn't exist.

INDIAN BLANKET

E very garden I care to own must contain flowers that supply dazzling, nonstop color from spring to fall with very little effort from me. One summer star is a carefree perennial that does all of the above without impinging on my sacrosanct cocktail hour. It's called Indian blanket or blanket flower.

ASK GRUMPY

Spotty Impatiens

Q. My impatiens have burnt orange spots on the leaves. What is it, and what can I do about it?
—Rena

A. Your plants have either necrotic spot virus or botrytis blight. If you find stunted leaves near the top of the plant, it's the virus, which is spread by tiny thrips. There is no cure. Just pull up the infected plants, and throw them out with the trash. If botrytis is the culprit, spray your plants according to label directions with a fungicide called Immunox.

Native to the South and Midwest, Indian blanket gets its name from the warm bands of yellow, orange, and red (reminiscent of those on an Indian blanket) that decorate its daisylike flowers. It grows happily on the beach as well as the prairie, so you know it thrives on neglect. Just give it sun and well-drained soil and put away the fertilizer and watering can. It loves heat, has no serious pests (not even deer), provides excellent cut flowers, and blooms continuously for months on end. This latter talent makes it a favorite for pollinators.

Although multicolored flowers are the norm, you can also buy Indian blanket with solid red, orange, or yellow blossoms. Most belong to *Gaillardia x grandiflora*, a group of hybrids that result from crossing *Gaillardia aristata* and *Gaillardia pulchella* to get bigger blooms, more colors, and better form. They can grow up to 3 feet high, but most people prefer shorter, more compact, and mounding selections.

Grumpy's favorites include 'Baby Cole' (yellow-tipped red flowers, 6 to 8 inches tall), 'Goblin' (red-orange flowers with bright yellow tips, 12 to 14 inches tall), the Commotion Series (flowers in many different colors with striking, fluted petals, 18 to 24 inches tall), 'Celebration' (red flowers, 14 inches tall), and 'Sunset Flash' (orange-red flowers with fellow tips, 14 inches tall).

HOW TO GROW

As I said, these guys are easy, easy, easy. Do not baby them. They need just full sun and well-drained soil. The easiest way to kill them is by overwatering, so once they're established, keep the soil on the dry side. Faded flowers quickly form seedheads. I cut them off to keep plants groomed and tidy, but they'll continue to bloom even if you don't.

ASK GRUMPY

Beach Blanket

Q. Is Indian blanket good for coastal gardens?
—Bea

A. Yes! Indian blanket is one of the few flowers that grow in pure sand, even on the beach.

IVY

hy is it wrong to give the right answer? This situation faces me just about every time my answer involves a vine called English ivy.

Here's the typical set-up. A reader says they have a large, bare, sloping area that's shady. It erodes when it rains hard. What can they plant to blanket the problem area and stop soil from washing away?

No, they can't plant grass. No grass grows in shade. They can't plant low, wide-spreading plants like creeping juniper (yuck), cotoneaster (barf), or thyme (very nice) either, because those want lots of sun too. They could plant mondo grass, provided their family includes at least 16 children willing to set out thousands of little sprigs. Or they could plant the one thing that is evergreen, thrives in shade, roots as it goes, and covers quickly. English ivy.

The firestorm begins the moment I put this answer in print. "Seriously, Grumpy? Ivy?" someone writes. "An invasive, exotic plant that takes over whole gardens. I expected more from you."

Sigh. No matter how much Grumpy gives (and it's stupendously huge, let me tell you), people always want more. Even when the plant I suggested is the right one.

True, English ivy (*Hedera helix*) can be very invasive if set loose in unmanaged areas. Not only do its long stems sprint along the soil surface, but also thanks to aerial rootlets the plant climbs anything and everything—trees, shrubs, walls, chain-link fences, junk cars, swing-sets, boulders, lampposts, outhouses, and abandoned stills (so tragic, this last one). The rootlets can loosen the mortar in masonry. On wood siding, rootlets and leaves trap moisture, leading to rot. And if there is a spider or snake that doesn't like hiding in a choking mass of ivy, I have yet to make its acquaintance.

Be this as it may, ivy need not be a ravenous monster. The key is controlling its spread by taking a couple of minutes a day to trim it. Don't let it spread into areas of the yard you can't reach. Don't let it climb above head height on trees or structures.

While the most familiar form of English ivy sports dark-green, five-lobed leaves, many variations exist. You can buy ivies with tiny leaves, heart-shaped leaves, curly leaves, and leaves shaped like bird's feet. Leaves can also be splashed with white or gold. Some folks are such big fans that they form ivy societies and collect and trade all the different kinds.

Sorry, ivy-philes, but Grumpy cannot join you. For every plant that exists, there also exists a society that extols it and wants you to attend regular meetings and shows. The famous Grump is much too busy for this. In the words of an old Mamas & Papas song, "It takes up all of your time to fall in love with Ivy."

ITCHING FOR THE TRUTH

Poison Ivy—Myth or Fact?

Poison ivy (*Toxicodendron radicans*) has afflicted people for so long that a lot of old wives' tales surround it. Fortunately, you have me, the Grumpy Gardener, to infallibly separate myth from reality. Let's examine the following beliefs.

"YOU CAN GET POISON IVY FROM YOUR PET."

FACT. If Goebbels, Barfy, or Fleabag has been romping through woods that's filled with poison ivy, urushiol, the plant's oil, will get on their fur and then transfer to you when you pet them. So you either have to give them a good bath (wear rubber gloves) outdoors or resolve never to pet them again. Or you could pet them using a broom.

"YOU CAN GET POISON IVY FROM SUPERMAN."

MYTH. Superman is a comic book character.

"YOU CAN GET POISON IVY FROM DRINKING MILK FROM COWS THAT ATE POISON IVY."

MYTH. Think about it. If this were possible, you'd have gotten poison ivy this way already, because no farmer with cows in the field can supervise what all the cows eat. Urushiol does not come out in the milk.

"POISON IVY IS CONTAGIOUS."

MYTH. Look, we're not talking smallpox here. Poison ivy is caused by an oil, not a virus. The only way to get it from a person is by touching the oil on their skin or clothing.

"SCRATCHING POISON IVY BLISTERS SPREADS THE RASH."

MYTH. The ooze that comes from the blisters is not urushiol, but rather the gunk your body produces as part of an allergic reaction. Only spreading the oil, not the ooze, can spread the rash.

"YOU CAN GET POISON IVY BY BURNING POISON IVY."

FACT. If you burn dead or living poison ivy, urushiol will contaminate the smoke. If the smoke contacts your skin, you'll get a rash. If you breathe in the smoke, you can suffer a horrible reaction all the way down to your lungs. So don't burn it!

"SOME PEOPLE ARE IMMUNE TO POISON IVY."

PROBABLE MYTH. I used to think I was immune as a kid, because my brother always got it and I never did. When I was 20, though, and convinced of my invincibility, I tore poison ivy off of a tree with my bare hands. To my amazement, I developed an agonizing rash and have been sensitive to this day. Like other allergens, urushiol may not affect you at first, but each touch puts your immune system on alert. You never know when the next touch will set it off.

"IT'S IMPOSSIBLE TO TELL POISON IVY FROM VIRGINIA CREEPER."

MYTH. Although they are both native vines that are often found together in the woods or garden, a close look distinguishes them. A poison ivy leaf consists of three ivy-shaped leaves attached at a single point. Leaves of Virginia creeper (*Parthenocissus quinquefolia*) consist of five leaflets arranged like fingers around your palm. Virginia creeper doesn't cause skin rashes, but it's an incredible weedy plant that can climb anything.

"POISON IVY AND POISON OAK ARE THE SAME."

MYTH. Poison ivy is a vine that occurs mainly east of the Mississippi River and grows abundantly in lowlands. Poison oak (*Toxicodendron diversilobum*) grows as a shrub or vine and is commonly found in uplands on the West Coast. Its deeply lobed leaves resemble those of an oak, hence the name, and cause skin rashes too.

"CALAMINE LOTION IS THE BEST TREATMENT FOR THE RASH."

MAYBE. For mild cases, good old, pink calamine lotion applied to the skin will dry up the rash and relieve the itching. So will the juice produced by crushing the stems of jewel weed (*Impatiens capensis*), a native plant often seen growing next to poison ivy in moist, shady spots. You'll know it by its showy, yellow-orange flowers in summer. Other remedies for mild cases include cold water compresses for 15 to 30 minutes; topical creams and ointments containing zinc acetate, zinc carbonate, or zinc oxide; and oral antihistamines. Severe cases may require the use of steroid medications prescribed by a doctor.

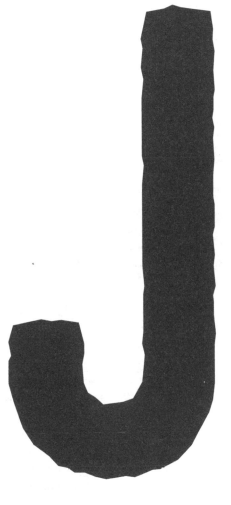

JAPANESE ANEMONE to JUPITER

JAPANESE ANEMONE

I f your September garden looks pooped, it's time to make it pop. One easy way to do that is to plant one of Grumpy's favorite perennials for late summer and early fall. Japanese anemone.

Japanese what? Don't feel bad if you're not sure how to pronounce it. Is it "Anna moans?" (You dang kids stop being mean to Anna!) Nope. It's "A-NEM-oh-nee." And believe me, anemone is not your enemy. It's easy to grow and puts on a great show. And in late summer, garden centers should have plenty.

WHY I LOVE IT

Japanese anemone (*Anemone x hybrida*) grows from fibrous roots that slowly form a spreading clump. From spring through summer, it remains a handsome mound of deep green, 3- to 5-lobed leaves that resemble grape leaves. Then in early fall, graceful, branching stems 2 to 4 feet high rise above the foliage bearing beautiful single or semidouble flowers of pure white, pink, or rose. A border of it in full bloom is prettier than Don Knotts in a wedding dress. Honest.

And the flower is just so cool! Start with a green eye in the center. Then ring it with golden stamens. Finally, add a backing of large petal-like sepals that remind you of dogwood blooms. The flowering lasts for several weeks—smack-dab in the down time between the peaks of summer blooms and autumn foliage, when your garden needs it most.

WHITE OR PINK?

Maybe it's because Grumpy is so pure of heart, but his favorite Japanese anemone has always been lily-white 'Honorine Jobert.' I can just imagine taking the white-gloved hand of the pristine Ms. Jobert, as I escort her and her parasol through the royal flower gardens of the French court before sitting down in all our magnificence and quaffing a chilled glass of Keystone Light. Could any experience be so divine?

You, however inexplicably, may prefer another flower color. May I suggest 'September Charm?' Its blossoms are pink—the perfect accompaniment for a glass of white Zinfandel poured right from the box. It's Grumpy's treat! Or go for 'Queen Charlotte.' It boasts semidouble pink blooms. How sweet—just like your wine.

HOW TO GROW

Give Japanese anemone full to part sun and moist, well-drained soil containing lots of organic matter. Plant from a pot in spring or fall. Plants in flower may need staking. If you want a full border of anemones, space plants 2 feet apart and let them fill in. Make more plants to keep or give to friends by dividing clumps in fall or early spring.

JAPANESE HONEYSUCKLE

Forgive me, but I'm terribly conflicted. I just walked by a plant that I love to see and smell in spring and hate to see anytime else. Japanese honeysuckle.

This rampant vine has probably engendered more fond childhood memories than any other plant. Remember when the sudden surprise of honeysuckle fragrance told you that spring was here? Remember pinching off the end of the flower, pulling the thread-like pistil through, and being rewarded with a drop of sweet nectar? No kid ever said anything bad about honeysuckle.

But kids grow up and then they see the real damage honeysuckle does. First sold in this country in 1823, Japanese honeysuckle (*Lonicera japonica*) found the Southeast very much to its liking. It quickly escaped cultivation and spread into woods and countryside. It has blanketed our landscapes ever since. Growing fast as a Gulf oil slick, it coils around trunks, branches, fence posts, sleeping Congressmen, and anything else within reach. It smothers plants below it and strangles trees and bushes it climbs. Today, it's common to see whole woods entangled in honeysuckle vines. Hope there are some Congressmen in there.

Trumpet-shaped and sporting long, spidery stamens, the showy flowers emerge white and then turn yellow with age. I've always thought that flowers turned yellow to show they'd been pollinated, but I don't know that it's true.

Because it is such a noxious weed, you'd probably think nurseries wouldn't sell Japanese honeysuckle. You'd be wrong. I just looked in a plant catalog and found four varieties for sale, including a variegated one and a purple-leafed one. These varieties are just as roguish as the species. As I do not wish to contribute to planetary decline, I'm not telling which nursery it is.

You can kill this vine by spraying it according to label directions with Brush Killer, but you must be careful not to spray any plant you don't want to kill. One way to get around this is to cut the top off a gallon milk jug and fill it with Brush Killer mixed per directions. Then scrunch as many of the stems and leaves into a ball as you can without tearing them from the plant and plunge them into the milk jug. Leave them there for a week. The plant will slowly absorb the chemical and die.

But do the sentimental Grump a favor. Don't dispatch honeysuckle while it's blooming. It's our childhood's scent of spring.

[RULE #20]

Choose the perfect tree for a small space.
People often ask me for a recommendation. My first thought is
Japanese maple; it's my second thought too.

—

JAPANESE MAPLE

veryone who knows how much Grumpy loves fall color knows how miserably depressed he is when he doesn't get a colorful show. Fall color where I live in central Alabama was awful recently. I called it "Fifty Shades of Mud." Yet one person in Tyler, Texas, showed me no mercy. Every 15 minutes, she posted a picture on Facebook of yet another glorious Japanese maple in her yard. Please, Sharon, in the name of all that is sacred and merciful, stop.

She would not. Sharon is the past president of the North American Branch of the Maple Society. Think about this for a minute. This is obviously a group of disturbed individuals who live, breathe, think, and dream about Japanese maples. The fact that she belongs to the "North American Branch" of this organization means that this fanaticism exists worldwide. What do we really know about these people?

Now don't get me wrong. I like Japanese maples (*Acer palmatum*). When a person asks me for my number one choice of a small tree for a small yard, my answer is always the same—Japanese maple. Its genetic diversity permits it to exist in more colors, shapes, and sizes than any tree I know. It can be upright. It can be weeping. It can be 30 feet tall. It can be 3 feet tall. You can grow it in the yard. You can grow it in a pot. Its leaves can be scarlet, crimson, burgundy, purple, orange, salmon, yellow, pink, or variegated. (And blue, if you spray-paint them, which I'm sure Sharon is doing right now.)

But not in my yard. I get dirt, taupe, sandstone, beige, cardboard, and mud. For example, I have a 20-year-old maple near the street called 'Osakazuki' that's supposed to display some of the prettiest fall color of all. This year, like every other year, it turned muddy red for two days and then brown.

This is so cruel. While she posts another photo of an incandescent maple in her yard. I can hear this Maple Maven cackling all the way from east Texas.

I have begged Sharon to stop her sadism, but she will not. She suggested that I become a member of the Maple Society, of all things. Next, she stated her intention to buy the empty house across the street from me and plant 150 Japanese maples there.

This is a person familiar with waterboarding.

But, as always, Grumpy will take the high road. I won't post pictures of my cat on Sharon's Facebook page every day or pepper her with invites to play Candy Crush Saga.

I will, however, remind this rabid Texas A&M football fan of the time I derided the Aggie Hort Department for introducing new Texas bluebonnets whose colors included pink and white. "What were [they] thinking when they took the blue out of bluebonnets?" I asked. "I mean, who wants a wildflower that fades in the fourth quarter?" Texas A&M promptly lost its next game in the final minutes, after leading for more than three quarters.

Justice served.

JUPITER

Need a tough, hard-to-kill evergreen to dress up your hotel, shopping mall, gas station, or highway median? Does Grumpy have that plant for you! Jupiter.

What's that, you say? You thought Jupiter was a planet? That's true, but it's also what lots of people call juniper (*Juniperus sp.*), a group of plants that include ground covers, columnar shrubs, and trees. They're very popular in arid places like California because they need little water. They also come in colors of blue, silver, and bright yellow. What Left Coaster can resist? In the Southeast, though, they look too commercial for my taste. I'll stick with Venus flytraps.

ASK GRUMPY

Entry Accent

Q. I need a small tree to accent the entry to my condo. Any suggestions?
—Sarah

A. A selection of weeping laceleaf Japanese maple would be perfect. These mounding, architectural trees grow slowly to about 8 feet tall and wide and are beautiful year-round. Fall foliage is magnificent scarlet, burgundy, orange, purple, and gold. Grumpy's favorite selections include 'Garnet,' 'Waterfall,' 'Inaba-Shidare,' 'Tamukeyama,' and 'Crimson Queen.'

KALE TO KUDZU

KALE

believe I wrote the first story about growing kale that ever appeared in *Southern Living.* It was the 1980s. As a result, an infuriated public nearly hauled me off to the pokey—all because I offered them insight and wisdom about this neglected, nutritious veggie.

I had recently moved from Maryland to Alabama and was dismayed that no grocery stores stocked this delicious winter green. No garden centers sold it. Whenever I'd ask, they'd reply, "Never heard of it. We have collards." So I ordered seed, planted kale in my garden, and presented kale to the South as if I were Moses descending the mountaintop, tablets in hand.

The reaction was less than positive. One letter read (people actually wrote letters then), "Mr. Bender, we do not need you to save us from our ignorance. Why don't you take your kale and go back to Yankeeland?"

All right, I admit I could have been less uppity in my tone. The Grumpy Gardener was not yet a revered and beloved source of gardening wisdom.

The funny thing is today Southerners are gaga over kale. You can buy it at Kroger, Publix, Piggly-Wiggly, Whole Foods, and even Wal-Mart. When you can buy it at Wal-Mart, you know it's mainstream. Kale is touted as a health food, supplying huge amounts of Vitamins A, C, and K (vital to being a successful kicker in the NFL), as well as lots of minerals and fiber. Love that fiber.

But why buy kale if you can grow your own? It's easy. This cool-weather green grows all fall and winter and tastes even sweeter after a frost. Here's all you have to do.

1. Start in fall with small plants from the garden center. (You can sow seeds, but then you must contend with snails eating the seedlings. Plus, your first harvest will be a month later.) 'Winterbor' kale features blue-green frilly leaves. Other popular kales include 'Redbor' (reddish purple frilly leaves with pink veins), 'Red Russian' (flat, gray-green leaves with purple veins—great for use as baby kale in salads), and 'Lacinato' aka 'Toscano' or "dinosaur kale" (thick, gray-blue, puckered leaves prized by chefs).

2. Set plants into fertile, well-drained soil containing lots of organic matter. Kale prefers sun, but tolerates light shade. Give each plant a drink of liquid fertilizer. Then sprinkle a handful of slow-release fertilizer (cottonseed meal or Espoma Garden-tone 3-4-4) around each plant. Water your kale plants every rainless day for two weeks to get them established.

3 Insect pests are fewer in fall, but white cabbage moths occasionally visit kale, leaving behind caterpillars to eat your precious leaves. You can protect your kale by draping it with floating row covers or spraying according to label directions with two natural insecticides—*Bacillus thuringiensis* or spinosad. You can get these at garden centers.

4 Harvest kale when plants are large enough by cutting off the outer leaves and letting the inner ones grow. That way, you'll be harvesting for months.

Should I still move back to "Yankeeland"? And should I take kale with me? The polls are now open.

KILLING YOUR JADE PLANT

Faithful Texas reader Marie asks, "My jade plant is several years old. It is thinning and dropping leaves. It gets water twice a week from the edge spray of the sprinkler system. What are your suggestions?" As always, Grumpy is the font of knowledge.

Jade plant (*Crassula ovata*) is one of our most popular succulents for growing either as a houseplant year-round or outdoors in warm weather months. "Succulent" means that it stores water in its plump, thick-skinned leaves and stems so it can tolerate months of drought. It's hard to kill a jade plant by underwatering it. It is, however, a simple task to kill it by giving it too much water. This rots the roots and your jade plant meets its maker. The surest sign of overwatering is when leaves fall off green.

You say your jade plant gets water from the sprinklers twice a week. Stop! A jade plant should not be watered on a preset schedule. Instead, water only when it needs it. You need to let the soil go nearly dry before watering again.

Having said that, a jade plant grown outdoors can thrive where summer showers are frequent, as long as the soil drains quickly and surplus water doesn't stay in the pot. The ideal scenario is a clay pot (because it's porous and "breathes") filled with gritty potting soil formulated for cacti and succulents. I also like to cover the soil surface with gravel to reduce humidity around the base of the plant.

Overwatering isn't a problem relegated to succulents. It's also a death sentence for many potted plants, indoors and out, that are routinely watered without checking the soil first. I've done it. Make sure you don't.

'KNOCKOUT' ROSE

Introduced in 2000, 'Knockout' rose quickly to become the best-selling landscaping plant in the country. It had everything—showy, continuous blooms; compact growth habit; tough constitution; and, best of all, no need to spray it for black spot disease. But now, nature has tossed green kryptonite at Superman. And 'Knockout' rose may get its bell rung.

Its nemesis is a virus that causes rose rosette disease. It is spread by mites so tiny that they literally blow in on the wind. When they feed on the rose, they transmit the virus. At this point, the jig is pretty much up.

An infected plant starts producing Medusa-like bunches of bright-red shoots. Flowers are distorted. The rose gradually dies back until it croaks. Down for the count.

There is no cure. Spraying will not help. You must pull up the infected rose, roots and all, bag it, and throw it out with the trash. If you don't, the virus may spread to other roses. All are susceptible. Sorry to ruin your day.

KUDZU

There's a good side to everything in life. Take tornadoes and trailer parks, for example. Why, if it weren't for the sight of trailers sailing through the clouds every spring, jumbo jets may never have been invented.

The same can be said for a true Southern icon, the kudzu vine. Oh sure, it swallows houses, engulfs junked cars, suffocates forests, enshrouds telephone poles, and blankets some of our countryside's prettiest propane tanks. But kudzu has a kinder side. Just ask the Harvard hamsters.

According to sources, researchers at Harvard looking for a drug to treat alcoholism discovered that golden hamsters given a kudzu extract

---

▶ ASK GRUMPY ◀

One-Two Punch

Q. When can I prune my 'Knockout' roses? They've gotten really big. Adrienne can't see out the window no more.

—Rocky

A. 'Knockout' rose can grow up to 8 feet tall and wide over time. The good news is that you can cut it back to the size you want at any time and it will still bloom. It's very thorny, so wear gloves when you do. If you forget, I know a good cut man.

showed a stunning reduction in their craving for alcohol—a result made even more remarkable by the fact that the study took place during the Super Bowl. Unfortunately, human trials proved somewhat less successful, because while the subjects drank less, they also became obsessed with running on exercise wheels.

But that doesn't diminish my admiration for this oft-maligned plant one bit. Did you know that every part of kudzu is edible? It's true.

1 You can cook the enormous tubers just like potatoes or grind them into a powder to thicken sauces and gravies.

2 Bees produce a delicious honey from the fragrant, maroon flowers that appear in August and look like lupines. You can also add the blooms to salads or use them to make jelly, syrup, or tea.

3 Deep-fried leaves are absolutely delicious and boast high levels of Vitamins A and C.

Why, if more people just ate the rampaging kudzu instead of complaining about it, we could significantly reduce world hunger. We might also uncover many things we thought had disappeared, like truth in government and Madonna's career.

I say turn kudzu into biofuel. It grows faster than bread-and-milk lines at grocery stores before a hurricane, doesn't need water or fertilizer, thrives on just about any soil, and you don't have to weed it, since it's the baddest weed in town. And should the world ever need more natural gas, you can feed it to cows, who will happily supply the gas.

Grumpians, I urge you to contact your Congressional representatives immediately and demand we plant more kudzu. It's tasty, nutritious, and full of energy. Plus, kudzu tonic has been used for centuries in China and India as an aphrodisiac. Considering that those two countries contain about 40% of the world's population, I'd say it works.

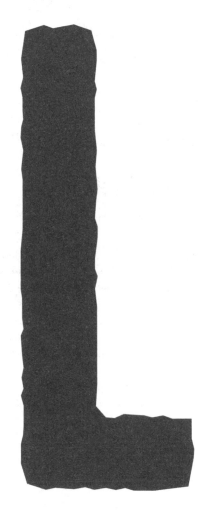

LADYBUGS TO LOROPETALUM

LADYBUGS

LADYBUG Q&A

Q. Ladybugs are invading my house! How do I get rid of them?

—Peggy

A. Fortunately, ladybugs are harmless, unless you happen to be an aphid. They come inside to visit because it's so warm and cozy there and everyone says you're the perfect hostess. But when you see dozens of them crawling on your windows, it (understandably) tends to creep you out. The best way to deal with them is to seal all windows and doors tightly to prevent their entry. Once they're inside, don't squash them or they'll leave a foul odor. Instead, use a handheld, portable vacuum cleaner to suck them up.

Q. I don't like to use chemical sprays in my garden. Can I buy and set loose some ladybugs to control harmful insects in my garden?

—Stacey

A. Yes, a number of websites specializing in organic gardening will sell you ladybugs. The problem is once you set them free in your garden, there is no way to keep them from flying off. Ladybugs work better in an enclosed space, like a greenhouse.

MEET MISS LANTANA

For Nonstop Color and Clouds of Butterflies,
Try This Tough and Showy Plant.

When newbie gardeners pray for the summer roast to end, somebody should tell them about lantana. Tougher than Clint Eastwood, lantana parties in heat, chortles at drought, and blooms in a slew of sunny colors from spring to fall. Plus, its nectar-laden flowers attract pretty butterflies like moths to a flame.

Lantana (*Lantana camara*) can be an annual (dying in winter) or a perennial (coming back after winter), depending on the selection and where you live. In general, it's winter hardy in the Lower, Coastal, and Tropical South (USDA Zones 8-10). Tough heirloom types like 'Miss Huff' (orange and pink flowers) can get big—up to 5 feet tall and twice as wide—but, frankly, that's a lot larger than most people want unless they live at Versailles. Fortunately, plant breeders have developed lower-growing, compact hybrids suitable for containers and small gardens. Plants in the Lucky series, for example, grow about 12 inches tall and 16 inches wide, while those in the Landmark series grow 15 to 20 inches tall and 18 to 24 inches wide. (A series is a collection of different colors.) Slightly larger offerings in the Bandana series grow approximately 24 inches tall and 30 inches wide. You need just a few plants to put on a show.

Rounded, flattened flower clusters about an inch across crown each plant. Colors include yellow, orange, apricot, pink, red, and white. Most plants combine two different colors.

Because the seedlings can be invasive in Florida, gardeners there should plant selections that set little or no seed, such as 'Gold Mound,' 'New Gold,' 'Carlos,' 'Lemon Swirl,' 'Pinkie,' and the Landmark series. Lantana performs great in pots, window boxes, and hanging baskets and also dials up the flower power in beds.

LAVENDER

We can grow many great plants in the South, but up until now traditional lavender hasn't been one of them. It didn't like our soil and climate and would collapse and die in a heartbeat. But now there's hope with a new lavender that's simply phenomenal.

Actually, 'Phenomenal' is its name. It's disease-resistant, tolerates heat and humidity, and is also deer-proof. Its purple blooms are extremely fragrant, not like those of the Spanish lavender (*Lavandula stoechas*) we've been forced to settle for in the South. They're good for cutting, making sachets, and so forth. Their high oil content makes them perfect for use in baking, cocktails, and other delectables.

Whom do we have to thank for this Herculean herb? Wholesale plant growers Lloyd and Candy Traven of Peace Tree Farm in Kitnersville, Pennsylvania. Lloyd recounts their discovery of 'Phenomenal.'

"We were doing custom propagation for a lavender farm," he says, "including varieties like 'Grosso,' 'Hidcote,' 'Munstead,' 'Edelweiss,' and others. Losing them by the thousands—EXCEPT one patch in one flat of 'Grosso' [the most widely planted kind in France and renowned for fragrance] that was glowing like a pulsar and thriving. We separated and watched and started selecting. Did trials alongside regular 'Grosso' and the other varieties in areas where we knew there was disease in the soil, and it simply does not die. Saw how incredibly UNIFORM it is. It has trialed all over the planet now...simply, a quantum leap in performance compared to any others."

'Phenomenal' lavender has been tested all over the South, including such prominent trial gardens as the Dallas Arboretum and the State Botanical Garden of Georgia, and passed with flying colors. It grows well in hot, sticky Florida, where other lavenders go to die. It grows 3 to 4 feet tall, 2 to 3 feet wide, with silvery-green foliage. It's hardy throughout the South (USDA Zones 5-10). Give it full sun and excellent drainage.

Drainage is the key. Don't expect great things if you plant it in wet clay. Lean, gritty soil is much better. Its need for good drainage makes it an excellent choice for growing in containers filled with good potting soil.

With luminaries like Grumpy going looney over this plant, you shouldn't have trouble finding it in garden centers this spring and summer. Go out and buy a plant—before I buy all of them for myself.

LAWNS

O kay, I've had it. For years, I've stood wimpily by as so-called "experts" and "opinion makers" launch assault after vicious assault on one of our most sacred and treasured institutions, the family lawn. I can stand by no longer.

To these sanctimonious pontificators, the lawn is an evil, horrible, awful thing, responsible for ecological ruin, stress-related illness, and the baffling ascendance of zombie shows. Only by downsizing the offending lawn or (preferably) eliminating it altogether, they decree, can we sinners be restored to righteousness.

What a load of composted cow manure.

Those bloggers, sloggers, and pettifoggers who so vehemently condemn the lawn would do well to contemplate the alternative. It wasn't so long ago that houses were surrounded by "swept yards," composed of lovely 100 percent dirt. When it rained, the yard turned into 100 percent mud, which was soon tracked through 100 percent of the house. But lawns put an end to the quagmire. Green grass cleaned up more towns than Wyatt Earp or Pine-Sol.

"But we're not living in the nineteenth century anymore," say the lawn-haters. "Lawns today are bad. They require too much water." Did you ever notice that most people saying this have in-ground swimming pools and bathtubs that fit four? Besides, where I live in the Southeast, it usually rains so much I can often go an entire year without watering my Bermuda grass.

Ask your
lawn service
what product
they're
applying.

*This way, you can
Google the product's
name so you know
what the potential
hazards are.*

Don't burn off
a dormant
lawn in
winter.

*It will look like an
asteroid struck your
yard. Not to mention,
the last time I set fire to
my dormant lawn, I
nearly burned down
my garage.*

One year, I stepped off my deck and fell into a kelp forest.

"Lawns are bad for the environment," insist the lawn-haters. "All that lawn fertilizer winds up in our groundwater."

"Hey," I reply, "ever visit a dairy farm? Those mounds you step in aren't anthills."

"But lawns are a monoculture," sneer the lawn-haters, "a mass planting of a single species susceptible to diseases and insects."

"You know what's great about a monoculture?" I counter. "You can care for it all in the same way. It's like Southwest Airlines flying nothing but 737s."

Then the lawn-haters get mad. "Lawns are high-maintenance!" they bellow, expecting me to cringe at their reckless use of the M-word.

"Oh really," I respond, "you mean like those mulched, 'natural' areas people stick out in front of their houses? The mulch decomposes, so you must keep spreading it. If you don't, you get more weeds than Ozzy Osborne still has brain cells. (That doesn't sound like a lot, but it is.) The fact is, it takes much less time to maintain 1,500 square feet of lawn than it does to maintain 1,500 square feet of annuals, perennials, bulbs, vegetables, herbs, or fruits.

"So what if your lawn takes a little work?" I ask. "In case you haven't noticed, most Americans move slower than the continental drift. We're overweight, diabetic, out-of-shape beanbags. But mowing the lawn is good exercise—a lot more exercise, may I add, than snipping a sprig of lavender or staring blankly at your mulch."

"Lawns are ultra-American," I conclude. "How can you claim to be 'green' when you bash the greenest symbol of freedom America has ever produced—the cherished lawn? The White House lawn is proof. It's a sacred place where kings, diplomats, Presidents, and dictators can mingle with the common man under the watchful eyes of the Secret Service. To stand there is to feel true

[RULE #23]

The secret to keeping your lawn green all summer is not cutting it lower than 2 inches.

Lawns mowed tall are less stressed by heat and drought, build more extensive root systems, and need less water and fertilizer.

kinship with George Washington, Thomas Jefferson, FDR, JFK, and the Scott's fertilizer people. It's thrilling."

But the lawn-haters will not be swayed. Which is why, dear Grumpians, if you believe as I do, you must let your voices be heard. Tell the world that it may no longer besmirch your loved one.

Stand by your lawn.

LEAF BLOWERS

D ear readers, you know that for years Grumpy has railed against the senseless and short-sighted act of raking or blowing fall leaves to the curb to be hauled off by the city to landfills. He has championed the environmentally friendly alternative of chopping them up with a mulching mower and leaving the leaf bits on the lawn to decompose and enrich the soil. Yet today, I am a fraud and lack all credibility. For if you drive by my house, you'll see the curb filled with leaves.

I didn't do it. But it is still my fault. You see, my wife, Judy, is a recently retired operating room nurse with a lot of energy. After she finishes mopping the floors, doing the laundry, sweeping the deck, edging the lawn, painting the front door, washing the car, and setting in motion a delicious, hot meal for later that day, she gets bored.

All the signs were there. I should have known. It was a nice, mild day. The perfect day for working in the yard after cleaning. Driving home one day, I had this ominous feeling that something dreadful would greet me when I reached our house.

There it was! OMG! Judy had used the leaf blower to deposit leaves from our lawn in the curb! She thinks it's no big deal.

I cannot live with this shame. But how to atone for my transgression? It was I who had left the leaf blower in plain view in the garage. I was Judy's enabler. I could offer to clean the toilets and empty out Jean-Luc's litter box as penance, but that would just encourage Judy to repeat her offense. There is only one logical thing to do.

Every time I drive away from the house, that leaf blower's going with me. Love the sinner; hate the sin.

LIVERWORT

hate liver. Hate it, hate it, hate it! Hate the way it looks, the way it smells, the way it tastes. That's why it's so weird that one of my favorite native wildflowers is called liverwort.

How is this possible? Well, first you have to separate "liverwort" into two words, "liver" and "wort." Whenever you see "wort" as the suffix of a plant name, it indicates the plant was used in traditional herbal medicine to treat some ailment—in this case, disorders of the liver. Did it work? I don't know. All I know is that liverwort doesn't smell, taste, or look nasty and is one of my favorite heralds of spring.

Native to woodlands of the eastern and central U.S., liverwort (*Hepatica americana*) is a low-growing, evergreen perennial reaching 6 to 9 inches tall and about 6 inches wide. The handsome leaves are divided into three rounded lobes. In late winter and early spring, clouds of beautiful, dainty flowers rise on slender stalks above the leaves. I've read the blooms can be light blue or pink, but mine bloom pure white. A new crop of leaves sprouts after the flowers fade.

Sharplobe hepatica (*H. acutiloba*) is a close cousin

to liverwort and looks quite similar. Its main distinguishing feature is that the lobes of its leaves are pointed.

Liverwort is a well-behaved, carefree little plant that deserves much wider use. It likes partial to full shade and moist, well-drained, acid soil that contains lots of organic matter. I haven't noticed any pests.

But good luck trying to find it at garden centers, despite the fact that it's easy to grow and propagate. In fact, it's hard to find in mail-order catalogs. Realizing, however, that your addiction to excellent service and information is an unquenchable craving the Grump has purposely cultivated, I have generously uncovered a mail-order source—in Canada. It's called Fraser's Thimble Farms, located on lovely Salt Spring Island in the Pacific Northwest, where I once traveled on a biking trip. They ship all over the U.S., so don't get your shorts in a knot. You'll find lots of different Hepatica species in their plant lists as well, including some really wild Japanese hybrids with double pink, red, blue, and purple flowers.

Give me liverwort or give me death! Just don't give me liver.

LOROPETALUM

Hedge Your Bets

Q. I over-trimmed our loropetalum hedge. I'm afraid I killed it. My wife is gonna kill me! What can I do other than hide?

—Allen

A. Well, if she's gonna kill you, it won't be because of the loropetalums. These tough plants adapt well to even bad pruning, so if you leave them alone, they'll fill out. FYI, the best way to keep hedges full and thick is to make them wider at the base than at the top, so sunlight reaches all of the leaves near the ground and the plants don't get leggy.

MANURE TO MOLE CONTROL

[RULE #24]

You know you're a gardener if
you consider a truckload of manure an
acceptable Mother's Day gift.

It's also great for birthdays and anniversaries.

MANURE

The soil of a great garden is like one of Grumpy's posts. It's loaded with manure. But slinging this stuff isn't as simple as it sounds (although it sure is fun). Use the wrong kind or misapply it and your plants could shrivel instead of thrive. Take a nice, warm seat as Grumpy gives you the poop on using nature's black gold.

FIRST A LITTLE HOUSEKEEPING

But before we step in up to our knees, we need to get something straight. There is only one correct way to pronounce "manure" and it is not "min-YER." Anyone who says "min-YER" has min-YER between the ears. The correct pronunciation is "muh-noo-er." Let's not speak of this again.

WHAT DOES MANURE DO?

It stinks—at least it does when it's fresh and you didn't grow up in a hut made of it (thinking Paris Hilton here). But it also contains three essential plant nutrients—nitrogen (N), phosphorus (P), and potassium (K)—not in high amounts but enough to do the job back in the day before components of inorganic fertilizers were mined or made from natural gas. By quickly returning livestock manure to the soil, farmers maintained the soil's fertility. Of course, this wasn't the ideal situation, as fresh manure can contain weed seeds, plant pathogens, and parasites. It can also burn plants.

Enlightened gardeners like you know that manure's best use is not as a fertilizer but rather as a soil conditioner. It is all organic matter (sweet!), which is the best stuff you can mix into clay soil to loosen it or sandy soil to hold it together. Its presence adds billions of beneficial microbes to soil, suppressing bad microbes and making nutrients available to roots. Plus, it increases the number of hardworking earthworms that stir and loosen soil.

SERVE UP THE RIGHT STUFF

Unlike human beings, livestock manure is not created equal. So let's grab our shovels and dig deep into the details of the three most widely available flavors—uhh, types.

Horse manure is often the most readily available, but it's relatively low in nutrients. Cow manure is the next most available and probably the best all-around as it contains a balanced level of N, P, and K in moderate amounts. Chicken manure boasts more than twice the nutrients of the other two and is considered "hot," since its elevated level of quick-release nitrogen can burn plants if you use too much. A friend once spread chicken manure on his lawn that was so fresh it still had feathers. His grass turned white. Then it clucking died.

COMPOST THAT ****

So don't use fresh manure! Use manure that has been composted for a year or so. The easiest way to do this is to mix it with straw or hay, pile it up somewhere out of the way, and leave it. Unlike fresh manure, composted manure doesn't smell or attract bugs. The composting process also generates heat that kills most weed seeds and pathogens.

ATTACK OF THE KILLER COMPOST

One thing that composting won't do is remove persistent pesticides that may have been applied to pastures where livestock were grazing. Joe Lamp'l, one of the good guys in this business and host of the PBS show *Growing a Greener World* discovered this the hard way.

He amended the soil in his new raised bed vegetable garden with copious amounts of horse manure he'd composted for a year. But instead of flourishing, his tomato, eggplant, pepper, and bean plants appeared stunted with distorted foliage. When Joe asked the farmer who'd supplied the hay for his horses if he'd sprayed anything on his grass, the farmer said yes—picloram. Picloram is an herbicide used to control broadleaf weeds. It's very persistent— it takes years to break down. In fact, even after passing through the digestive tract of a horse and being composted for a year, it was still killing broadleaf plants. The lesson here—before adding livestock manure to your garden, make sure it comes from pastures that haven't been sprayed.

BAGGED MANURE—COSTS MORE, LESS RISKY

Don't have horses, cattle, or chickens nearby? Not to worry—composted manure is readily available in many forms at your garden center. Sometimes it's in bags, like Black Kow.

Behind every good gardener is a lotta Black Kow.

Buying composted manure in bags costs more. But at least you know it doesn't contain weeds and herbicides. Sometimes, composted manure even comes in tea bags you can use to make manure tea.

I'm not kidding. My friend in California, rancher Annie Haven, produces two manure-based soil conditioners from organically raised, grass-fed livestock called Authentic Haven Brand Natural Brew. You steep the little bags in water, just like tea bags, brew a few gallons of manure tea, and then water your plants with the magic elixir.

Have a cup! It's jolly good! Grumpy takes his with a little milk.

MARIJUANA LOOK-ALIKES

Did you see the video of the guy in Georgia who said police raided his home after they mistook the okra he was growing for marijuana? Okra doesn't look like pot to me, but maybe it does to a cop hovering 60 feet above in a helicopter.

The poor guy thought the police were after his okra plants, but the camera kept shooting pictures of the plant they really thought was Mary Jane—chaste tree (*Vitex agnus-castus*). Neither he nor the cops knew what it was. This just underscores the importance of knowing your plants, so you don't get hauled off by Miami Vice. Here are four popular plants often mistaken for weed.

—1—
CHASTE TREE

Yep, this is what got Mr. Perry into deep doo-doo with those detectives. I sure hope it isn't a giant marijuana tree, because I have one in my front yard. (Hey, you kids, stop stripping that foliage!) Without the flowers, chaste tree does indeed resemble marijuana. The leaves of both are palmately compound.

Chaste tree has 5 to 7 narrow leaflets, and Happy Plant has 7 to 9. Far from getting you high, chaste tree has the opposite effect, as you might guess from its name. During the Middle Ages, monks used an extract from its seeds to decrease libido and remain pure. Maybe they should have just smoked pot.

— 2 —

JAPANESE MAPLE

Japanese maple (*Acer palmatum*) is one of our most popular, small, ornamental trees. People love its weed-shaped leaves that change from green and burgundy in summer to blazing red and orange in fall. If this one is illegal, half of the South will be moving to Amsterdam.

— 3 —

SPIDER FLOWER

Like pot, spider flower (*Cleome hassleriana*) is a Southern passalong. Only legal. This heat-loving annual sure doesn't appear legal before it blooms. The leaves look like they'd set you free. Spidery stamens peek from pink and white flowers giving away its identity. Hope yours blooms before "Law & Order" shows up.

— 4 —

TEXAS STAR

Right after college, I lived in an apartment complex where an Asian lady kept a little garden. Every morning, she was out watering, weeding, and cultivating. I marveled at her dedication until I figured out what she was growing—pot! It looked just like it. What foolhardiness, I thought, considering at least a half-dozen cops lived in the complex. Why, I bet she brought the seeds from Vietnam!

Then the plants bloomed. Huge, star-shaped, scarlet flowers atop the stems. Could this be the infamous "Panama Red?" No, it was a species of native hibiscus related to okra called Texas star (*Hibiscus coccineus*). I called off the DEA.

WHAT HAVE WE LEARNED?

We have learned that some of our favorite vegetables and flowers can cause armed police to drop out of the sky and haul off your fanny to the slammer. To prevent this, we have also learned it is vitally important for you to authoritatively identify and defend your questioned plant, as in, "Hands off my Vitex! Can't you recognize an obvious member of the Verbenaceae family?"

To help you point out the manifest differences between your plants and ganja, print out a photo of real marijuana from the Internet. Unfortunately, Grumpy cannot supply a photo, as he has never encountered a marijuana plant in his life. Not until next summer's vacation to Colorado, anyway.

Rocky Mountain high, Colorado. Rocky Mountain highhhhhhhhhh. . . .

Resolve that the only mimosa you will enjoy
in your garden is the one you can drink.

Yes, I know you just loved climbing the mimosa trees in Grandma's yard. The
sweet flowers were so pretty. But did you have to pull up thousands of its seedlings
or gaze at a tree that was so ugly in winter it belonged on Mount Doom? No.

MIMOSA

When anyone asks me what's the best time to prune a mimosa, my instinctive response is, "Any time you can find a chain saw."

That's judgmental of me, I know, but heck, that's pretty much my job. And mimosa is one of those plants you either love or hate. I hate it now. But I used to love it.

Why, when I was a kid, at the nadir of sensibility and good taste, I thought mimosa (*Albizia julibrissin*) was the prettiest tree in the world. Its leaves were like ferns. Its flowers were pink puffballs. And it bloomed in summer when few other trees did.

Judy, my wife, who notices very few plants, has fond childhood memories of mimosa too. She remembers climbing up in her neighbors' trees to smell the fragrant flowers. I think they smell faintly of gardenias.

HOW IT ALL BEGAN

Native to the Middle East and Asia, mimosa was brought to this country in 1785 by the famous French botanist André Michaux, who planted it in his botanic garden in Charleston, South Carolina. It grew quickly into a vase-shaped, flat-topped tree, 30 to 40 feet tall, and it loved the Southern climate. The flowers, attractive to butterflies, hummingbirds, and colonial gardeners ranged in color from nearly red to deep pink to flesh-pink to white. On one roadside near my home, there is a row of them, each a different color.

I really like the white, but I've never seen it for sale. The various colors are due to genetic variation with pink being dominant. Where I live in Alabama, the trees usually start blooming in June and continue for several weeks into July.

SO WHY DO I HATE MIMOSA NOW?

Two reasons. First, like almost all fast-growing trees, mimosa is notoriously short-lived, is subject to many pests, and will die on you in a heartbeat. When people ask me the best way to get rid of a mimosa, I tell them to make it the focal point of their landscape and it will be gone momentarily.

Second, after the flowers fade, the tree grows hundreds of 6-inch-long, bean-like, brown seedpods that hang from every branch. The seedpods persist all winter, even after the tree has dropped its leaves. Few trees look as ugly or more forlorn.

But wait! It gets worse! Each of those pods is filled with seeds. Each one of them germinates somewhere, even in cracks in the pavement. Plant one mimosa in the yard and soon every house in the neighborhood has two or three mimosas—coming up in the fence, the middle of a bush, or by the satellite dish.

Mimosa adapts to almost any well-drained soil, laughs at heat and drought, and does not mind if you spray-paint the trunk white, hang tires from the branches, or park your pickup on top of its roots. In hort class, we called it a "pioneer species," because if you disturb the land, remove native vegetation, and open the tree canopy to light, it's one of the first trees to appear. That's why you see it growing along just about every highway and country road in the South. Northerners, be glad it doesn't like your cold winters, but with global warming, who knows how much longer you'll be free?

NOT FOOLING ME

Recently, a new kind of mimosa was introduced to the gardening world, a purplish bronze leaf selection called 'Summer Chocolate.' The hype over its undeniably pretty foliage and pink flowers was overwhelming. Many of you probably bought one and are enjoying it right now. But not me.

Any mimosa that flowers is going to produce seeds and lots of them. And if a thousand seedlings come up in my yard, I don't care if they have green leaves or purple leaves. They need to be eliminated with extreme prejudice.

Thus, my advice about when to prune a mimosa tree remains the same—whenever you can find a chain saw.

[RULE #26]

Remember the best way to get even with someone who has slighted you.

Give them a flat of rampaging mint to plant in their garden. Soon it will be sprouting in their foyer and taking over the goldfish bowl. Before you do this, though, make sure your houses are separated by at minimum an interstate and preferably an ocean.

MISTLETOE

Kiss Me, You Fool!

Q. We can't find any mistletoe in our trees this year. Can I plant it in my wooded Tennessee backyard so I can get a kiss for Christmas next year?
—Leila

A. My, my, my, Miss Leila! You only get kisses at Christmas? Alas, mistletoe is a parasitic plant that grows high up on tree branches, not in the ground. Birds that have eaten the berries plant it up there, and people in the country use rifles to shoot it down. If you can't shoot straight or the local mistletoe has vanished, you can always buy sprigs at nearby garden centers and Christmas shops or online at mistletoe.com. Grumpy suggests that you preserve a few for later use so you won't have to go a whole year between smooches.

MOLE CONTROL

A few years back, reader Beth Winslett Fontenot emailed me: "We've recently discovered that we have MOLES tunneling through our yard! My yard looks like it has varicose veins! Any thoughts on getting rid of them?"

Of all the critters that gardeners rail about, moles top the list. Unlike their look-alikes, voles and mice, moles aren't rodents but belong to a class of mammals called insectivores. This means that they don't eat and damage plants the way the others do.

Then why do gardeners hate them so? Because in pursuit of a subterranean diet that consists of earthworms, grubs, snails, slugs, and ants, they dig shallow, dome-shaped tunnels just under the soil surface, pushing up mounds of soil along the way and ruining pristine lawns. Their turbo-charged metabolisms force them to consume up to 100 percent of their body weight

(2 to 3 ounces) every day, usually in the hours near dusk and dawn. I have no idea how they spend the rest of their time, but suspect much of it goes to texting and social media.

If mole tunnels are crisscrossing your lawn at this moment, you can take solace in the fact that it means you have good soil. Moles don't like compacted rocky or clay soils because they make for hard digging and skimpier meals. They prefer the soft, fertile soil also favored by garden plants and earthworms. Did you take solace? No, I thought not.

How do you get rid of moles in your yard? Forget most of the homemade remedies you've read about on the Internet, like clogging the mole's intestines by feeding it Juicy Fruit gum, assassinating it with poison peanuts, or suffocating it by hooking up your car's exhaust pipe to the tunnel system. These don't work.

The best, most effective solution for the average homeowner is a mole trap. One that I really like is the steel Mole Eliminator Trap available online from gemplers.com. It looks mean. It IS mean—but only to moles. If you set one of these in an active mole tunnel and a mole comes scurrying through it, well...heaven just gained one more mole.

The key is to locate an active tunnel. In searching for food, a mole typically uses one main tunnel in your yard and then builds shorter side tunnels that lead to nowhere. To locate an active tunnel, use your shoe to mash down a 6-inch section of tunnel. Then come back later and see what's happened. If the damage is repaired, you've found an active tunnel. Carefully following directions, place the trap into this tunnel and gleefully await the carnage.

Pressing down onto the trap with your foot sets it. When the mole comes along, he pushes up soil against the plunger, springs the trap, and scissor-like blades give him an extremely close cut. Pull up the trap and dispose of the body in a respectful way while playing church music.

ASK GRUMPY

Lanky Mums

Q. My garden mums are 3 years old and have become quite leggy. If I cut them back after they finish blooming, will they fill out?
—Teri

A. Some mums get very leggy over time. Cut them back to the ground in late fall, and then cut them back by half around July 4 of the following summer. They'll still bloom, but they'll be shorter and fuller.

NAKED LADIES TO NUTTALL OAK

NAKED LADIES

You've all seen them—front yards of neighbors surreptitiously adorned during the night with flamingos, crows, cows, and mules to mark the arrival of an auspicious day. But as for Grumpy, you can save those things. When I open my eyes on my birthday morning and look out from my window to the dawn's early light, I want to observe one thing—the garden filled with naked ladies.

I understand that will be difficult. My birthday is in January and it's cold. But if I wish—wish very, very hard—something magical may greet me.

Of course, Grumpy isn't talking about human naked ladies. He's a happily married man and, except for episodes of *Game of Thrones* that he watches through the cracks in his fingers pressed tightly to his face, never thinks of those. No, I'm referring to special bulbs passed along from friend to friend and gardener to gardener that decorate our gardens every August.

Named for their habit of popping up in the garden as leafless stalks, naked ladies (*Lycoris squamigera*) stand about 2 feet tall and open whorls of lavender-pink trumpets in late summer. Folks also call them magic lilies and surprise lilies because they emerge overnight without warning, usually following a good rain.

Don't confuse naked lady with its cousin, spider lily (*Lycoris radiata*), another heirloom favorite in the South. Spider lily is red, appears about a month later, and is better suited to warmer climes (USDA Zones 7-9). Naked lady likes less heat and more cold and does well in USDA Zones 5-8. Both send up foliage in fall after the blooms fade. The leaves hang around in winter and disappear in spring.

This explains why both are such carefree, long-lived plants. They need water only when their foliage is present, which just happens to be the wettest time of the year. After the foliage dies down, they need no care at all.

Left to itself, naked lady spreads to form ever-expanding colonies by way of bulblets that calve off from the mother bulb. When you come upon a sweep, it means either they've been there since the Turtles ruled the pop charts (circa 1880) or someone has compulsive trowel disorder (CTD). Send Grumpy any amount of cash you can afford over $1,000 as we search for the cure.

Speaking of searching, this dissertation on naked ladies undoubtedly has you panicked over where to procure them. (I'm talking about bulbs here. Sorry, Senator.) Southern Bulb Company (southernbulbs.com) is an excellent source. Fall is the time to plant. Surround yourself with naked ladies.

NANDINA

One of the first of many commands my wife gave me after we got married was to rip up all the nandinas in front of my house. "It makes the house look abandoned," she stated. "If you don't do it, I will."

Now that's a threat an experienced gardener like Grumpy loves to hear because I know what it takes to tear out an established clump of nandina. A big-butt backhoe. We don't have one.

This is because regular nandina (*Nandina domestica*), also known as "heavenly bamboo" for no fathomable reason, grows a nearly impenetrable network of stout roots that keeps expanding every year. Over time, a small clump grows into a thicket the approximate size of Delaware. Extracting a clump using a pick or shovel goes about as fast as chiseling your way out of Alcatraz. Plus, every little piece of root you leave behind grows another plant. Thus, when my lovely bride threatened to treat the nandina with extreme prejudice, I responded compassionately.

"Have fun!"

Over the course of a weekend, the nandina clump shrank with the speed of an Antarctica ice sheet calving off ice cubes. The nandina won. It always wins.

THE PLANT WE LOVE TO HATE

That's precisely why so many people hate this import from Japan. It's too easy to grow. It grows in sun. It grows in shade. It grows in any well-drained soil. No pests bother it, not even deer. It laughs at droughts. Winter cold is its only obstacle. Below zero temps kill it to the ground. Then it grows back.

RUSH TO JUDGMENT?

But wait a second. Why should a plant be hated just because any moron can grow one? Morons need gardens, too. Plus, nandina does have some good points. In the South, it's evergreen. The attractive green foliage turns burgundy and scarlet in winter. And no plant produces showier clusters of bright red berries in fall and winter. They're the best berries for holiday decorating because they're firm and dry, and they last for months. Many people use them to create striking wreaths. As for Grumpy, I ingeniously place clusters inside heirloom cobalt blue Milk of Magnesia and Bromo Seltzer bottles. My work will be on display next Christmas at the Guggenheim in New York.

TRY THE NEWER NANDINAS

While you may hate easy plants, nurserymen love them. They've gone to considerable trouble in recent years to develop nandinas that grow much shorter than the typical 6 to 8 feet and don't spread. What's the attraction? Compact, dense shapes and attractive foliage, like several found in the

Southern Living Plant Collection (southernlivingplants.com). 'Blush Pink' grows only 2 feet tall and wide—perfect for massing under low windows or planting in containers. New foliage emerges bright pink before turning green. In fall and winter, the leaves turn bright red. 'Flirt' nandina stays even smaller. Its new foliage emerges deep red. If you're worried about seedlings sprouting everywhere, relax—most new ones bear few or no berries.

Don't be a heavenly bamboo hater. It just diverts your attention from what's really important. For example, right now your kid's driving that backhoe. He just destroyed your garage.

NARCISSUS *(See also Paperwhites, page 171)*

A faithful reader, Cathy, wants to know what she should do with her paperwhite narcissus. She writes, "I grew paperwhites in water for Christmas and they were beautiful. They are still in the tall vase with their leaves turning yellow. What can I do with them until I plant them outside this spring?"

Grumpy's 110 percent Guaranteed Always Correct Answer: Paperwhite narcissus are almost exclusively grown as forced bulbs for the holidays. The reason is that they don't need any winter chilling to bloom. Just stick the bulbs' butts in water or moist soil and they'll blossom indoors in a couple of weeks.

However, paperwhites aren't very cold-hardy, making them a poor choice for most gardens. They won't take winters colder than those in Zone 8. Even where Grumpy lives in Zone 8A in central Alabama, they're marginal. They tend to bloom very early (January) and the inevitable winter freezes turn them to slop. They're much better in the mild-winter areas of the Coastal South and Florida in Zone 9. In fact, they're such reliable winter bloomers in Beaufort, South Carolina, that people there call them "Beaufort snow."

So...if you live in Zone 9, you can plant the bulbs outside after they finish blooming indoors, making sure not to cut off the foliage until it turns yellow. Elsewhere, chuck 'em. Buy new paperwhites next December.

[RULE #27]

The most common reason plants fail to bloom is not enough sun.

The second most common reason is parking your RV on them. Park on the blacktop.

———

Just because a plant is native, that doesn't make it better.

Some of the weediest plants around, such as Virginia creeper, hackberry, silver maple, trumpet creeper, and river oats, are natives that will take over. Choose the right plant for the spot, no matter its origin.

NATIVE PLANTS

People love native plants. They praise their beauty, ease of care, and how gentle and loving they are to the environment. As opposed to evil plants from Europe, Asia, and Africa, native plants are always well-behaved and a better choice. Or are they?

No. They are not. Esteemed members of the jury, the prosecution calls your attention to Exhibit A—the showy evening primrose (*Oenothera speciosa*).

First off, this native plant has a stupid name. Its pretty pink flowers open during the day, not the evening. You've undoubtedly seen large sweeps of it blooming by the highway in spring and early summer. And many of you have said, "That's so beautiful, I think I'll dig up some and bring it home." This is a bigger mistake than bringing home Charlie Sheen for a family cookout.

This low-growing thug spreads by seed and also by roots that know no bounds. It sort of disappears in summer—it's sneaky. Then the next spring, it sprouts everywhere and consumes your entire garden. One seed germinated in my flower border years ago, and I've been battling this menace ever since. But, hey, it's native, so I guess that's OK.

I now present to you Exhibit B—our native redbud tree (*Cercis canadensis*). People love its lavender-purple spring flowers, and they should. But honestly, can there be a weedier tree? This thing ranks right up there with non-native mimosa (*Albizia julibrissin*) and native black cherry (*Prunus serotina*) in the incredible number of seedlings that spring all around it. Every year, I pull up hundreds around mine. But, hey, it's native, so I guess that's OK.

Presented for your inspection, Exhibit C—a lovely native vine called Virginia creeper (*Parthenocissus quinquefolia*). "Virginia creep" would be more like it.

Granted, this vine does have some good points. Its five-leaflet leaves (folks often confuse them with those of poison ivy) turn brilliant red in the fall. And its blue-black fruits feed the birds. But this latter point is where the trouble starts. Birds poop out the seeds; seedlings come up everywhere.

Thanks to adhesive discs, Virginia creeper climbs anything—fences, walls,

PVC, concrete, telephone poles, the walking dead, anything. It easily grows 30 feet a year. All the while, its roots—sometimes thick as ropes—spread far and wide, often sprouting new plants 20 feet away from the mother vine. But hey, it's native, so I guess that's OK.

Let's wrap up our case with Exhibit D—the infamous horsetail (*Equisetum hyemale*). This ancient survivor from the Carboniferous Age spreads by spores, not seeds, and consists of slender, hollow, green tubes several feet high. It likes water and is often planted near ponds. But be warned—its roots must be absolutely, completely cut off from the outside world or else it will conquer the outside world. Pots planted with it cannot have drainage holes. Beds planted with it must be surrounded with steel edging or feet of paving. But hey, it's native, so I guess that's OK.

THE VERDICT

"We, the enlightened, esteemed, and unbiased jury, having examined all the evidence, find that native plants are NOT always better than those from foreign lands. While many native plants such as sourwood trees, native azaleas, and Virginia bluebells are to be treasured, a surprising number of native plants are invasive, weedy, destructive, and a pain in the hiney. Therefore, we encourage the gardening public not to dogmatically eschew all non-native plants but to choose the right plant for the right spot, regardless of its origin."

Case closed.

NUTGRASS *(Nutsedge)*

If you have lots of nutgrass in your lawn, blame yourself. Nutgrass (not true grass, but a sedge) thrives in sickly lawns that are underfed, poorly drained, watered too much, and mowed too short. Stop all that. Grow a thick lawn mowed no shorter than 2 inches, and let the good grass crowd out the nutgrass. In the flower and veggie garden, pull any plants as soon as they sprout and spread a 2-inch-thick layer of mulch over the top. Pulling plants early keeps them from spreading by seeds, roots, and tubers (nuts) left in the ground.

How to kill it: In the garden, suck it up and pull it. Pull some every day. Hoe out seedlings before they get 3 inches tall. Stick to it. Persistence works. In the lawn, treat according to label directions with Image containing imazaquin. Make sure it's labeled for your type of grass.

NUTTALL OAK

ny discussion of great shade trees for home gardens must start with oaks. Oaks are tough, adaptable, long-lived, strong-wooded, and tolerant of heat, cold, and drought. Most are also beautiful. But as with any large group, some oaks are gems while others are losers. Let's talk about a relatively little-known gem that is getting rave reviews for its looks and ease of growth— Nuttall oak, also known as Texas oak.

Native to the American Southeast, Southwest, and Midwest, Nuttall oak (*Quercus texana*) is quickly replacing some other oaks, such as pin oak (*Q. palustris*), red oak (*Q. rubra*), and Shumard red oak (*Q. shumardii*), because it combines their good points while lacking their weaknesses. It quickly grows into a pyramidal tree 40 to 60 feet tall with a strong central leader. It accepts most soils, even alkaline or wet ones. It drops all of its leaves cleanly in late fall. Nuttall oak leaves plenty of headroom beneath its branches, making it an excellent lawn, patio, or street tree. It doesn't develop surface roots and won't invade water lines.

Maples are rightly recognized as the best shade trees for fall color, but Nuttall oak is no slouch. Its deeply lobed leaves turn bright red in mid- to late fall, usually after those of the maples have dropped.

Now you may think that a tree with a nutty name like Nuttall oak would be hard to find at garden centers and nurseries. Not necessarily, young Skywalker. Because of the tree's quick growth and pleasing shape, wholesalers like growing it and retailers like selling it. You just have to ask for Nuttall oak by name. It's a good choice for USDA Zones 5-9, which includes all of the South except tropical South.

DON'T PLANT THIS

Probably the most widely planted oak is pin oak (*Q. palustris*), named for the fact that before people made pins from steel, they made them from pin oak. (This is the kind of interesting trivia you just won't find in other books!) Pin oak owes its popularity in landscapes to its fast growth, pyramidal shape, and red fall foliage.

Unfortunately, it also suffers from two major flaws. First, its lower branches hang all the way to the ground, making it impossible to walk, mow, or park a car beneath it. Second, it absolutely requires acid soil. If your soil is the least bit limey, pin oak's leaves will be yellow in summer instead of green. The lack of chlorophyll responsible for the yellow means the tree can't make food from sunlight, so it slowly starves to death. Even lime leaching from nearby concrete can cause this.

Take Grumpy's advice. Plant Nuttall oak instead. It's the oak you want.

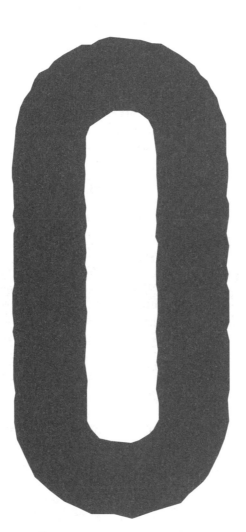

'OKAME' CHERRY ^{TO}
ORGANIC GARDENING PRODUCTS

'OKAME' CHERRY

I f you're snowbound, afflicted with cabin fever, can't wait for spring to get here, or simply have two eyes and a brain, I have the tree for you. It's a vision of beauty even pinker than the Women's March—'Okame' cherry.

Wonder how to pronounce the name? Just imagine you're calling out to Joseph Stalin. "Oh, Commie!"

'Okame' is a hybrid between Taiwan flowering cherry (*Prunus campanulata*) and Fuji cherry (*Prunus incisa*). From the former, it inherited heat tolerance, low-chill requirement for blooming, early flowering, fast growth, and deep pink flower color. From the latter, it received increased cold-hardiness. This makes it one of the finest ornamental trees for the South. It blooms great in Kentucky. It blooms great in Florida. For those who live elsewhere, it blooms well in USDA Zones 6B through 9B.

You can always count on 'Okame' to be one of the first trees to bloom every year. In my Alabama neighborhood, it's usually in full bloom by Valentine's Day.

This tree eventually grows 20 to 25 feet tall and wide with a tidy, rounded or oval shape. It's a good candidate for lawn, street, patio, and courtyard planting. Plant it in a sunny spot with well-drained soil. Do any necessary pruning after the flowers fade. In fall, you'll get a bonus—the leaves turn a nice orange-red. And you can force cut branches into early bloom indoors in winter.

'Okame' cherry is rather short-lived, as most flowering cherries are. You can get maybe 20 to 25 good years out of it. So don't plant it for your grandchildren. Be selfish and plant it for you.

ASK GRUMPY

Honor Your Roots

Q. I have two live oaks in my front yard that are more than 30 years old. They have developed large surface roots approximately 4 inches in diameter. I checked with a tree service, and the guy said that they could be horizontally scalped. I would appreciate your comments.
—Darel

A. The only thing that should be scalped is that numskull with the tree service! Scalping or cutting the roots of large oaks would most certainly kill them. If you want level ground under the trees, one thing you can do is spread a layer of bark or pine straw mulch between the roots. Do not spread soil—that, too, would smother the roots and kill the trees.

Don't add just one okra plant to your garden.

Southerners cannot get enough of okra. Plant four plants for every family member. Add one for each pet. Add two for every relative whose first name is actually two names.

———

OKRA

This Iconic Summer Staple Proves That Southerners Really Are Pod People

N o veggie is more closely identified with the South than okra. Related to hibiscus (you can tell by the flower), okra loves our long, hot summers. We love its delicious seedpods fried, roasted, grilled, pickled, and used in soups, stews, and gumbos. Don't let the pods grow more than 4 inches long before cutting, however, or they may get too tough to eat. Regular cutting also extends the harvest into fall. At the end of the season, let the pods at the top fully mature and dry until you can hear seeds rattling inside. Cut off the top 3 feet of each stalk, spray-paint it gold, and use it for indoor decorating. Now that's tasteful!

OLEANDER

O h, that won't grow here." How many times have aspiring gardeners had their hopes dashed by such a blanket statement? The fact is just because you don't see something growing in your neighborhood doesn't mean it won't. Oleander (*Nerium oleander*) is a good example.

Native to the Mediterranean region, this shrub has so much going for it. It's evergreen. It's easy. It's tough. It offers weeks of beautiful single or double flowers in a huge range of colors, including red, pink, peach, yellow, and white. The only thing that holds it back is tenderness to cold.

Because many people see oleander growing at the beach, they think it won't take frost. They are wrong. More than 25 years ago, I bought a small pink oleander at a garden center on Pawley's Island, South Carolina, while on a family vacation. I took it home to Maryland. When I moved to Alabama, that oleander came with me. It's blooming this very day. And I've learned how much cold oleanders can really take.

Twenty degrees. That's how cold it can get without causing any damage to flowerbuds or foliage. At 10 degrees, flowerbuds die and leaves get burned. At 0 degrees, the plant will probably die to the ground and then regrow. Because mine grows in a big pot, I take it inside the garage when night temps drop into the teens. But especially hardy selections, such as 'Hardy Pink' and 'Hardy Red,' bend the barriers. I've seen an established, 10-foot-tall, pink oleander in full bloom growing in front of a house in Moundville, Alabama. I know it's been there for years.

GROWING CONDITIONS

Other than winter cold, almost nothing bothers oleander. Just about any well-drained soil will do—acid or alkaline. Once established, it's very drought-tolerant. It also withstands wind and salt spray, which is why it's a favorite for coastal planting. It needs little fertilizer. Give it full sun.

PESTS

Very few pests assault it, except for oleander caterpillars. Moths lay eggs on the undersides of the leaves. The eggs hatch into voracious bright orange caterpillars with tufts of black hairs. Severe infestations can defoliate a plant. To prevent this, spray your plant according to label directions with B.t. (*Bacillus thuringiensis*)—sold under a variety of names, including Dipel—a bacterium that is harmless to people, pets, and most insects, but lethal to caterpillars.

PRUNING

Oleanders can grow 10 to 20 feet tall if you let them, so here are some basic pruning guidelines. Prune these shrubs immediately after their flowers fade. This will encourage new, fresh growth and you may get more flowers. (Some oleanders rebloom; others don't.) Older oleanders may get woody and bare at the bottom. Rejuvenate them by cutting off one-third of the oldest trunks at ground level in

ASK GRUMPY

Help Wanted

Q. Can oleander stay indoors all year? The guy at the home-and-garden center says yes.
—Connie

A. Not unless you live in a greenhouse. (They need full sun in warm months.) Do bring it inside to a cool, well-lit room for winter if temps drop to 15 degrees or below. Take it outside after your last spring frost. You can grow it this way for decades. Grumpy's potted oleander is more than 30 years old and recently received a membership invitation from AARP.

spring over a three-year period. Don't want to prune? Buy a dwarf selections, such as 'Turner's Carnival.' It grows only about 4 feet tall.

Isn't oleander poisonous? Why, yes, the sap is. Despite this, hardly anyone gets poisoned, because the leathery leaves and stems are thoroughly unappetizing, unless you're an oleander caterpillar. The Grump did hear of Boy Scouts getting poisoned by toasting marshmallows over a campfire using oleander sticks for skewers. My advice? Don't do this.

ORCHID

Ice Isn't Nice

Q. I received an ice cube orchid about two years ago that hasn't flowered since. What can I do to get it blooming again?

—Marvell

A. Ice cube orchids sound like tiny ice sculptures but are really moth orchids watered by letting ice cubes melt atop the soil to "prevent overwatering." This is a dopey idea. First, moth orchids come from tropical Southeast Asia, where ice is foreign. Ice could damage the tender foliage and roots. Second, slowly dripping ice cubes don't water plants very well. A moth orchid needs the humidity provided when its bark soil is drenched with room temperature water that drains quickly and is reapplied once the soil dries. To get your orchid blooming, give it bright light and temperatures around 70 degrees. Twice a month, water the correct way and then feed with a liquid 20-20-20 fertilizer mixed to half strength. What's that? Your friend says ice cubes have always worked for her. Great. The next time she uses them, I'm bringing tequila.

ORGANIC GARDENING PRODUCTS

I know some of you think Grumpy is in bed with the big chemical companies, but nothing could be further from the truth. Judy will let Jean-Luc, our cat, sleep with us, but absolutely nobody else. Helping gardeners sleep more soundly these days is a wide range of nature-based pest control products, some even made by the big chemical companies. Here are a few of Grumpy's favorites.

FERTILIZER

Ever since Grumpy was a wee lad starting out in the nursery business, he had a deep appreciation for the Espoma line of organic fertilizers and other products. The fertilizers, which combine the target plant with the word "tone" in the name (Plant-tone, Holly-tone, Rose-tone, Tomato-tone, etc.), are long-lasting, slow-release products that won't burn plants or leach away with the rain. They derive their nutrients from natural sources like feather meal, poultry manure, alfalfa meal, and cocoa meal. They also contain a host of beneficial soil microbes that help plants more readily absorb the nutrients. Espoma products are easy to find in garden centers and big box stores. Try them.

INSECTICIDE

Oil may power the world, but it's a death sentence for bugs. That's because bugs don't have lungs. Instead they breathe through tiny openings in their bodies. Clog up these openings with oil and the bugs suffocate and croak. That's the idea behind EcoSmart Garden Insect Killer. It combines natural oils from cloves, rosemary, peppermint, and thyme, so it's completely safe around people and pets. It kills and repels ants, beetles, spider mites, aphids, caterpillars, whiteflies, and other garden pests. It dispatches eggs and larvae too. You can find this and other EcoSmart products at garden and home centers.

FUNGUS AND DISEASE CONTROL

Bayer (the same company that makes Bayer Aspirin) may be about the largest purveyor of garden pesticides in the world, but it also has a line of natural pest control products called Natria. One of them that I really like is Bayer Advanced Natria Disease Control. It employs a strain of beneficial bacteria to control the fungi that cause black spot, powdery mildew, dollar spot, rust, leaf spot, and other diseases. It did a good job in my garden last year. It comes in a spray bottle for spot treatments and a hose-end sprayer to cover larger areas. Both bottles are ready-to-use, so there's no mixing. Look for Natria at garden and home centers.

[RULE #30]

Don't rake up the fallen tree leaves on your lawn.

Run them over with a mulching mower. The ground-up particles will filter down to the soil, enrich it, and attract earthworms. Or bag the chopped leaves and use them to mulch your planting beds. They look great and stay put.

———

LAWN WEED KILLER

Eliminating broadleaf weeds from your lawn is difficult to do with nature-based products, because most do not translocate. In other words, you can spray the foliage and kill the weed to the ground, but the active ingredient will not travel into the roots and kill them. Perennial weeds like dandelion, plantain, clover, and thistle just grow back. Ortho Elementals Lawn Weed Killer uses an iron chelate called iron HEDTA (hydroxyethylenediaminetriacetic acid), which kills perennial weeds to the root by overdosing them with iron. Fortunately, it doesn't kill grass, although it may temporarily discolor it. Some may quibble about this product being "organic" because while iron is natural, the iron chelate is manufactured. But Grumpy hasn't heard of any problems with it. My quibble is while I think this is great for killing weeds growing in cracks of my sidewalk, I can't imagine stooping over to spot-spray a whole yard filled with hundreds of weeds. Chiropractors would be lined up around the block! Garden and home centers sell this too.

GRUMPY'S BUZZ KILLER

A paper wasp confronted me last summer on my screened porch. My first thought was to grab the Raid, but all I had at hand was a spray-bottle of Pledge orange oil furniture cleaner. My second thought was, "Oil kills insects and wasps are insects, so meet your maker, wasp!" I sprayed the wasp and it dropped like a stone! Dead in about 15 seconds. I subsequently discovered that orange oil does a fine job on cockroaches, ants, and other household bugs.

Because the label on the Pledge bottle doesn't list pest control as an accepted use, I can't formally recommend that you spray bugs with it on purpose. However, say you have a dingy dining room table that needs to be cleaned and revitalized. Just as you spray it with Pledge, a wasp or roach barrels into the spray. Omigosh! It's dead!

Accidents will happen.

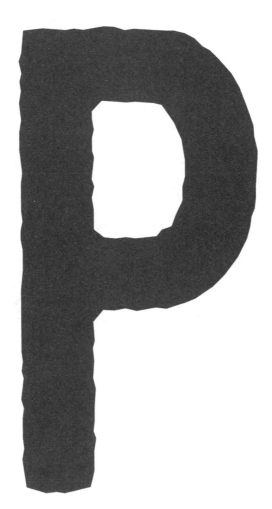

PANSIES *to* PRAYING MANTIS

PAPERBUSH

I t's 15 degrees on this January morning—so cold that when I look through the window at my bird feeder outside, even the chickadees chickadon't. Yet I know that in just a few weeks one of Grumpy's favorite winter shrubs will fill the garden with fragrant, golden orbs of happiness—paperbush.

Paperbush (*Edgeworthia chrysantha*) gets its name from the high-quality paper made from its bark in its native China. In the South, it languished in obscurity for years until nurseries discovered it's incredibly easy to force into early bloom. Winter flower and garden shows then made it a mainstay of their displays. Every gardener who sniffed its perfume and gawked at its blooms wanted one. Because it's easy to grow and its cuttings root in a snap, voilà! Gardening had a new star.

This shrub is unique in that it looks like it's blooming for weeks before it actually does. Plump flowerbuds slowly expand as the days grow longer, so that by mid-February in Grumpy's neck of the woods (north-central Alabama) any mild weather starts them popping. Bloom clusters a couple of inches across consist of many fragrant, tubular blossoms that are white outside and golden inside. They might remind you of the blooms of winter daphne (*Daphne odora*), a relative, but paperbush is much easier to grow than winter daphne.

Even if paperbush didn't bloom, it would make a handsome shrub. Dark blue-green leaves, about 4 inches long and half as wide, cloak the plant from spring to fall. They remind me of rhododendron and anise. And glorioski—deer don't eat them.

Carefree and pest-resistant, paperbush grows rapidly to 6 to 12 feet tall and wide. It likes moist, fertile, well-drained soil in full sun or light shade. Like winter daphne, lack of cold-hardiness limits its use to mild winter areas—USDA Zones 7-9. Sorry again, Alaska!

HOW TO SELECT A PAPERBUSH

Just plain vanilla paperbush is plenty to love for most people, but here are some special selections you might want to consider for your garden.

'Akebono.' ('Red Dragon'). Orange-red flowers! Grumpy has a small one that's yet to flower. It's less vigorous and more finicky than the others. I suspect it's really a selection of a different species, *Edgeworthia papyrifera*.

'Gold Rush.' Bright yellow flowers, moderate growth rate, grows 6 feet tall and wide in 10 years.

'Hawkridge Selection.' Yellow flowers, compact form, slower growth, 4 feet tall and wide in 10 years. Good choice for small spaces.

'Nanjing Gold.' Large, very fragrant, yellow flowers, 8-inch-long leaves, 8 feet tall and wide in 10 years.

'Snow Cream.' Yellow flowers, very vigorous, fast growth, 12 feet tall and wide in 10 years.

PAPERWHITES

People love growing paperwhite narcissus because they bloom indoors in fall and winter without any soil or special treatment. You just nestle the ends of the bulbs into a container filled with an inch or so of gravel or glass beads, add water up to the bottoms of the bulbs, and place it in a sunny spot. BUT—one night you'll hear a tremendous crash and run downstairs armed with a badminton racquet in case there's a burglar, only to discover that the dimmer indoor light and warmer inside temps have induced the flowers to grow so tall they've pulled over the container and smashed it on the floor. To prevent such a heart-stopping disaster, once the bulbs sport green shoots at the tips about 1 to 2 inches tall, replace the original water in the pot with a mixture of 1 part gin or vodka to 7 parts water. This results in paperwhites that are one-third shorter but three times happier. Bottoms up!

[RULE #31]

Don't ever let anyone "top" your shade trees.

If someone offers this service, smear him with chicken grease and give him five minutes alone with your pet gator. Topping—cutting off the tops—ruins trees forever and serves only to pad the perp's wallet. Tree toppers prey on the elderly; so don't let your parents get taken, either.

PASSALONG PLANTS

"Dear Steve Bender,

I have looked forward to your columns in SL for years and years, every single month. Your humor and cut-to-the-chase style makes me laugh out loud sometimes. This is brown cotton, a boll sent to me by a dear friend I grew up with in Desha County, Arkansas. We were cotton farmers, so Marion knew I'd love this beauty.

I have planted the seeds now for 2 years and this is from my 2015 "crop" (5 plants in my backyard beds).

Even if you look at it and throw it away, thought you'd enjoy feeling the fiber and seeing its lovely champagne color!

With gratitude for your great knowledge,

Judy Roberts"

Judy, the Grump may be the most cantankerous, disagreeable curmudgeon on Earth, but how could you think he would ever throw away such a precious gift? Never! Gestures of these sort are de rigeur among true gardeners, the most generous people in the world. They take so much pleasure from the noble art of growing things that they share their treasures without a moment's thought.

This was the motivation for *Passalong Plants,* the book I co-authored with Felder Rushing in 1994. (It's still available on Amazon!) We wanted to tell the stories of wonderful, weird, and singular plants you can't find at Lowe's or Home Depot. The only way they survive in gardens today is by being thoughtfully shared—friend to friend, generation to generation. The best part of the transaction is that each time you look at a shared plant growing in your garden, you remember when you got it and the person who gave it to you.

Passalong plants grow all over my garden. I have Louise's variegated Solomon's seal and heart's-a-bustin bush, crinum lilies from Jenks and Greg, pearl bush and spider lilies from Celia, Margaret's gardenia, old mums from Jason, Jane's Japanese maple, Margaret's irises, and red buckeyes I grew from seed mailed by a fellow in Colorado. Envelopes have arrived filled with seeds of opium poppies, larkspur, love-in-a-mist, moon vine, and four o'clocks. Each came with a story.

The brown cotton sent by Judy is a Southern heirloom that predates the Civil War. Several versions of it exist, each slightly different. There are also a couple of green cottons still being grown. The Southern Exposure Seed Exchange is a great mail-order source.

Thank you, Judy, for your kind words and even kinder gift. I'll grow it and share it with others.

PAWPAW

Walk down the fruit aisle at your grocery store. Almost all the fruits you'll see—apples, peaches, pears, plums, citrus, figs, cherries, mangoes—come from trees native to other continents that traders and settlers brought here centuries ago. One delicious tree you won't see is native to the entire Eastern United States. The pawpaw.

During a recent visit to West Virginia to visit my brother and his wife, Grumpy found himself biking down a wooded trail next to the old C&O Canal. I began noticing groups of small trees 15 to 25 feet high with large leaves that had begun turning yellow. "Pawpaws!" I bellowed with uncontrollable joy. "Anybody here besides me ever eaten a pawpaw?"

Nope.

Backwoods folks in Appalachia certainly ate pawpaws wherever they could find them. Check out the lyrics of this old song I remember from childhood:

> *Pickin' up paw-paws, puttin' 'em in her pockets,*
> *Pickin' up paw-paws, puttin' 'em in her pockets,*
> *Pickin' up paw-paws, puttin' 'em in her pockets,*
> *Way down yonder in the paw-paw patch.*

Why have so few people today partaken of this native fruit? Two reasons. First, its thin skin bruises easily, making it difficult to ship. Second, ripe fruits rot within a couple of days unless you freeze them. So, one's best chance at eating a pawpaw is to grow a pawpaw tree at home.

Which would be a good idea even if a pawpaw never fruited. In the wild, pawpaw (*Asimina triloba*) grows in the woods as an understory tree and spreads by root suckers to form thickets or "pawpaw patches." But you can train it to a single trunk. It forms a highly ornamental small tree with a pyramidal to rounded form. Leaves turn banana-yellow in fall. It has no pests that I know of—not even deer—and unlike most fruit trees, needs no spraying or special care at all.

Pawpaw flowers are weirdly compelling. About 1 to 2 inches wide, the reddish purple blooms consist of three petals and three sepals and hang on short stems just beneath the branches. Their main pollinators? Flies. This means flies are good for at least one thing in this world. Clusters of oval to oblong fruit, 3 to 6 inches long, ripen in fall, turning a greenish yellow. Since they're roughly the same color as the leaves most of the time, they can be hard to spot, unless you know what to look for.

Why would you want to eat a pawpaw? Because, quite simply, no other fruit boasts its flavor or texture. The taste combines notes of banana, mango, pear, and melon. The soft flesh melts in your mouth like egg custard. (You do need to spit out the large, brown seeds, though.) Besides eating pawpaws fresh, you can puree the flesh and add it to all sorts of things—bread, shakes, smoothies, ice cream, cakes, and pies. Pawpaws are high in potassium and anti-oxidants too.

As I said before, pawpaws aren't that fussy. Plant them in fertile, well-drained soil that contains plenty of organic matter. They like full shade or half-sun, half-shade. Planting two different named selections, such as 'Mango' and 'Taylor,' produces better crops and tastier fruit. You can order trees online from Just Fruits and Exotics. You can even order fresh pawpaws from Earthly Delights.

Just don't leave them in your pockets.

[RULE #32]

Don't get upset when plants die.

It's not failure—it's an opportunity. Think of it as the Big Guy looking down on your garden and saying, "Oh, you're going to grow that again? Here, let me kill it so you can try something new and more interesting."

PERSIMMONS

Most people familiar with persimmons know them as orange, Ping-Pong ball-size fruits that drop from the tops of tall American persimmon trees (*Diospyros virginiana*) in fall. They also know that if you eat a native persimmon before there's been a hard frost, your mouth will draw into a pucker the likes of which you haven't experienced since your husband last gave you Jane Seymour Open Hearts Jewelry for Christmas. (Shudder.)

Japanese persimmons aren't like that. Most selections bear tomato-size non-astringent fruits that are sweet from the get-go. The flesh of the persimmons starts off firm and crisp, like an apple, then grows soft and juicy as it ages.

Need more convincing? Unlike most other tree fruits, Japanese persimmons need no spraying. Bugs and fungi don't bother them. Plus, their large, glossy foliage turns brilliant orange and red in the fall.

My favorite selection of Japanese persimmon is a self-fruitful one called 'Fuyu.' What I love about a 'Fuyu' fruit is that except for the cap on one end that attaches to the stem, you can eat the whole thing. It doesn't have a core, like apples or pears, or a stone, like peaches and plums. It only rarely has seeds, and these occur only if it cross-pollinates with a nearby American persimmon or a different selection of Japanese persimmon.

What does 'Fuyu' taste like? The closest approximation I can think of is papaya, but it really has a delicious, sweet flavor all its own. Judy (Grumpy's extremely better half) loves Japanese persimmons so much that I have to race her to our tree every fall. Last year, our 10-foot-tall tree delivered 30 pounds of fruit!

Two other selections whose fruit you'll sometimes see at the supermarket are 'Hachiya' and 'Tamopan.' The first bears large, acorn-shaped fruit. The second looks like a big, flattened tomato with puffy lips and a big smile. Unlike 'Fuyu,' they remain puckering until fully ripe.

Fall, winter, and spring are good times to plant Japanese persimmons in the South. Here are some of the basic facts you'll want to know.

Size: About 25 feet tall, 30 feet wide

Light: Full sun

Soil: Well-drained

Prune: Prune young trees in spring to open up the center of the trees and provide well-spaced branches aiming outward. Pruning is seldom needed after that.

Nutrition: Japanese persimmons are an excellent source of Vitamins A, C, and B6 and also dietary fiber. Two a day keep the Ex-Lax away!

Pests: Family members that pick all the fruit, leaving none for you.

Growing zones: Upper through Coastal South (USDA Zones 6-9)

ASK GRUMPY

Heat Lovers

Q: I purchased some starter pepper plants from the local hardware store and planted them directly into rich organic mushroom compost. They are budding, but I am not noticing a lot of foliage growth. What am I doing wrong?

—Daphanie

A: Pepper plants love the heat. In cool weather, they don't do much. Mushroom compost works fine as a soil medium but contains few nutrients. Peppers are heavy feeders, so to get plenty of foliage and fruit, you need to fertilize regularly. Try feeding your plants with some Miracle-Gro or Espoma Garden-tone.

PET-DEADLY PLANTS

A recent email from a reader telling of the tragic death of her dog after consuming the seed of a sago palm set me to thinking: "How many garden plants out there are toxic to dogs and cats?" A simple Google search revealed an astonishing answer—literally hundreds and hundreds. In fact, looking through my garden, it was hard to find a plant growing in it that wouldn't sicken or kill these pets if certain plant parts were ingested.

That begs the question: Why are cats and dogs still running around in our neighborhoods? Given the ubiquity of pet-toxic plants, shouldn't all of them be poisoned and dead by now?

No. The reason is that most plants toxic to cats and dogs don't look palatable and don't taste good so pets ignore them. Azaleas are a great example. They're found in just about every yard where they will grow. And they can be lethal to dogs and cats if consumed. Why don't we find stacks of dog and cat corpses surrounding every azalea in the yard? Because dogs and cats don't eat them. They may pee on them, but they don't eat them.

The plants you need to worry about are ones that produce a berry, fruit, seed, nut, or flower that looks tasty to animals and is capable of severely sickening or killing pets. (FYI, many of them have the same effect on you.) Here are eight.

—1—
CASTOR BEAN

Ricinus communis. This striking plant is prized in the South for its bold, exotic foliage and colorful seedpods. Unfortunately, all parts of it are extremely toxic to animals, particularly the seeds. They contain a substance called ricin, more powerful than cyanide. Say sayonara to any pet that eats one.

—2—
CHINABERRY

Melia azedarach. Chinaberry is a weedy tree imported from China that grows practically anywhere it's cold-hardy. Clusters of fragrant, lilac-colored flowers in spring give rise to yellow, berrylike fruits in summer and fall that turn soft and squishy when they hit the ground. Farewell, Fido, if he eats them.

—3—
FOXGLOVE

Digitalis purpurea. One look at the magnificent, stately spires of this biennial tells you why it's so common in our gardens. Trouble is, every part of the plant is extremely toxic to pet and pet owner. Don't decorate your salad with the flowers—or Fluffy's food bowl either.

[RULE #33]

It's easy to keep dogs from digging up your flowers.

Get rid of one or the other.

———

HEAVENLY BAMBOO

Nandina domestica. Heavenly bamboo is a very popular landscape shrub because it grows in sun or shade, is nearly impossible to kill, and bears large clusters of bright-red, long-lasting berries in fall and winter that are great for holiday decorating. If your pet eats too many of them, however, your next Christmas gift could be a jar of ashes.

— 5 —
LILIES

Lilium sp. Fans of dead cat jokes will appreciate this one. Lilies—all kinds of lilies—are no danger to dogs, but lethal to cats if ingested. Hmmmm. I have a 20-year-old, cantankerous, neurotic cat whose cacophonous yowling every two hours during the night is driving me insane. I think he needs a little gift to reassure him that he's loved. What will it be? Oh, I don't know. A lily?

MILKWEED

Asclepias sp. How can this be? How can this American wildflower, the sole source of food for the larvae of our treasured monarch butterflies, be so dangerous to our beloved cats and dogs? Sorry, I don't make up this stuff, I just report the facts. And the facts say that all parts of a milkweed plant are potentially fatal if ingested by dogs and cats. So if you're adding milkweeds to your garden to see more monarchs, you may be seeing fewer bundles of love.

> ASK GRUMPY

Raining Pinecones

Q. Right now, I have about a ton of pinecone "petals" in my yard from squirrels gnawing on the cones. Raking them up is murder on my back. What do you do with them after you rake?

—Joan

A. Squirrels love to eat the seeds in the pinecones at this time of year. When this happens with my trees, I rake up the pinecone scales and use them to mulch my beds. It looks good and works well.

— 7 —
SAGO PALM

Cycas revoluta. Treasured for its handsome, feathery fronds, this shrub has separate sexes that are easily distinguished when they flower. The male produces a conical structure covered with pollen from the center of the fronds. He's no threat to pets. Females, however, produce a rounded structure that develops egg-shaped, red or orange seeds. One seed can kill your pet. Moral of the story—never trust a female.

— 8 —
YEW

Taxus sp. Widely grown group of needleleaf, evergreen shrubs bearing bright red, soft, juicy fruits that look yummy. In Bowser's tummy, they can kill.

PLASTIC FLOWERS

It's Plastic? Fantastic

Q. I dug up a huge clump of pampas grass and now see two oil pipes sticking out of the ground. What plants can I use to hide them that cost next to nothing, need no maintenance, and bloom 365 days a year?

—Charles

A. There is only one answer—plastic flowers. They're cheap, don't require watering, don't need fertilizer, never stop blooming, and last forever. Best of all, they come in bizarre colors that real flowers don't offer! You can have blue poinsettias, purple daffodils, orange hydrangeas, and golden geraniums. Remember, though, that good design requires flowers to be seasonally appropriate. Don't display poinsettias in summer or geraniums in winter, or people will think you're clueless. (Okay, I'm just kidding. No real plant meets all of your requirements, so I'd use boxwood or 'Yewtopia' plum yew to hide the pipes.)

POINSETTIA

Okay, how many times have you heard people say something like this? "Be sure to keep poinsettias away from children and pets, because they might eat the leaves and get poisoned."

Poinsettias are NOT poisonous. The milky sap might not look appetizing (which is why very few sentient people would actually eat the leaves), but it won't kill you. In fact, you could eat 500 leaves and the worst you would suffer is a stomachache. That's nothing compared to the suffering of the poor plant that donated the leaves.

Look, I'm not suggesting adding poinsettia leaves to your mesclun salad, but there are far more toxic plants around your house and garden (dieffenbachia, angel's trumpet, azalea, castor bean, mountain laurel, rhododendron, hydrangea, Japanese yew, oleander) and you don't give those a second thought.

No one has ever died from eating a poinsettia. The KGB has never bumped off an enemy agent by feeding him a poinsettia. Stop spreading this stupid myth! And while you're at it, stop repeating that Tiger Woods was raised by tigers in the woods! (He was raised by a very nice panda.)

POPPIES

The poppies that do best in heat and humidity are annuals that flower in spring, set seed, die, and then come back from seed the next year. Examples: Iceland poppies, Shirley poppies, and Grumpy's favorite, opium poppy (*Papaver somniferum*). Yes, the latter is the same kind that villagers in Afghanistan grow for opium. It's also the one that Dorothy, the Tin Man, the Scarecrow, and the Cowardly Lion ran through to get to the Emerald City—AND the one you eat on poppy seed rolls that make you fail your drug test to be a Wal-Mart greeter. It's still legal to sell the seeds though.

[RULE #34]

Old and dry potting soil will not absorb water.

Fix this by slowly pouring water containing a drop or two of liquid detergent into it and stirring with a stick or spoon. It will absorb water from then on.

PRAYING MANTIS

Looking for an unusual pet? One that doesn't bark, shed, or need shots or a litter box, and it will look you straight in the eye with obvious affection? You need a praying mantis!

An insect for a pet? Why not? Can you honestly say pet rats, hedgehogs, toads, hermit crabs, ferrets, and encyclopedia salesmen are any weirder? No, you cannot.

About 2,400 species of mantises exist worldwide, ranging in size from tiny ones about an inch long to giants more than 5 inches long. You instantly recognize them by their triangular heads with two bulbous eyes and their folded, spiny forelegs held in a "praying position," hence the name. Their swiveled heads can turn 180 degrees to watch you, which is both cool and makes you glad you're much bigger than they are. These ambush predators usually wait motionless on a leaf or branch that matches their color for an unsuspecting bug to walk by, then seize it with their forelegs and devour it headfirst. ("Dibs on the brains!")

Although mantises are often praised as beneficial insects for eating a raft of destructive insects such as flies, caterpillars, beetles, and roaches, in truth they're garden-neutrals. They'll eat anything they can overpower, including bees, butterflies, small lizards, and (horrors!) even hummingbirds. And if a prehistoric one the size of a Boeing 747 gets loose because an Antarctic volcano melts the glacier it has been trapped in for tens of thousands of years, humans are on the menu too. A famous documentary film produced by the Defense Department in 1957, "The Deadly Mantis," conclusively proved this, as the 200-foot-long mantis first gobbled down two teenagers at a dance and then attacked a school bus and dined on its terrified passengers.

Fortunately, this only happened once.

The three most common mantises in the United States are the European mantis (*Mantis religiosa*), the

---

[RULES #35 & #36]

The best time to prune spring flowering trees and shrubs is right after they bloom.

If you wait until summer or fall, you'll cut off a lot of the flowerbuds for next year. Examples: forsythia, azalea, quince, spiraea, lilac, and Japanese magnolias.

Power company pruning crews are not artists.

If they say they're going to prune your trees, assume they will do so in the ugliest way possible—though they generally wreak less destruction if you're there as a witness.

Chinese mantis (*Tenodera sinensis*), and the Carolina praying mantis (*Stagnomantis carolina*), which is native to the South. The latter is usually green, but can be brown. Females grow 2 to 3 inches long, and males a little smaller. Its egg case looks like a tiny loaf of bread. Each one of those chambers contains a baby mantis just waiting to meet you.

Another common one is a giant introduced from China, the Chinese praying mantis (*Tenodera aridifolia*). It grows up to 5 inches long, and can be green, tan, brown, or a combo of these colors. The egg case of the Chinese mantis looks like a blob of hardened foam.

One myth about praying mantises Grumpy would like to dispel is that immediately after mating, the female bites off the male's head and eats him. While this does occur on occasion—like when she's really hungry or he forgets her birthday—this is by no means the rule.

Now that you desperately want a pet praying mantis, how do you get started? Where does one go to find a tiny mantis leash or chew toy? Fortunately, websites abound that can help you purchase mantis egg cases, mantis cages, mantis food, and mantis treats. Try Mantis Pets or The Praying Mantis Shop. And don't worry about mantises biting you—they won't do that. Well, except if they're as big as a 747. Then all bets are off.

HOW TO TOP
A POT

One problem with growing plants in a container is keeping potting soil from washing out over the rim when you water. So add a thin layer of mulch to the soil up to the pot's rim. You can use gravel or tumbled glass, but Grumpy's favorite is plain old pine bark mini nuggets. Mulching also gives a nice, finished look.

‹‹‹‹‹

ASK GRUMPY
Puny Pumpkins

Q. I'm trying to grow prizewinning pumpkins. I started seedlings in a tray and then transplanted them to big containers. The last transplant caused them to wilt completely. How can I minimize shock?
—Isabel

A. Forget about growing those 800-pound behemoths. You can't do that in containers. Each giant pumpkin plant needs about 400 square feet of garden, and you get only one pumpkin per plant. Instead, sow seeds of small-fruited kinds (5 pounds or less) such as 'Small Sugar,' 'Jack Be Little,' and 'Baby Boo' directly into the pots in spring.

QUEEN ANNE'S LACE TO QUISQUALIS

QUEEN ANNE'S LACE

Some people will stop at nothing to get a wildflower named after them. Take, for instance, that notorious schemer, Queen Anne of England (1665-1714). Whilst sewing some lace like proper queens always do, she just happened to prick her finger with the needle, causing a single drop of royal blood to fall upon the white linen. She immediately called her press secretary and ordered him to brief the chroniclers of the day about this momentous event.

The press secretary, Sir Sean Spoofer, held up the stained fabric in front of the assembled press and asked, "What flower does this remind us of?"

"Wild carrot!" replied the scribes in unison.

"From now on," decreed Spoofer, "this blossom shall be known hither and yon as 'Queen Anne's wild carrot.'"

"'Queen Anne's lace' would be a prettier name," piped up a pamphleteer in the crowd. "Ladies like lace, ya know."

"He's right," remarked a nearby diarist. "Clearly, 'Queen Anne's lace' is a most gracious name that evokes the beauty and elegance of Her Majesty."

"Shut up!" hollered Spoofer. "Don't make me clear this room! The name is official. Queen Anne's carrot. This briefing is ended." Clutching the lace that was now named a carrot, he stormed from the room, fell through a trap door secretly triggered by the Queen listening through a peep hole, and was never seen again.

"Idiot," she muttered.

Now you know the rest of the story.

The reason the press shouted out, "wild carrot" in the first place is that Queen Anne's lace really is a carrot, albeit a grossly inferior one culinarily speaking. Only a few genes separate it from our cultivated carrot, *Daucus carota sativus*, that we prize for its large, sweet root. The smaller, woody root of Queen Anne's lace is edible if you're a starving English peasant. We are not, so we grow it for its flowers.

Queen Anne's lace is a biennial. It grows carrot-like foliage the first year. The second year, flat-topped flower clusters appear atop 3-foot stems in June. The inflorescences are called umbels. Each tiny flower is attached by a pedicel to the same points on the stems. One or two flowers in the center of an umbel may be purplish red, although I have not seen this. After the umbel fades, it curls up into a clump of seeds that resembles a bird's nest. Seeds disperse widely and germinate readily before the plant dies. This explains how Queen Anne's lace has become naturalized across most of the United States.

Ah, you noticed I said "naturalized," like a "naturalized citizen." Queen Anne's lace is not native to this country but to Europe. Oh no! This makes it an invasive, exotic weed destined to destroy our ecosystems!

Well, I think the prettiest flower in a summer meadow is no big threat. It makes a nice cut flower. Lots of butterflies dine on its nectar.

There's an abandoned, foreclosed house across the street from me where people stopped mowing months ago. Weeds have taken over, tall enough to hide Sir Spoofer. Perhaps I shall sneak over at night and sow some Queen Anne's lace. Should someone question my motive, I'll just say I'm planting carrots.

'QUEEN MUM' AGAPANTHUS

Also called lily-of-the-Nile, 'Queen Mum' Agapanthus is one of those plants people see while on vacation in California, Florida, and along the Gulf coast that they fruitlessly covet because it won't take their cold winters back home. In this regard, 'Queen Mum' rules! It's hardy down to 10 degrees. In late spring and summer, 3-foot stems rise from clumps of strap-like leaves crowned by clusters of white and violet-blue flowers the size of softballs. This perennial is great for flowerbeds and containers. It needs full to part-sun, tolerates drought, and deer won't eat it. If it still won't take winter in your area, grow it in a pot and take it indoors.

ASK GRUMPY

All Hail the Queen

Q. This summer, I cut seedheads of Queen Anne's lace. Is this plant invasive? Would it be crazy to sprinkle the seeds in my garden now?

—Jill

A. Queen Anne's lace (*Daucus carota carota*) may not be native, but this sister of the carrot is one of Grumpy's favorite early summer wildflowers. It's biennial, growing foliage the first year and then flowering, setting seed, and dying the second. Sow seeds now or in spring for flowers the next year. One seedhead per garden is plenty. If too many seedlings sprout, just pull up the ones you don't want—no problem. When you see the pretty blooms of the ones you left, you'll go bonkers. But leave the inedible roots for Bugs Bunny to enjoy.

QUINCE

One of the first plants to bloom every year is flowering quince. It blooms so early, in fact, I'm loathe to call it a spring-blooming shrub. Depending on the mildness of the winter, it can start as early as January. Thanks to the fact that most of the U.S. has decided to skip winter this year, it's probably blooming now in your neck of the woods or soon will be.

Flowers appear before the leaves and put on a spectacular show. They may be single, semidouble, or double in colors of white, pink, red, salmon, orange, or multicolors. You can enjoy them in the yard, clip blooming branches for display, or clip budded branches and place them in water-filled vases to watch the flowers open indoors.

Unlike its cousin, the fruiting quince (*Cydonia oblonga*), flowering quince (*Chaenomeles speciosa*) is grown mainly for flowers, not fruit. However, some selections do bear small, hard, delightfully aromatic fruits in fall that you can smell from far away. The fruits contain lots of pectin, making them good for jelly or preserves provided you add copious amounts of sugar. Reliably fruiting selections include 'Apple Blossom' (light pink flowers), 'Cameo' (double salmon), 'Texas Scarlet' (tomato red), and 'Toyo Nishiki' (white, pink, and red). Planting two different selections for cross-pollination gives a bigger crop.

Flowering quince is found in so many gardens because, in addition to its lovely blooms, it's easy to grow and hard to kill. Deer won't eat it. Leaf spot may defoliate it by midsummer in humid areas, but that won't reduce flowering the next year. It likes full sun and well-drained soil. Adapted to USDA Zones 4-9, it grows 3 to 8 feet tall and wide depending on the selection. Prune it immediately after it finishes blooming.

ASK GRUMPY

Quince Question

Q. I live in North Carolina, and the weather has been unusually warm. My quince bush has already bloomed. Will it flower again in the spring?
—Jean

A. Sorry, but flowering quince, like many spring-blooming shrubs, produces only one crop of flowers a year. Any bloom that opens in winter is one less flower in spring. There's nothing you can do but sigh. I'll sigh too.

QUISQUALIS

G rumpy's loathing for plant taxonomists knows no bounds. Like the masons, taxonomists are a secret society that operates in the shadows. Its members get to decide the botanical (Latin) names of plants—the genus and the species. Only once they assign such names to plants, they feel free to change them about every three years so that the gardening public has no idea which plants to ask for at the garden center.

For example, coleus and aster used to be named just that. You could go to a nursery and say, "I want a coleus and an aster" and you would be shown those two plants. This made taxonomists furious, so they changed the genus names to *Solenostemon* and *Symphyotrichum*, respectively. This really toasts my aster.

And now, I'm really mad. The concept for this book requires me to talk about at least one plant or gardening activity for every letter in the alphabet. Have you any idea how hard it is to find multiple plants whose names start with the letter "Q"? I racked my brain for hours before I finally found a fourth one: *Quisqualis indica* aka "Rangoon creeper."

Native to Burma, Malaysia, New Guinea, and the Philippines, Rangoon creeper is a very cool plant. Translated from the Latin, *Quisqualis* means "Who?" and "What?" This is because it confused early botanists. In youth, it is shrubby. As it ages, it becomes a scrambling vine.

Fragrant, tubular flowers up to 3 inches long appear on the end of stems in summer. Blossoms start out white and then age to pink and finally red.

Because it's native to the tropics, Rangoon creeper isn't very cold-tolerant. It's fully hardy in USDA Zone 10. In Zone 9, it may die to the ground in winter and come back from the roots. Elsewhere, you'll have to grow it in a pot you can bring inside for winter or root a cutting in fall that comes inside too.

Unfortunately—yet predictably—*Quisqualis indica* no longer exists. The evil taxonomists discovered I was looking for another "Q" plant and just changed the name to *Combretum indicum*. What a sorry lot they are.

But am I just going to sit here and let them ruin my book? Nay! I say, nay! As Edmund Burke observed, "The only thing necessary for the triumph of evil is for good men to do nothing."

Quisqualis indica lives in this book. *Combretum* be damned.

RHODODENDRON ᴛᴏ RUBBER MULCH

RHODODENDRON

There is a rhododendron in my backyard. Her name is 'Caroline.' She's purty! Unfortunately, growing rhododendrons in the South can be quite a challenge, unless you follow Grumpy's expert advice.

But before we get to that, let me dispel some confusion you may have about rhododendrons. People talk about rhododendrons and azaleas as two different groups of plants, but in fact, all azaleas belong to the genus *Rhododendron*. Our native azaleas, also called wild honeysuckles, are upright, airy, deciduous shrubs, often with fragrant flowers. Their Asian counterparts, like 'Hershey's Red' and 'Formosa,' are dense and mounding, non-fragrant, with evergreen leaves from 1 to 2 inches long. They usually grow from 3 to 8 feet tall and wide.

For our purposes, "rhododendrons" refers to those plants with large, evergreen leaves up to 6 inches long. They get bigger than azaleas, 8 to 12 feet tall and wide (although I've seen our native Catawba rhododendrons towering 30 feet tall in the North Carolina mountains). Rhododendrons have much bigger flowers than azaleas, bloom later, and are open, not dense.

You with me so far? Good. Now here's how to grow rhododendrons in the South.

KEYS TO NOT KILLING YOUR RHODODENDRON

1 Choose heat-tolerant kinds. The world's most glorious rhododendrons grow in Seattle, Ireland, England, New Zealand, and other places in the Goldilocks zone where it's not too hot, not too cold, but just right. We don't live there. We need rhodies that tolerate long, hot summers, such as 'A. Bedford' (lavender-blue), 'Anah Kruschke' (reddish purple), 'Anna Rose Whitney' (deep pink), 'Belle Heller' (white), 'Caroline' (orchid-pink), 'Roseum Elegans' (lilac-pink), 'Cynthia' (rosy-crimson), 'Nova Zembla' (red), Southgate Series (various colors), and 'Vulcan' (brick-red). Rhododendron Society folks turn up their noses at such "common" types, but in Grumpy's never-humble opinion, a live common plant beats a dead special one.

2 Pay attention to the soil! Rhododendrons need moist, acid, loose, well-drained soil that contains a good bit of organic matter. This is why they're hard to grow here. Most Southerners have either acid, clay soil or alkaline, clay soil. Rhododendrons hate both because clay drains slowly and roots rot. Rhododendrons also hate being dropped into a turkey fryer, but I doubt that happens very often. Once burnt, twice shy.

3 Plant a little high. No, I don't mean you should be a little high. This ain't Oregon. Grumpy means you should plant your rhododendron so that the top of its root-ball sticks about 1 inch above the soil surface. Then

cover the exposed root-ball with mulch. This improves drainage and aeration around the root-ball. No weed required.

4 Provide light shade, especially in the afternoon. Plant rhododendrons in the dappled light beneath tall pines and hardwoods. Don't plant in deep shade or the plants won't bloom.

ROACHES

any books have been written detailing what a woman really wants from a man.

According to various authors, female priorities include:

- Love
- Companionship
- Children
- Financial Security
- Emotional Support

Of course, this is wrong. What a woman wants most of all from a man is the willingness to squash a bug.

Let one spider, ant, millipede, or roach crawl across the floor and a typical woman will immediately respond with a bone-rattling, "EEEEEEEEE!!!! Kill it!! Kill it!!"

Any man who fails to take appropriate action will never pass on his genes to the next generation.

WE'VE BEEN BUGGED

The Grump knows this firsthand. My son recently complained from his lair in the basement, where he has elevated the pursuit of sloth to a fine art, that he could hear little skittering noises coming from the drop ceiling above his head. So I lifted one of the panels, stuck my head up to see what was going on and...

LORD, HAVE MERCY!

It was like a scene from *Aliens*. Big, black roaches everywhere. Hundreds of them coming to kill us. "Roaches," I said solemnly. My wife immediately grew nauseous, fled up the stairs, and ordered me to kill them. Kill them all!

Considering that I'd already passed on my genes, you might think I could refuse. No way. As Judy has explained to me numerous times when I threatened to disobey, I have to sleep sometime.

THIS IS WAR

So I opened my arsenal of products dedicated to killing whatever frightens or grosses out women (for example, my death stalker scorpion door knocker) and selected the perfect weapon for the job—Bengal Tiger Gold Roach Spray. This stuff quickly flushes out and kills adult roaches. It also contains a growth regulator that stops baby roaches from maturing and laying eggs. Cool.

I lifted up a square of drop ceiling, hit the button, and fogged the entire area under it. Worked like a charm. In just a few minutes, no more skittering. Roaches dead. Hundreds of bodies belly-up. Cool.

NOT SO FAST

When I proudly proclaimed the triumph of man over vermin to Judy, I expected her unqualified affirmation and respect. Instead, she said, "So you're just going to leave them there?" I didn't see her point at first, but then she reminded me, "You have to sleep sometime."

Uhhh. Not cool. The worst part of the job was about to begin.

LOCK AND LOAD

I gathered my equipment—mask, ladder, flashlight, and vacuum cleaner with a long hose. I proceeded to lift ceiling tiles at various points, determine where the dead roaches were, and suck them into the vacuum cleaner. Some were so big, it sounded like sucking up marbles. I also vacuumed up a lot of roach poop, which isn't nearly as fun as it sounds.

Please, please don't let the vacuum bag explode, I prayed.

In addition to roach remnants, I sucked up big spiders, vicious-looking wasps, broken drones the government sent to spy on us, and extraterrestrial bugs I've yet to identify. At least they're all dead.

Finally, the terrible job was done. My basement ceiling is now debugged. Judy is happy and that's really good news. Because I have to sleep sometime.

ASK GRUMPY

Roasted Rhubarb

Q. I moved from Wisconsin to Georgia and discovered to my dismay that no one grows rhubarb here! Why not?

—Lars

A. Because rhubarb doesn't like our short, mild winters in the south. It needs long, cold ones. In the Lower South (USDA Zone 8), you can grow it as an annual, though. Set out divisions of 'Victoria' rhubarb in the fall for a winter-to-spring harvest.

ROCKY POT

T hanksgiving is all about family and friends—enjoying the day with the ones we love. To his dismay, however, the Grump has discovered that many of you are leaving out one member of the household—the one that lives in your attic. This Thanksgiving, let's all make a point to invite Rocky and his squirrelly friends to dinner. Or better yet, let's make them dinner.

I realize that some of you less fortunates have never enjoyed the privilege of dining on native squirrel. How sad. Not only is the meat delicious (just ask Bear Grylls), but it's a completely renewable, self-sustaining resource. Fact is, squirrels reproduce faster than we can eat them, thanks to all the people who set up bird feeders and end up feeding our furry, flea-bitten friends instead. By consuming more squirrels, we are being good stewards of the planet and leading the way to a more diverse and satisfying dinnertime experience.

At this moment, you're undoubtedly asking yourself: "How do I prepare squirrel?" Well, to the squirrel itself, you say, "If you're not tender, I'm using the blender!" (High-protein squirrel shakes are ideal for body-builders, athletes, and, well, your cat.) Rocky will find this amusing.

To the cook in your house, you say, "I just found a whole lot of tasty squirrel recipes on the Grumpy Gardener!"

In the interest of full disclosure and mainly to avoid a lawsuit, I admit these recipes come from *Backwoods Bound*, where you can find a whole slew of delicious Rocky recipes: Bacon-Wrapped Squirrel, Cajun Squirrel, Chicken-Fried Squirrel, Squirrel Cacciatore, Squirrel in Cream Sauce, and Squirrel Stew. The one I'm going to present here, Squirrel Creole, is gamey enough for the football crowd, yet tailored to the refined palate.

Of course, you wouldn't dream of serving a dish like this unaccompanied by the perfect wine. My buddy Scott Jones (www.jonesisthirsty.com), former Food Editor and wine expert at *Southern Living*, recommends a full-bodied Syrah.

Thanks, *Backwoods Bound*! If only you'd been around to advise Miles Standish at the first Thanksgiving, a lot of innocent turkeys might have been spared. And our attics would be a whole lot quieter!

Squirrel Creole

4 squirrels, cut into pieces	⅛ teaspoon cayenne pepper
2 tablespoons canola oil	2 (14.5-ounce) cans tomatoes,
1 clove garlic, minced	chopped
1 green pepper, chopped	Salt and pepper to taste
1 medium onion, chopped	1 cup brown rice, uncooked

Season meat pieces with salt and pepper, lightly brown in oil.

Combine remaining ingredients and mix well.

Spoon into large casserole dish, arranging meat pieces on the top.

Cover and bake at 325 degrees for 1½ hours or until meat is tender enough to fall off the bone.

BUT, GRUMPY, MY GROCER DOESN'T STOCK SQUIRREL! WHAT, OH WHAT, SHALL I DO?

It's hard to believe, but many supermarkets (obviously under the thumb of Big Turkey) fail to offer squirrel. This is not a problem for hunters, however, and it should not be for you. Did Miles Standish go to Publix for his turkey? He did not.

Should unenlightened local ordinances prevent you from discharging firearms at suburban wildlife, try a squirrel trap. I find sunflower seeds and peanut butter to be excellent bait. If they don't work, try a 220V electric line squirrels can chew through and short out all the power to your home. No squirrels can resist that!

RUBBER MULCH

The world's resources may be finite, but the supply of stupid ideas will never run out. A stupid idea currently making the rounds is solving the problem of millions of used tires piling up by grinding them into little pieces and using them as garden mulch. Hey, what could possibly go wrong?

Rubber mulch didn't start out as a gardening product. It found its niche as a bouncy, soft surface for children's playgrounds. Yes, research showed that if a kid fell onto rubber mulch from 6 feet up on a jungle gym, he was less likely to be injured than if he fell on rocks, concrete, broken glass, or sharp steel spikes.

But as the number of children's playgrounds is miniscule compared to the number of houses and gardens out there, the rubber mulch folks turned their attention to suburbia. "Let's get moms and dads all over America to spread ground-up tires all over their landscapes," they said. "It'll be YUGE!"

But to do this, they had to tout the benefits that rubber mulch has over natural mulches like pine bark, shredded hardwood, and pine straw. Here are some of the selling points they came up with.

1 Rubber mulch promotes recycling—and provides an excellent model for recycling all of those spent fuel rods piling up at nuclear plants. ("Give your garden that special glow!")

2 Unlike natural mulches, rubber mulch doesn't decompose, so it's "sustainable." It doesn't add any nasty organic matter to the soil the way bark and pine straw do.

3 Rubber mulch keeps the soil surface cool by trapping all of the sun's heat atop it where your feet are.

4 You can get rubber mulch in almost any color imaginable. What's your favorite color? Bright red? Teal? Blue? Why not use a different color in every garden bed? Zowie!!!!

LET'S SPREAD A LITTLE TRUTH

Not gonna sugarcoat it for you. Grumpy HATES rubber mulch. It's stupid and it stinks—literally. On a hot summer day, it smells like hot tires. Don't know about you, but Eau de NASCAR is not a fragrance I enjoy wafting through my garden.

Secondly, colored mulch looks horrible. Put down purple or orange mulch in your yard and you might as well wear a T-shirt that reads "Ig-nant & Do'nt Care."

Thirdly, natural mulch slowly decomposing over time is a GOOD thing. Adding organic matter to the soil loosens it, increases nutrient and water retention, and feeds earthworms and beneficial soil microbes.

Finally, rubber mulch isn't a healthy choice. Like everything else, it does break down, and when it does, it leaches a witch's brew of heavy metals and toxic chemicals into the soil and ground water. Rubber mulch is also a fire hazard—it burns at a much higher temperature than natural mulches and belches toxic smoke.

Forget rubber mulch. That extra bounce it puts in your step just ain't worth it.

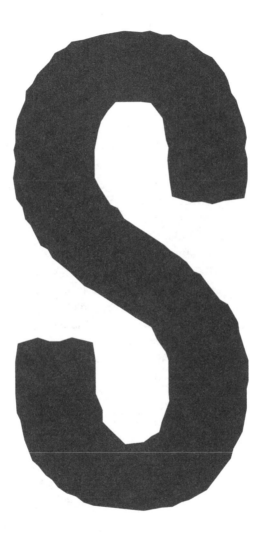

SASSAFRAS TO SYCAMORE

SASSAFRAS

One of the Grump's favorite native trees for fall color is sassafras. Its peachy-orange leaves help make autumn the favorite season of all discerning gardeners. But if you're at all worried about shrinkage, guys, you might want to steer clear.

Native to the eastern U.S., sassafras (*Sassafras albidum*) stands out for a couple of unusual qualities. First, it expresses (and you'll want to remember this term to impress your friends that you really are into book learning) foliar trimorphism. This means that its leaves have three different shapes. Some are oval; some have two lobes and look like either right-handed or left-handed mittens; and some have three lobes. All three appear on the same tree. Feel free to slip this term into casual cocktail party conversation. "Hey, Don, just love that tie. Is it just me or is foliar trimorphism going crazy this year?"

Second, all parts of the tree are aromatic—just tear a leaf and sniff it. Sassafras tea is a traditional country drink made from boiling the bark of sassafras roots. Grumpy thinks it tastes like root beer, which logically, it should. I remember as a kid making it with my dad, feeling a little guilty about digging up those roots and skinning them. I hope the tree had plenty more.

What I didn't know at the time was that sassafras tea made this way contains a potentially dangerous, naturally occurring compound called safrole. A couple of cups during your lifetime won't hurt you, but regular consumption has been linked to liver cancer and something even worse— testicular shrinkage. The Grump assures you he drank only one cup. Fortunately, you can now buy sassafas concentrate with the safrole removed at the grocery store. This means the only legitimate excuse for shrinkage is that the pool water was very, very cold.

Most sassafras trees are understory plants in the woods, quickly growing 20 to 25 feet tall, although they can eventually grow 40 feet or so. Young trees have bright green bark. This makes them easy to spot in winter woods. Successfully transplanting one from the wild isn't easy, because the roots are sparse and stringy. The smaller the tree is, the more luck you'll have. I wouldn't dig a tree any taller than 4 feet. Some garden centers carry sassafras grown in containers.

Sassafras likes full or partial sun, although you'll get better fall color in full sun. Give it moist, acid, well-drained soil that contains a good bit of organic matter.

Here's an interesting tidbit for those who constantly battle pests. Japanese beetles find sassafras leaves irresistible, so if you have lots of Japanese beetles where you live, woe is you.

On the other hand, deer don't seem to like sassafras foliage. Pick your pest.

SNAKES

O ver the course of countless conversations with Southerners throughout the years, one truth stands heads and tails above the others. Southerners, especially females, love snakes. Realtors will tell you that when it's decision time to buy a house or not, the deal-breaker for women is not granite countertops, size of the closets, number of bathrooms, or the floor plan. It's "Does the yard attract snakes? 'Cause I can't live without lots of snakes."

This being the case, it behooves everyone thinking of selling a house to put a plan into action to attract as many snakes as possible. Here are five easy strategies to follow to turn your yard into the neighborhood's serpentarium.

Don't cut the grass or trim the bushes. Let the whole yard grow up a verdant jungle. Excessive vegetation provides cover for snakes, hiding them from predators such as hawks, owls, dogs, cats, possums, honey badgers, old guys with metal detectors, and velociraptors. It also provides cover for rats, mice, voles, and other rodents that are the favorite food of many snakes. The more rodents your yard harbors, the more snakes will arrive to dine.

Leave bowls of smelly dog food and cat food outside. This will be a clarion call for hungry rodents who, once sated, will multiply faster than Stephen Hawking. Snakes relish tender, young rodents and will thank you for this generous gift.

Throw pieces of junk that collect water into the yard, like old tires, empty cans, and satellite dishes. Summers are hot down here, and snakes need to drink periodically. Show them how much you care for their comfort and well-being.

Use chicken wire instead of hardware cloth to seal openings into your backyard chicken coop. The openings are big enough to let most snakes crawl through unimpeded. Snakes love chicken eggs and don't worry about cholesterol.

They'll gulp down as many as they can fit—along with a chick or two.

Fail to seal up possible entry points into your house that will allow snakes to slither into your basement, garage, crawlspace, attic, or (my personal favorite) the bathtub. Snakes are cold-blooded, so their body temperatures reflect the conditions of their surroundings. If it's hot as Hades outside, they may seek cool shade inside. If it's cold, they'll seek out warmth. Who knows, a female snake may decide your house is the perfect place to raise a family. It worked for you, didn't it?

No snakes in your yard yet? Don't despair. Think of your yard as the baseball field in *Field of Dreams*. If you neglect it, they will come.

SOIL

Gumbo-licious

Q. We're moving from the Northeast to South Carolina, and people say we'll have "gumbo" soil. What will I need to add to allow me to grow flowers?

—Mary

A. In the garden, "gumbo" isn't an okra-based soup with added crawfish. It's blackish soil composed of very fine silt that becomes gummy when wet. Because it drains poorly, many plants turn up their noses at it. The best solution is to mix in lots of organic matter such as chopped leaves, ground bark, and composted manure before planting. Season with peat moss to taste.

SPANISH MOSS

ts flowers are puny, its foliage dull, and it lies upon the landscape like a boy in his hammock. Yet this indolent plant, this Spanish moss, sums up all that is Southern. Watch its listless sway, and in the cobwebs of its being you will smell fried okra, tread sugar-sand beaches, cuss no-see-ums, and keep time to a gospel choir.

Neither Spanish nor moss, Spanish moss (*Tillandsia usneoides*) acquired its name through an exchange of ethnic insults. Early French explorers counseled Native Americans to call it "barbe Espagnol" or "Spanish beard." Greatly offended, the Spanish countered that the proper name was "cabello Francès" or "French hair." Native Americans apparently thought better of the French, so "Spanish beard" won out. Political correctness finally prevailed in the 18th century. Swedish botanist Carolus Linnaeus named the species *usneoides*, which means "looks like moss." Thus "Spanish moss" was born.

Spanish moss occurs primarily in mild Coastal Plains from the Carolinas down to Louisiana and Texas and as far south as Argentina and Chile. Although it tolerates drought and brief stretches of cold, it flourishes in the Lowcountry, where humidity hangs like wash on a line.

An epiphyte, Spanish moss relies on trees only for support. Chlorophyll allows it to turn sunlight, water, and carbon dioxide into nourishing carbohydrates. Grayish scales, called trichomes, covering the leaves also trap minerals and nutrients that flow down from tree canopies following a rain.

The plant propagates in two ways. Birds and the wind carry moss fragments from tree to tree where they lodge and grow. In addition, tiny yellowish green or blue flowers produce wind-borne seeds that snag in the fissures of tree bard. Live oak is a favorite host, but the plant also targets bald cypress, pond cypress, black gum, water tupelo, pecan, and red cedar. Individual strands may stretch 25 feet.

ASK GRUMPY

Shear Disaster

Q. My spiraea was full of blooms, and then my husband sheared it into an ugly box. It was the focal point of my yard, and he took off nearly 2 feet! Can anything be done?
—Liz

A. I suggest the two of you make an appearance on Dr. Phil to address serious gardening issues that threaten your relationship. As for the spiraea, it's a tough plant that will soon return to its former lovely shape. But just to make sure, enroll your hubby in Pruners Anonymous.

Through the years, people found many practical uses for Spanish moss. Early settlers mixed it with mud to caulk their cabins. Doctors took advantage of its antibacterial qualities and prescribed extracts to treat diabetes. Because it "breathes" well and stays cool, it was a favorite material for stuffing mattresses in the hot, humid Lowcountry. It is still prized today for filling fine upholstered furniture. Spanish moss is also a popular decorative mulch for pots. Zapping freshly gathered moss in the microwave for three minutes before using it kills the chiggers it often harbors.

No matter how we choose to picture the South, Spanish moss insinuates its way into every image. It is, said writer James J. Kilpatrick, "an indigenous, indestructible part of the Southern character; it blurs, conceals, softens, and wraps the hard limbs and hard times in a fringed shawl."

SQUASH

Every winter when I was a kid, my mother would bake butternut squash for dinner. It looked yucky—like an alien's head split down the middle with a pool of butter in place of the brains. Mom said I had to sit at the table until I ate it. Once, I sat there 4 months.

But eventually, after only about a half-century, I came around. My wife, Judy, who in very irritating and unreasonable fashion insists I try something before I declare I hate it, fixed us a baked butternut squash. I looked at it fearfully, chugged a couple of quick bourbons, and tried it.

Glorioski! It tasted good! The next week, she baked an acorn squash. I liked that too. Clearly, my mom was wrong for not making me sit there 5 months.

The worst thing you can say to a kid when trying to force food down their throat is, "It's good for you." That means it tastes awful. But kids don't read the Grumpy Gardener, because their brains haven't fully developed. Yours has. Therefore, you will not shrink back in horror when I say that squash is very nutritious. A single serving of butternut squash, for example, contains high amounts of Vitamins A, B, C, and E, plus calcium, magnesium, and potassium. Why, that's even more nutritious than beer!

There are two main classes of squash—summer squash and winter squash. Summer squash, like yellow crookneck and zucchini, have thin skins, mature in summer, and don't store well. Winter squash have thick skins, mature in late summer and fall, and keep a long time if stored in a cool, dry place. You can eat it all winter. It isn't as easy to grow as summer squash in the Deep South (USDA Zone 8 and below), but it's cheap to buy. Muy importante.

Winter squash comes in lots of types. In addition to the acorn and butternut types that generally weigh 2 to 5 pounds, try the similarly sized spaghetti squash. Spaghetti squash gets its name from nutty-tasting flesh that forms spaghetti-like strands. You can substitute them for pasta.

Then there are really big winter squashes, like 'Hubbard' and 'Blue Hubbard.' They tip the scales at 12 to 15 pounds, enough to feed the entire customer service department of your cable provider. Wow—if my mom had fixed that, I'd still be sitting at the table!

HOW TO KILL
STINKBUGS

To keep stinkbugs from destroying your tomatoes, peppers, cucumbers, etc., fill a wide-neck vase halfway with water, and add two or three drops of liquid detergent. Place the vase under any stinkbug you see, and flick it into the vase. The detergent will keep the bug from escaping the water, and it'll drown. So satisfying!

-⟨⟨⟨⟨⟨-

SYCAMORE

Champion of the oppressed and wrongfully vilified, Grumpy stands ready to shine his Beacon of Truth on any misunderstood plant. Today, he happily parts the gloom enshrouding what is arguably the most striking native shade tree in winter—the Brobdingnagian sycamore.

"Brobdingnagian" means big, and if you don't get the reference, you must have been shooting spitballs at your friends when your 8th grade class read *Gulliver's Travels*. A mature American sycamore (*Platanus occidentalis*) may stand 120 feet tall and 80 feet wide. Its stout trunk and massive, spreading limbs make it a dominant force of living architecture. And its impact is only magnified when it drops its leaves in fall.

Sycamore grows fast. Planted in moist, fertile soil, it can easily add 2 to 3 feet a year in the Southeast. "Moist" is key. Sycamore relishes the deep alluvial soils deposited by streams, creeks, and rivers. When you spy a line of sycamores snaking through the woods in the countryside, you can bet it mirrors the route of a hidden stream.

Spotting a sycamore is easy in winter. Its bark is whiter than the population of Iceland. When lit by the sun, the trunks simply dazzle. It gets this way by shedding big flakes of its old, gray-brown bark in autumn like a snake sloughing off its skin. The bark gradually dulls to greenish gray by summer, and in fall the cycle begins anew.

Large, lobed leaves give sycamore a coarse texture in the summer landscape. Fall color is usually uninspiring, but sometimes, the leaves can turn a nice buttermilk-biscuit brown.

For a kid, sycamore is just about the best climbing tree around. The bottom branches are usually low enough for you to grab and pull yourself up, and the main limbs up the trunk are sturdy and conveniently spaced. Grumpy spent many a happy hour climbing sycamores as a young'un, pondering such mysteries of life as quantum mechanics and how come instant coffee takes time to make.

That said, a sycamore is not a tree you want in a small yard. It will swallow the whole thing. Sycamore is best when given plenty of room to spread. Don't plant it in the strip between the sidewalk and curb, either, unless you like sidewalks that double as skateboard ramps.

SAVING SICK SYCAMORES

Folks shy away from planting sycamores for two main reasons. First, the tree is somewhat messy. It does regularly drop twigs and flakes of bark. If you can't stand this, don't buy a sycamore, buy a flagpole.

Second, two maladies commonly affect the foliage and you have to inspect the leaves carefully to determine which is the culprit. Anthracnose is a fungal disease that attacks young sycamore leaves just after they've unfurled in spring. This usually follows a spell of cool, wet weather. The leaves develop brown streaks that first follow the veins and then expand to fill in between. Infected leaves drop. There really isn't much you can do to curtail anthracnose on big trees, other than raking up and burning fallen leaves.

Unlike anthracnose, leaf scorch begins with leaves turning brown between the green veins. It usually shows up in mid- to late summer and results from drought. (Sycamore likes moist soil, remember?) Badly scorched leaves drop. The best way to prevent

[RULES #37 & #38]

Never pile dirt over the exposed roots of a mature tree, especially an oak.

The roots will be smothered, and the tree will croak. If you want to cover roots to level the ground, use something light that lets the air through, such as pine straw or bark mulch.

Beware of big trees that are hollow inside or have mushrooms growing on them.

They'll probably fall down on something precious, like your Big Green Egg or your house. Take preemptive action now.

—

this is by planting in good, moist soil and watering during extended dry spells. Also, don't plant sycamores where their branches will extend over hot pavement.

FOOLISHLY QUESTIONING GRUMPY

"Huh?" some of you are saying right now. "I see sycamores planted near hot pavement all over downtown." No, you don't. What you're seeing is a sycamore look-alike called the London plane tree (*Platanus x acerifolia*). This hybrid is more tolerant of city pollution and poor, compacted, dry soil than sycamore. But the bark isn't as white in winter—more of an olive-cream. To distinguish sycamore from London plane, look at the seed balls hanging from long stems. On sycamores, the seed balls are solitary; on London planes, they come in pairs.

WHERE TO BUY SYCAMORE

Many nurseries (hereabouts anyway) sell sycamores, so you shouldn't have any trouble finding one. If you need quick shade, have plenty of room, and like to climb, it's the tree for you. While you're up there, see if you can solve the mystery of instant coffee. It's haunted me for years.

[RULE #39]

When planting a tree or shrub, dig the hole
no deeper than the root-ball.

*The key is to make it three times as wide. Use the excavated soil
to fill in around the roots. Then water thoroughly, mulch over the top,
and enjoy an adult beverage.*

———

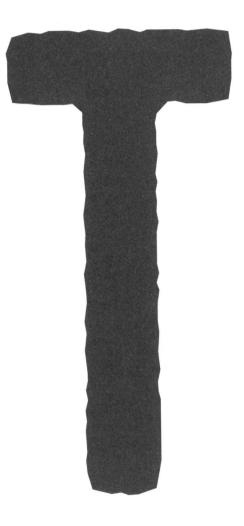

TEN TROUBLESOME PLANTS TO TRILLIUMS

TEN TROUBLESOME PLANTS

We all lead busy lives (except for you, you bum, and you know who I mean), so we can't afford to waste a single minute on something that just doesn't work. This applies to gardening. How many times have you toiled and fretted over a plant that wasn't worth a Ramen noodle? You and everyone else need to stop that. Grumpy is here to help. I present to you ten finicky plants that ain't worth the trouble trying to grow in the South.

—1—
AFRICAN DAISIES

Just about every spring flower expo I attend features tables filled with gorgeous African daisies (*Osteospermum sp.*). The growers eagerly await my "ooh" and "ahh." Then I pose the Question That Must Not Be Asked: "How well do they bloom in summer?" Faces fall. Ritual suicide swords are unsheathed. We all know the answer: They don't. African daisies quit blooming in hot summer weather, which in the South starts in May. They won't bloom again until maybe October. And then, they won't survive a cold winter. So I'm going to give space in my garden to a plant that just sits there for 90 percent of the time? African daisy, you ain't worth the trouble.

—2—
DROOPING LEUCOTHOE

You'd think an evergreen shrub native to the South would grow well here, wouldn't you? Not so with drooping leucothoe (*Leucothoe fontanesiana*). Growing 2 to 4 feet tall and wide, this mounding plant is often planted in sweeps, on banks, or in combination with azaleas, rhododendrons, and hollies. But I swear, I can hardly remember a time I've seen it where it looked the least bit presentable. It's terribly prone to leaf spot diseases and apparently feels life is just too hard. Drooping leucothoe, you ain't worth the trouble.

—3—
GARDEN VERBENA

Hybrid garden verbenas make spectacular color displays on garden center benches each spring, offering clustered rings of flowers of just about every color. You buy them and plant them and they look great for two weeks. Then you notice their leaves turning yellow or silvery, as tiny, sucking insects drain sap and nutrients from the leaves. This insect attack happens almost all the time and cannot be halted. Stems turn brown and die. Renowned Pennsylvania nurseryman Lloyd Traven said it best: "Verbena—when you absolutely MUST have thrips." Garden verbena, you ain't worth the trouble.

— 4 —
GERBERA DAISIES

The very existence of gerbera daisies (*Gerbera jamesonii*) makes me think we ought to expand our categories of herbaceous garden flowers to annuals, biennials, perennials, and dailies. No flower is more spectacular in the garden center. No flower dies so quickly in your garden. Being from South Africa, where the climate is the opposite of ours, it doesn't like our soil, rainfall, and humidity. If it isn't planted in rich, perfectly drained soil, it quickly rots and dies. Gerbera daisy, you ain't worth the trouble.

— 5 —
HYBRID TEA ROSES

Go to a meeting of a rose society today and the first thing you'll notice is a sea of white hair. These are the lone survivors of a once-mighty nation of rosarians who pledged they'd grow hybrid teas until it killed them. For most, it has. Has there ever been a stiffer, more graceless, more troublesome garden plant than a hybrid tea rose? People plant them in rows of equally spaced shrubs, each accompanied by a name marker. They look like headstones in a cemetery. "Who's buried beneath that rose?" I wonder. Hybrid teas are plants for dedicated masochists. Japanese beetles devour them. Black spot and mildew denude them. You must water, fertilize, and spray, spray, spray. Take away the flowers and they're just thorny, ugly plants. Hybrid tea roses, you ain't worth the trouble.

— 6 —
JAPANESE PAINTED FERN

Japanese painted fern (*Athyrium niponicum pictum*) is the world's most beautiful fern. It is also a royal pain to grow. It requires rich, moist soil loose enough to dig in with your hands. It's totally intolerant of both drought and root competition

ASK GRUMPY

Knocked-Out Roses

Q. I've watered and fertilized my roses, but they give only one or two blossoms at a time. They actually bloom better during our Houston winter. Can you tell me what is wrong with them?
—Garry

A. You probably have hybrid tea roses. These popular plants often go nearly dormant during the peak heat of summer and flower production declines. But if you keep watering and fertilizing them, the flowering should increase this fall. And cheer up—most people (especially those poor souls who live in Minnesota) would love to see roses in winter.

from other plants. In summer, you must water it nearly every day and still it never looks as good as the day you bought it. Japanese painted fern, you ain't worth the trouble.

— 7 —
PEACH

Do you recoil at the thought of spraying pesticides over and over again on something you're going to eat? Then don't plant a peach tree. Let me list a fraction of the pests that plague this tree—peach tree borer, white peach scale, fruit moth, brown rot, peach leaf curl, canker, leaf spot, scab, birds, and squirrels. If you don't spray, you're not going to harvest edible fruit—period. And even if you do, peach trees don't live very long. So why bother? Peach tree, you ain't worth the trouble.

— 8 —
PLUME COCKSCOMB

Plume cockscomb (*Celosia argentea*) often makes the covers of seed catalogs, due to its fiery colored spears of blossoms. And I'm sure that somewhere in this country where it doesn't rain all that much and the air is dry, it lives longer than a quark in the Large Hadron Collider (physicists are slapping their knees at that one). Not in the South. Here it'll give you a couple of weeks of half-hearted mediocrity and then collapse and rot following a tropical downpour. Plume cockscomb, you ain't worth the trouble.

— 9 —
SOURWOOD

It really pains to me to place sourwood (*Oxydendrum arboreum*) here, because it's a wonderful native tree that I love nearly as deeply as Dogfish Head 90-Minute IPA. It bears sprays of creamy white flowers in summer that make a delicious honey. It follows that up with scarlet fall foliage that simply glows. But while it grows happily

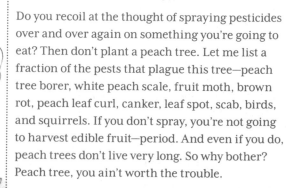

[RULE #40]

...BASIL, CHIVES, OREGANO AND DILL...

Simon & Garfunkel sang about parsley, sage, rosemary, and thyme for a reason.

It's because they're very easy herbs to grow. They also could have mentioned basil, chives, oregano, and dill, but that probably would have messed up the song.

[RULE #41]

There's an easy way to prevent insect and disease problems.

Start with plants that are naturally pest resistant. If you're growing tomatoes, look for the letters VFTNA after the selection name. This tells you your plants resist the most common tomato diseases. To locate other resistant plants, consult The New Southern Living Garden Book, *edited by yours truly.*

---

in the woods, it doesn't like most other places. I planted a memorial sourwood for my father at the botanical gardens. It looked great on Friday. On Monday, it wilted and died. For. No. Reason. I planted another. Same thing happened. I loved my father and this wasn't nice. Refusing to give up, I planted a third at the edge of the woods in my backyard. In two years, it has grown 2 inches. In good soil. If you have a nice sourwood already on your property, cherish it. But plant one from the nursery? Sourwood, you ain't worth the trouble.

— 10 —
SUMMER SQUASH

Summer inevitably brings Grumpy the same anguished entreaties: "My summer squash have nice, green leaves and lots of flowers, but I never get any squash. Why?" Grumpy feels your pain. It happened to me too. See, squash produces both male and female flowers; only females set fruit. But a lot of times, the vines produce only male flowers. Mine did that for about two months until I ripped them up in frustration. Why do some squash plants produce both sexes and some just one? Nobody knows. Summer squash, you ain't worth the trouble.

ASK GRUMPY

Thanks for Nothing

Q. My Thanksgiving cactus has lots of new growth. It bloomed profusely for my mother but won't for me. In mid-September, I put it in a room where it gets no light after dark, but it still has no buds. What's wrong?

—Jill

A. Thanksgiving cactus usually flowers a few weeks earlier than Christmas cactus. Long, dark nights and cool temperatures bring it into bloom. Grumpy leaves his plant outside in the shade from spring until fall and then brings it inside before frost when it's showing buds. It always blooms profusely. Don't give up on yours yet. it could still flower after Thanksgiving.

[RULE #42]

To keep birds from pecking
holes in your ripe tomatoes, hang red
Christmas balls on the vines.

This drives them nuts!

—

TOMATO HATERS

y friends, I have something shocking to tell you. My name is Grumpy and I hate fresh tomatoes.

I cannot tell you how hard this secret has made my life. Every day I live a lie. Telling people you hate fresh tomatoes is like saying you hate giggling babies or that you loathe the prospect of world peace.

Thus, you lie. You conceal. You pretend. You dissemble. You squirm. When people pluck a ripe cherry tomato from the vine, pop it into their mouth, and suggest you do the same, you squeal with false delight and flee like the French in WWII. When people place a dish of freshly sliced tomatoes in front of you at the dinner table, you exclaim, "Golly, those are simply too beautiful to eat!" All the while, you're thinking, "Barf! Vomit! Hurl! Get me outta here!"

Grumpy doesn't hate all tomatoes. Only uncooked ones. He loves tomatoes on pizza. He loves tomatoes in pasta sauce. He even made the most delicious spaghetti sauce he's ever tasted from 'Roma' tomatoes he grew in his own garden. But he doesn't like them raw. He also recoils from the smell of fresh tomato juice. And he asks you to understand.

No one taught Grumpy to dislike fresh tomatoes. It wasn't a choice. Grumpy was born that way. Because of this, he suffered derision, humiliation, and discrimination from an intolerant society that won't accept someone who's "different." Yesterday, I was served a cheeseburger at the Atlanta airport that came with a tomato slice on it even though I specified, "No tomato." I know what the restaurant staff was thinking. "We don't want your kind in here."

Why? Am I so unlike you? If you prick me, do I not bleed? If you serve me a Michelob Ultra, do I not look insulted and pour it over your head? Yes! Yes, I do!

A LITTLE HELP FROM MY FRIENDS

Hating fresh tomatoes is so lonely. You want to shout to the world, "This is who I am!" but you dare not. So, you act like one of them. When they serve you a fresh tomato, you pretend to eat it, wait for them to glance momentarily away, and then quick-as-lightning squirrel it away inside your napkin, shove it in your pocket, and say, "Yum!" Then you desperately grab another napkin in case they offer you one more.

Until last week, I thought I was the only fresh tomato hater in the world. Then I attended an event at P. Allen Smith's place in Arkansas, where garden bloggers from all over the country convene to share ideas and post embarrassing photos of each other on Facebook. We were having salads at lunch when I spotted fellow blogger Christopher Tidrick who hails from Illinois, do something extraordinary. He carefully extracted all of the fresh tomatoes from the greens, and pushed them off to the side of his plate.

OMG!!!!!!! Another fresh tomato hater! Grumpy is not alone!

I wept uncontrollably. At last, at last, somebody understands.

"You don't like fresh tomatoes?" I blubbered incredulously.

"No, I never have," he responded.

Then an even bigger miracle than world peace happened. "I don't like them either," chimed in Ohio blogger Kylee Baumle. OMG!!! The sea had parted. It was the beginning of a movement!

Chris, Kylee, and I know we're not the only fresh mater haters out there. There are millions of us in hiding, but most people don't know it. We could be your neighbor. We could be your pastor. We could be your Army buddy. We could be your high school teacher. We could be your pool boy. We could be the chatty girl who does your nails. We could be the doctor who checks your prostate.

It's time for us to come out from the cupboard. Fresh mater haters demand our right to be treated as equals in society. Join Chris, Kylee, and Grumpy as we proudly proclaim to the whole world, "We're here, we're weird, and we count!"

Oh, and I hate fresh cucumbers, too.

HOW TO PLANT
A TOMATO

Buy a tall, leggy plant. Strip off the bottom foliage so just three or four leaves remain at the top. Dig a hole deep enough so when you place the plant in it, only the leaves and an inch of stem will show above the soil surface. Fill in thoroughly with soil and water. Roots will form all along the buried stem.

‹‹‹‹‹‹

TOMATO Q&A

Q. I'm growing 'Juliet' and 'Sweet 100' tomatoes. They've been very prolific up to this point, but after the heavy rain we've had, the ripening fruits burst open like in the movie *Alien*. What's causing this?

—John

A. When it rains a lot over a short period, tomato plants pump a lot of water into the ripening fruits. But tomato skins can't grow fast enough—they split open and people faint. Fortunately, the effect is temporary, so you won't have to blow up your ship to save Earth like Ripley did in the movie.

Q. It gets so hot here in Dallas that tomatoes won't grow. Have any advice on tomatoes that can take the heat?

—Bob

A. Yours is a common complaint throughout the lower half of the South. The problem isn't that the plants won't grow. It's that the flowers won't set fruit if it's too hot. What you need to do is plant heat-tolerant selections that don't mind Venus-like temps, such as 'Arkansas Traveler,' 'Solar Fire,' 'Heatwave,' 'Cherokee Purple,' and 'Sunmaster.'

Q. Why won't my tomatoes turn red? This is keeping me up at night.

—Deanna

A. Look on the bright side, Deanna. At least now you can watch Jimmy Fallon in real time. Not a comfort? Then consider these reasons why tomatoes can be slow to ripen: First, if it's still early summer, your plants may need a few more weeks; second, unseasonably hot weather or a heavy fruit-set can stress your plants and delay ripening. Spreading a 1-inch layer of mulch under your plants will help by cooling the roots and keeping them moist. The bottom line: Be patient.

TRILLIUMS

Among all the woodland wildflowers of eastern North America, trilliums rank high among people's favorites. Named for their three-petaled spring flowers sitting atop whorls of three leaves, they're found all the way from northeastern Canada to central Alabama and Georgia (USDA Zone 8). White trillium (*Trillium grandiflorum*) is both the showiest and easiest one to grow. That's why I just planted some and you should too.

I got my plants from a remarkable nursery in West Virginia called Sunshine Farm & Gardens, a 60-acre refuge atop a 3,000-foot mountain smack in the middle of nowhere. Actually, that's not true. It's just outside the little town of Nowhere and a few miles from Lost-as-Hell and Black Hole. It's operated by plantsman extraordinaire Barry Glick, who in between moonshine runs to Nowhere grows more than 10,000 kinds of plants, most of them legal.

I became acquainted with Barry some years ago when *Southern Living* did a story on hellebores. Hellebores are Barry's passion and he has 6 acres of them blooming every March, many his own hybrids. But his plant selections go way beyond that. He's a great source for Grumpy's favorite native plants, including Virginia bluebells (*Mertensia virginica*), merrybells (*Uvularia grandiflora*), Indian pink (*Spigelia marilandica*), liverwort (*Hepatica sp.*), and about 10 different kinds of trilliums. If you're looking for ginseng (*Panax quinquefolius*), he has that too, along with that legendary Appalachian delicacy, ramps (*Allium tricoccum*).

White trillium grows 12 to 18 inches high and features brilliant white blooms 3 to 4 inches across in early to mid-spring. As blooms age, they take on pink tones. The plant likes dappled to full shade and moist, acid, woodsy soil containing lots of organic matter. I planted mine at the edge of my woods in soil liberally amended with chopped up oak leaves. The foliage dies down in the heat of summer, but to keep the roots spreading, water the area every once in a while during extended droughts. A few handfuls of organic fertilizer sprinkled over the bed in spring will help too. Happy plants form ever-expanding colonies, giving you more bang for your precious buck.

Although Barry sells a lot of plants wholesale to nurseries, fortunately he ships to average Billy Bobs and Wilma Janes, too. The plants come as bare roots wrapped in moist moss with detailed planting instructions.

If you'd like to tour wooded hillsides blanketed by thousands of hellebores, trilliums, and other flowers, you can visit Sunshine Farm & Gardens whenever the truck driver you hitched a ride with dumps you off unceremoniously at Renick, West Virginia, and says, "This is as far as you go." Barry requests that you call first to make sure the revenooers have departed.

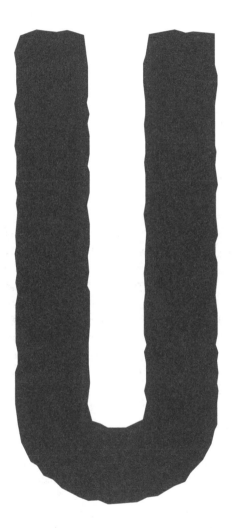

UGLY AGNES TO UVULARIA

[RULE #43]

Answer smartly when a person asks what you think of their ugly yard.

Try "That's really something!" or "I've never seen that before!" or
"Who would have thought of that?" Never say, "Bless your heart."
If you do, they'll know you think it's ugly.

—

UGLY AGNES

One of the privileges of being the Grumpy Gardener is getting to rail against plants that I hate for some reason. I find no shortage of plants to do so, as you have no doubt discovered by reading this book. One odious plant provides multiple reasons to condemn it. Ugly Agnes.

Now, if you're named Agnes, please don't take offense. I am not suggesting that girls named Agnes are ugly. Even if I were, the chance that someone named Agnes would be reading this is now quite remote. A common name in centuries past, its popularity in the United States crashed in the last 200 years. According to ourbabynamer.com, Agnes fell from spot #37 in 1839 to #1,272 in 2015. Why? Perhaps it's because "Agnes" sounds too much like "agony." Or maybe it's because the name is derived from the Greek word "hagnos." Many mothers fear naming a daughter Hag, lest it become prophetic.

"Ugly Agnes" is my nickname for a terrible evergreen shrub named thorny elaeagnus (*Elaeagnus pungens*). This fast-growing, nearly impossible-to-kill monster is frequently used as a sheared hedge or a screen to block unpleasant views—like more elaeagnus growing behind it. And if you're willing to shear it every seven minutes, it will do a serviceable job. Fall behind on your pruning, though, and you will rue the day.

Left to its own devices, Ugly Agnes grows 15 to 20 feet tall and wide. It does this by way of naked shoots, some more than 6 feet long, that skyrocket off above the foliage in all directions, evoking the image of Medusa. Flower arrangers like to cut these for use in their work, but that's like emptying Lake Michigan with a teaspoon. You can't do it fast enough.

Eventually, these shoots clothe themselves in leathery leaves that are dark green on top and silvery underneath. In fall, tiny flowers release a sweetly fragrant perfume reminiscent of vanilla. You think Ugly Agnes is finally cleaning up its act. No. The flowers give rise to small, red fruits with brown specks. Birds eat the fruits and spread seeds hither and yon. Heat, salt, and drought tolerant, Ugly Agnes grows just about everywhere it's cold-hardy (USDA Zones 6-10)—on the beach, on roadsides, at shopping malls, in the woods—and even deer won't eat it. How wicked can one plant be?

Each winter, Grumpy scours his patch of deciduous woods for spots of green—Ugly Agnes seedlings coming up—and quickly decapitates them with his pruners. They originate from a plant next door that employed its shoots to climb into an oak overlooking a scenic dog mud-wallow. Its branches dangle from a limb about 20 feet up and laugh at me. I'd like to sneak over one night and cut it down, but the stupid dogs always bark.

I'm stuck with Ugly Agnes.

UGLY SPUDS

Spud Ugly

Q. I recently dug up my sweet potatoes and was very surprised by what I got. Even though the potatoes tasted delicious, they were the ugliest things I have ever seen! What did I do wrong?

—Lori

A. First, console yourself with the fact that ugly sweet taters that taste good are better than beautiful taters that taste awful. Your soil is probably responsible. Like most root crops, sweet potatoes prefer loose, light soil. If yours is heavy or rocky, the roots can turn "spud ugly." To avoid having a repeat performance, lighten your soil by working in lots of organic matter before planting. Or just embrace their repulsiveness and start an Ugly Spud Contest. Your sweet potatoes can win—or at least get Miss Congeniality. Grumpy believes in you!

UNFORGIVEN

A while back, I sheepishly admitted to the world that my cat hunts hummingbirds. He stealthily crouches at the foot of my 'Lady in Red' salvia, waits for an unsuspecting hummer to show up, and pounces.

He's successful too. I've found little piles of green feathers at the base of the plants to prove it. He undoubtedly finds ruby-throated hummingbirds to be that rare delicacy that warrants spending endless boring hours of doing nothing waiting for a bird to show up.

On the other hand, cats, like elected officials, regularly spend endless boring hours doing nothing, so maybe it's just another day for him.

AN UNSPEAKABLE ACT

The Grump felt badly for the hummingbirds, but then my cat did something unforgiveable. In his wanton lust for another tiny winged treat, he leaped up into the air, came down on my salvia, and broke it. One whole branch gone, just like that.

Well, you'd better believe I lectured him severely. Consuming a hummingbird is one thing. Destroying my salvia is quite another. I told my felonious feline in no uncertain terms that he was never again to repeat this outrageous behavior.

I had no doubt he understood.

Thus, imagine my sense of betrayal when I returned home from work yesterday to find three more broken salvias and two broken angelonias! This brutal crime had his paw prints all over it.

Subsequent lab tests revealed innocent salvia DNA on his fur.

CRIME AND PUNISHMENT

I will not stand idly by while this remorseless, uneducable villain destroys my flowers. Therefore, unless one of you reading this can convince me otherwise, frontier garden justice may be served. My fur ball is a serial salvia killer who must be stopped, even if that means paying the ultimate price.

Of course, I could sentence him instead to watching every minute of the next presidential debates. But that would be cruel and inhumane.

UVULARIA

You're probably surprised to find a story about *Uvularia* in here. "I thought this was supposed to be a gardening book," you're thinking. "Why am I reading about that hangy-down thing in my throat?"

The answer is that I am not writing about your uvula—as delightful as that would be—but a genus of charming woodland wildflowers native to the Eastern and central United States. Commonly known as merrybells, *Uvularia* are woefully underrepresented in American gardens.

Big merrybells (*U. grandiflora*) is the showiest of the group, in my estimation. Featuring upright, leafy stems up to 2½ feet tall with downward-pointing, narrow leaves, they remind one a bit of Solomon's seal (*Polygonatum sp.*). That's good enough, but what really warms my heart's cockles are the bright yellow, bell-shaped blooms that dangle from the upper stems in spring. Twisted petals form blossoms 2 inches long. Good companions to hostas, ferns, trilliums, wild ginger, liverwort, and other shade-tolerant plants, merrybells spread by rhizomes to form colonies, but seldom present a problem.

Two other merrybells species you'll run into if you're lucky are wood merrybells (*U. perfoliata*) and little merrybells (*U. sessilifolia*). The former grows 2 feet tall with pale yellow flowers; the latter reaches about 18 inches tall with nodding, yellow blooms.

Winterthur Museum and Gardens in Wilmington, Delaware, boasts the most spectacular display of merrybells I've ever seen. They're planted beneath a grove of ancient hardwoods, many of which lack side branches below 30 feet. This location hints at the growing condition merrybells like—high, light shade plus moist, well-drained soil replete with copious organic matter.

If you're having a problem with your uvula, I'm very sorry not to have addressed it here. But this is a gardening book. Perhaps you should direct your query to the American Uvula Society. They'd love to hear from you.

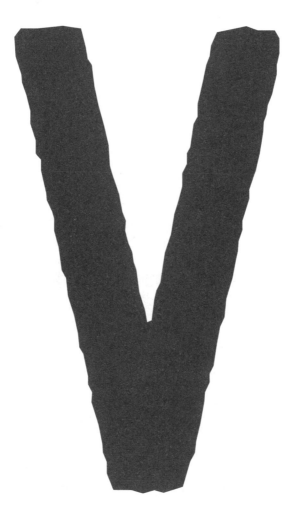

VEGETABLES FOR FALL to VOLE WARS

VEGETABLES FOR FALL

For about a month-and-a-half, I've been staring at my burned-up flower bed out front, a board-certified cemetery for parched petunias, crispy coleus, and immolated impatiens. What should I do with it now that autumn is almost here? Use it for burning garbage? Well, that may be OK in the trailer park where you live, but here in lovely Shangri-La Low-Tornado Mobile Home Estates, Judy and I take pride in our yard. That's why instead of setting fire to plastic milk jugs and old cans of paint thinner, I've decided to plant a fall vegetable garden. I don't have a whole lot of space—about 20 feet long and 6 feet wide. So I need veggies that give maximum return for the ground they take up. I also want something that's easy to grow, comes up quick, lasts long into the fall, and pleases my sophisticated palate.

That means one thing. I'm planting salad greens. The ones I've planted so far are a mesclun mix, gourmet lettuce mix, arugula, and 'Bloomsdale Long-Standing' spinach. I also threw out some radish seed, just for kicks. It's been warm here (cooling off at night, thank God), and the mesclun, lettuce, and radishes are up in less than a week. I'm counting on warm weather to get them going and cooler weather in the months ahead to make them crisp and sweet. Once the seedlings get a couple sets of leaves, their first meal will consist of a liquid organic, slow-release fertilizer. Should slugs and snails threaten, I'll counter with iron phosphate, which, unlike most slug baits, is labeled for use around vegetables.

Now some of you are undoubtedly upset with Grumpy for growing mesclun in the middle of such a nice trailer park and considering calling the cops. Before you do, turn off the Jimi Hendrix and your lava lamp and listen. You're confusing mesclun with mescaline (a hallucinatory chemical contained in a Mexican cactus). Mesclun is a mixture of savory salad greens, such as rocket, radicchio, endive, escarole, and mustard. A bag of this stuff in the grocery store costs a fortune—probably as much as mescaline (although Grumpy has no idea!), which is a good reason to grow it yourself. Some folks like to sow salad greens in a solid block. I prefer to do it in rows, because I've slanted the rows to make them look artsy. Spinach seeds are pretty big, but the seeds of lettuce and some other greens are tiny. If you want them to come up, just barely cover them with soil. I dug a shallow furrow for each row, sprinkled in the seeds, and then sprinkled a couple of handfuls of potting soil over each furrow and gently watered. It worked.

Seedlings will come up crowded in some spots and lonely in others. At some point, you have to thin plants to several inches apart, but with salad greens, nothing goes wasted. Throw the thinnings right into the salad bowl and enjoy.

If Grumpy's salad garden performs well this fall, Grumpy will let you know about it. If it doesn't, he will remain silent and sullenly burn some garbage.

VICIOUS VINES

Vines can be beautiful additions to the garden, but some of them are rampaging monsters. Here are five you should NEVER plant if you value your home, your environment, and your sleeping cat.

— 1 —
JAPANESE HONEYSUCKLE

Few childhood memories are as sweet as the scent of honeysuckle blooms or the single drop of nectar stolen from each flower. Japanese honeysuckle (*Lonicera japonica*) would be a treasure if only it would stay put. But it won't.

From plants first sold as ornamentals by East Coast nurseries, Japanese honeysuckle can now be found growing wild in three-quarters of the U.S. This fast-growing, twining vine spreads by berries eaten by birds and by suckers. It turns woodlands into impenetrable thickets. In high-rainfall areas like the Southeast, it's nearly impossible to eradicate. I consider it, Chinese privet (*Ligustrum sinense*), and kudzu to be the South's three worst landscape weeds.

— 2 —
JAPANESE OR CHINESE WISTERIA

I know, I know—wisteria in bloom is just so beautiful. It's deliciously fragrant too. How could Grumpy be so boorish to label it a monster? Because I've seen what both of these Asian species, *Wisteria floribunda* and *Wisteria sinensis*, can do. Tear off gutters. Bend iron railings. Strangle trees. Smother entire woods and hillsides.

Asian wisterias spread by seed, runners, and suckers. They'll grow as tall as whatever they're growing on. If they get loose in your yard, watch out. The only way I know to kill one is to cut through the trunk near the ground and paint the cut end with Brush-Killer according to label directions. Fortunately, there is a nice, friendly, native wisteria you can plant—American wisteria (*Wisteria frutescens*). Unlike its cousins, it's well-behaved and doesn't destroy things. Look for a selection called 'Amethyst Falls' at the garden center.

— 3 —
ORIENTAL BITTERSWEET

I keep urging our editors at *Southern Living* not to run holiday photos of bittersweet wreaths on doors, bittersweet boughs on mantels, bittersweet branches on gates, and bittersweet draped around pumpkins, but so far, no luck. Its bright-red seeds and yellow seed capsules make such a pretty picture! How could something so pretty be evil?

Easy. Unlike our relatively tame native American bittersweet (*Celastrus scandens*), Oriental bittersweet (*Celastrus orbiculatus*) is a thug. Birds eat the seeds and spread them everywhere. Suckers from the roots shoot up yards away from the original plant. Its thick, sinewy branches throttle small trees and climb as far as they can reach. If you buy a bittersweet wreath for the holidays, please seal it inside a plastic trash bag when you're through with it and put it out with the trash. To kill an Oriental bittersweet growing in your yard, treat it as recommended for wisteria.

— 4 —
PORCELAIN BERRY

I remember the first time I saw porcelain berry (*Ampelopsis brevipedunculata*) in my woody ornamentals class in college. I was awestruck. No plant has prettier berries! Berries start out yellow, progress to pale lilac, then deep magenta, and finally end up bright blue. Often all four colors are present in the same cluster. Whoa.

Woe is me—and you! For you see, as with bittersweet, birds love the berries of this ornamental grape from Asia. They gobble them all, poop out the seeds, and every seed germinates. With its thin, pliable stems, porcelain berry doesn't crush structures or plants. But I've seen it draping 60-foot trees in Pennsylvania. It's the kudzu of the North.

— 5 —
VIRGINIA CREEPER

So far, all the monster vines have been alien invaders. Now it's time to put the hurt on one of our own—our native Virginia creeper (*Parthenocissus quinquefolia*). This vine doesn't twine, but uses small, root-like tendrils to climb straight up anything—bark, steel, concrete, chain-link fences, PVC. Anything. And it grows fast.

I know it's not PC to criticize native plants whose

ASK GRUMPY

Living Fence

Q. I have an unsightly chain-link fence. What pretty, fast-growing vines could I use to turn it into a living fence?

—Marty

A. You need evergreen vines that bloom and grow fairly dense. Good candidates are Carolina jessamine (*Gelsemium sempervirens*), Confederate jasmine (*trachelospermum jasminoides*), and Armand clematis (*Clematis armandii*). All three are also fragrant.

pretty berries provide food for birds (notice the pattern here?), but I'm growing to hate this vine. Seedlings sprout everywhere in my yard, runners tunnel below the soil and come up 20 feet away, and the vines get on everything. Virginia creeper's one redeeming virtue is its brilliant red fall foliage. That ain't enough. Get it outta here!

VINEGAR

Some organic gardeners tout horticultural vinegar (20 percent acetic acid) as a natural herbicidal alternative to the popular weed killer Roundup. Grumpy does not. For one thing, vinegar this strong is very caustic and can cause serious damage to skin and eyes. Like Roundup, it isn't selective—it damages the leaves and stems of all plants it touches. Unlike Roundup, however, it isn't taken down to the roots, so tough perennial weeds may grow back. Horticultural vinegar also strongly acidifies the soil—some plants might not like this. Its best use is for killing weeds in the cracks of sidewalks and driveways, but beware: Repeated use can actually dissolve concrete.

Therefore, it you're going to use vinegar in the garden, I suggest restricting yourself to cider, white, red wine, balsamic, or rice wine vinegar. Not to pour on your weeds. To drizzle on your salad.

[RULE #44]

Fruiting veggies such as tomatoes, peppers, melons, and squash need full sun.

For partial sun or light shade, choose leafy greens, such as lettuce, mustard, and spinach.

HOW TO GOOSE
YOUR VIOLAS

Violas and pansies planted in fall could use a little boost in early spring. Pinch off any old flowers to prevent seed formation, and then apply a slow-release, organic fertilizer and soil conditioner such as Dr. Earth Bud & Bloom Booster (4-10-7). $8.50/4-pound box; planetnatural.com

VIOLETS

iolets are such sweet, little wildflowers that it's hard to believe that anyone other than North Korea's Dear Leader would want them dead. But believe it or not, Grumpy regularly receives requests for advice on how to eradicate these gentle plants. Has the world gone over to the dark side?

This entreaty from Anne in Kentucky is typical: "My front lawn has been taken over by violets. What would be the best way to get a nice grassy lawn back? I assume I will have to use some sort of weed killer. Thanks so much!"

Violets are weeds? Well, yes, they are, if they're growing somewhere you don't want them to. Dooryard violet (*Viola sororia*), the South's most common type, frequently invades lawns and gardens in both sun and shade. If you see one plant this year, next year you'll see a dozen. Then a hundred. Then a thousand. Then a veritable sea of violets will fill your yard. The prolific fiends nearly choked out my beautiful lawn of native mosses. I dug up buckets of them.

Dooryard violets spread so quickly because they're sneaky. They don't just develop seeds from the pretty, blue, purple, or white flowers you admire in spring. Most seeds come from weird, pale flowers resembling mung bean sprouts that hide at the soil line under the foliage. They sow seeds all summer without the need for pollination.

Each seed that sprouts grows a thick root called a rhizome that looks like a tiny horizontal carrot. Even if you dig it, any piece of the root left in the ground grows another violet. This root also makes the violet resistant to most weed killers available for home use such as Weed-B-Gon. Spray the leaves and they'll flop over for a week or so, but then they'll stand right back up and laugh at you.

However, I recently received a communiqué from Monterey Lawn & Garden Products about a weed killer called Spurge Power. In addition to killing tough weeds such as spurge *(duh)*, oxalis, ground ivy (creeping Charlie), and many others, Spurge Power purportedly KILLS violets! But like doubting Thomas, until I see it with my own eyes, I shan't believe.

The only sure way to control them is to dig up every one by the roots. You might want to start this morning, Anne. Or you could just relax, pour yourself a glass of wine, surrender to the inevitable, and let the violets take over. Observe their heart-shaped leaves. Heart = love.

VOLE WARS

Faithful reader, Jean writes: "Voles have eaten my entire patch of hostas, any bulbs other than daffodils, and one year ate my monkey grass one little clump at a time. Why do they eat such nice plants? How can I get rid of them? Can I mail them to you?"

Grumpy's insightful response: The easy answer is that voles prefer any plant you consider valuable and/or irreplaceable. Thus, they will always eat your hostas, toad lilies, plants with fleshy, juicy stems, and just about any bulb, corm, or tuber besides narcissus (which poisons the little slobs). The Grump appreciates your offer to ship him boxes of voles for Christmas dinner, but frankly they're so small it takes forever to prepare them. Hmm...maybe I could do something like hot wings.

SURE-FIRE CONTROL METHODS

Voles are related to lemmings (and thus perfect for lemming-meringue pie). Like lemmings, their populations explode suddenly and then fortunately die off. Cats are one reason. Ketchup, my oldest cat, is an expert vole-hunter. (Ever try voles with ketchup? Mmm...sounds delish.)

Other than cats, two things I've done to limit vole damage is to plant susceptible plants inside cages of hardware cloth and to scrape away any mulch or plant debris from the base of the plant. Voles love to burrow underneath the mulch where they can't be seen by predators. If you're planting bulbs, plant bulbs that voles and other rodents don't eat, such as daffodils, glory-of-the-snow, grape hyacinth, snowdrop, snowflake, Spanish bluebells, squills, and alliums.

WHAT DOESN'T WORK

Over the years, I've tried poison peanuts (they don't look like peanuts), animal repellent, vole traps, and spreading gravel around. None of these has had any appreciable effect on the vole population or the damage they do.

WEEPING WILLOW _to_ WINTERIZING

WEEPING WILLOW

Weeping willow, you will be shocked to learn, is a terrible tree. The only kind of place it should ever be planted is on the banks of a pond or lake with nothing else around. Keep the owner's house, driveway, sidewalk, pool, water lines, septic tank, pet cemetery, and all the neighbors' houses at least a zip code away. Refusing this advice courts disaster.

Let me be blunt (I'm known for this)—if you plant a weeping willow in the 'burbs, the best you can hope for is that it will die quickly.

Fortunately, for a number of reasons, there's a good chance of that.

First, it grows very fast. On the face of it, that might seem like a good thing, but fast-growing trees—think willows, poplars, silver maple, mulberry—are the products of aggressive, wide-spreading, shallow root systems that crack pavement, damage foundations, protrude above the soil, and invade water lines. The wood of just about any tree that grows lightning-fast is weak and breaks very easily in storms.

Second, weeping willow needs lots of water. This is why it looks its best near a body of fresh water. It's also why its roots snake into sewer lines and septic tanks, giving you a wonderful surprise when you flush the first time in the morning. Planted in drier soil, it sulks, looks ratty, and practically dons a sign that reads, "Cut Me Down Now."

Third, it grows too big for most residential lots—50 feet tall and even wider. Its branches sweep the ground, which means it's probably gonna swallow your entire yard. And unless you regularly prune the pendulous branches to head-height, forget about lounging in your hammock under there.

Finally, this sorry tree is a target for a plethora of insect and disease pests. The list is too long for me to recount. You can't control them. You can't stop

[RULE #45]

Never grow watermelons on a fifth-floor balcony, for obvious reasons.

them. Which is why you'll never encounter an ancient, 500-year-old weeping willow. It died 485 years earlier.

Therefore, let us resolve to consign this tree to the only place it belongs. Beside a large body of fresh water. With nothing else around.

WINTER HAZEL

If you're like Grumpy, you can't stand eating sauerkraut pumpkin pie more than three nights a week. You want variety in your garden, too. Sure, azaleas, boxwoods, and 'Knockout' roses are nice, but you deserve more. You want something new, something exciting—something that shouts to the world, "I am superior to you, you horde of dullards!"

Buttercup winter hazel (*Corylopsis pauciflora*) fits this description. If you can grow this deciduous shrub, you should. Let me elucidate why.

1 Pendulous chains of small, fragrant, bell-shaped, soft yellow blossoms appear in late winter or early spring before its leaves. It blooms a little later than forsythia, daffodils, and flowering quince. Its ethereal beauty is especially evident when combined with early purple rhododendrons and azaleas.

2 It's a good size for the home garden. Unlike some loropetalums, winter honeysuckle, pyracantha, and cherry laurel, this refined bush won't gulp down your house. It grows 4 to 6 feet tall and wide, never gets out of hand, and seldom needs pruning.

3 It's easy to grow if you live in USDA Zones 5-8. It likes sun or light shade and moist, well-drained soil. No pests that Grumpy knows of bother buttercup winter hazel, not even deer.

4 Its leaves, which resemble those of the hazel nut, turn soft yellow in fall.

5 Cut branches are very good for forcing into early bloom indoors in winter.

6 Nobody else in your neighborhood will have one, so your rank in society will rise to elite levels.

In a sane world, garden centers all over would sell it. But since most customers don't know what the heck buttercup winter hazel is, they don't ask for it and most garden centers don't stock it. (The good ones do.) Fortunately, you can order one online from one of Grumpy's Certified Purveyors of Geeky Plants, such as forestfarm.com or diggingdog.com.

You're very welcome.

WINTERIZING

F reeze warnings often come out late in October, meaning my impatiens will soon look like applesauce. Annuals turned into disgusting slime aren't the only damage cold weather can bring. Here are five quick ways you can head off winter's Armageddon.

— 1 —

BRING IN YOUR TENDER PLANTS

If you live where it freezes, bring indoors pots of tropical and semitropical plants you've summered outside, such as passion vine, Chinese hibiscus, bougainvillea, tree fern, mandevilla vine, clivia, princess flower, plumeria, and the like. It only takes a single night of 25 degrees for most of these to kick the bucket. Spray them first with horticultural oil or insecticidal soap to make sure they don't bring pests and their eggs with them. Indoors, give them as much light as you can. Don't worry if a few leaves quickly yellow and drop. The dimmer indoor light means the plant doesn't need them now. Don't feed these plants until spring, and be careful not to overwater—plants in winter grow slowly and don't need as much water.

— 2 —

CLEAN UP YOUR DEAD SUMMER VEGETABLE GARDEN

Limp tomato, pepper, squash, and cucumber plants still bearing sad, little fruits are on the ropes. Don't leave the carnage there. Those lifeless-looking plants still have plenty of live stuff on them—insect eggs, mite eggs, bacteria, and fungus spores. Remove every bit of these summer vegetables, and throw them away.

— 3 —

PROTECT YOUR CLAY POTS

Clay pots absorb and release water—they "breathe"—which is why plants grow so well in them. But when wet clay pots freeze, they develop small cracks that eventually become big cracks and the pots shatter. Either bring clay pots indoors for winter or store them outside in a dry place where they won't get wet.

— 4 —

TURN OFF YOUR SPRINKLER SYSTEM

Admit it—you've had it on automatic all year, set to turn on at 4 a.m. But it isn't July anymore, plants and your lawn don't need the water they once did, and if the sprinklers come on while it's freezing, you'll wake up to a yard that bears a striking resemblance to Siberia—or even worse, Minnesota (just kidding, Golden Gophers).

— 5 —
MULCH OVER MARGINALLY HARDY PLANTS

Who among us hasn't tried to cheat Mother Nature by overwintering something that isn't fully cold-hardy in our area? I'm talking angel's trumpet, banana plant, calla lily, elephant's ear, amaryllis, lantana, ginger lily, gladiolus, canna lily, agapanthus, and so on. One way to make this happen is to wait until after a hard freeze, remove all dead leaves and stems, and cover over the top of the plant with several inches of insulating mulch. Grumpy uses his mulching mower to chop up fallen leaves and pine straw, but you can also use hay or ground bark.

New Houseguests

Q. After bringing several tender potted plants inside for the winter, I heard my cat, Musky, making an eerie, howling noise. I walked around the corner and saw her playing with a green anole lizard. I almost had a heart attack! Thankfully, I was able to catch it and release it safely outdoors, but then three more surfaced to entertain Musky. Do you have any suggestions about preparing outdoor plants for interior overwintering? I do not want any more pets.

—Ellen

A. I'm glad you and Musky spared the lizards. They eat a lot of harmful bugs. Obviously, before bringing any plant inside, you and Musky need to do a thorough lizard search. Then spray all leaf surfaces and stems with horticultural oil to kill any insect or mite hitchhikers and their eggs. Finally, place the plants in shade for a week or two before they go indoors so they can adjust to lower light.

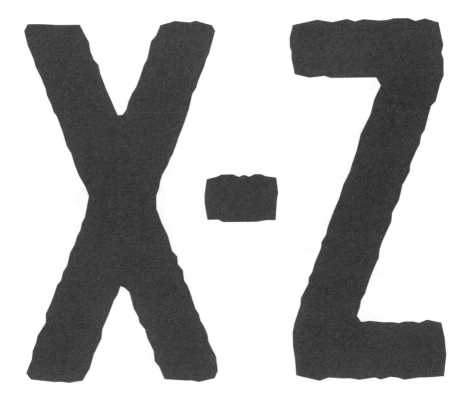

X-Z

XERISCAPING *to* ZZ PLANT

XERISCAPING

How well I remember the luncheon I attended years ago with the staff of *Sunset* in their lovely garden in Menlo Park, California. I was working on the first *Southern Living Garden Book*, a Southern adaptation of the famous *Sunset Western Garden Book*. As we sat around the table sipping Chardonnay from their own wine cellar (a lunchtime tradition there in the heady days of robust print journalism), their Garden Editor, Kathy Brenzel, asked me what I thought about a growing trend called "xeriscaping." Alas, I was less than diplomatic.

Poking a fork at my organic, locally sourced, mixed-green salad, I said, "Xeriscaping is just a fancy term for landscaping with rocks."

Crickets. Bug eyes. Raised eyebrows. Finally, Kathy piped up, "No, it is not." I asked for more Chardonnay. These people are going to stone me, I thought. Might as well go out with a buzz.

Xeriscaping, for those who don't know, is a term derived from the Greek word "xeros," which means dry. It promotes a way of gardening that minimizes the need for water that doesn't come from rain. It makes perfect sense for people living in arid regions like the American Southwest and Rocky Mountains that receive less than 30 inches of rain a year. Or for people like me, who just hate watering because it's boring.

Not everyone speaks Greek, of course, so many in the South call it "zero-scaping." Like I implied at my *Sunset* lunch, they imagine the practice calls for a garden blanketed with white gravel and sporting an agave or two. Beach town residents have this down to an art. Sometimes they'll plant a single plastic saguaro cactus wearing a Margaritaville shirt. Obviously, too much booze in the blender.

Succulents like cacti, agave, yucca, sedum, and ice plant are logical candidates for a xeric garden, but you don't have to make your garden look like Arizona. Plenty of trees, shrubs, perennials, annuals, and lawn grasses that commonly receive 50 inches of rain annually in the humid Southeast can get by with less. Chaste tree, crepe myrtle, ginkgo, cape plumbago, oleander, windmill palm, pearl bush, Japanese pittosporum, camellia, holly, boxwood, nandina, lamb's ears, blue fescue, bearded iris, and rosemary are but a few.

Xeriscape enthusiasts often target lawns for reduction or elimination because of their supposed gross water demands. While a lawn's size should meet your needs, there's no need to think of it as a water hog, provided you choose the right grass. Bermuda, buffalograss, and Zoysia are well-adapted to drought. I never water my Bermuda lawn and the guy across the street never waters his Zoysia. Last year, they endured a summer drought in which not a single raindrop fell for 90 days. They're nice and green today.

Even if your garden usually receives sufficient rainfall to sustain it, there is

[RULE #46]

Know the surest way to kill a plant.

Make it the focal point of your garden. It will die immediately.

no advantage to wasting water. Conserving it, on the other hand, makes you feel enlightened. You can do this by choosing drought-tolerant plants; planting in good soil containing lots of organic matter that retains necessary moisture while letting the excess drain away; designing your garden so that rain drains down into the soil rather than running off; mulching beds to retain moisture and reduce runoff; using garden hoses, soaker hoses, and drip irrigation to water rather than sprinkler systems; and minimizing areas of solid paving in your yard, so water penetrates the soil, instead of flooding storm drains.

Kathy, I've come back over from the Dark Side. Xeriscaping is more than landscaping with rocks. Can I get a refill on that Chardonnay?

X-TRA, X-TRA, READ ALL ABOUT IT!

ots of plants are called "everblooming," but when you get them home you find out the story is a bit different. Some skip a week; some skip a month. Now, however, I present a truly exxxxxtraordinary, everblooming plant that has never missed a day in the 25 years I've had it. It's crown of thorns.

Crown of thorns (*Euphorbia milii*) is a small, woody shrub named for the sharp, half-inch-long thorns that cover its main stems. Some people claim that its branches were cut to make the crown the Romans put on Jesus. I rather doubt this for several reasons. First, the plant is native to Madagascar—a 'fer piece from Calvary. Second, its thorns are too short to do the job the Romans wanted. Finally, if you're looking to make a crown from a thorny shrub or tree in the Holy Land, the place abounds with better, more exxxxcruciating choices.

Anyway, don't let the thorns put you off. My plant has never stuck me. Why? Because like the genius I am, I pick it up by the pot, not the stems.

My crown of thorns plant started out in a 3-inch pot. I bought it a quarter-century ago to combine with other low-water plants in a small, stone container I called "A Desert in a Dish." That 6-inch-tall wonder bloomed from day one. I eventually transferred it to its own pot. It now stands an exxxxxxxxxceptional 30 inches tall and is blooming as I type.

The true flowers are inconspicuous, but like poinsettia (another species of *Euphorbia*) they're overshadowed by colorful bracts that resemble petals. Red is the usual color, but I've also seen pink, yellow, orange, and white.

Thai Giants are hybrids presumably bred in Thailand that grow about as tall as regular crown of thorns, but have flowers, thorns, and leaves twice as big. They also boast a wide range of colors and color combinations. The Giants can be spectacular, but I prefer the species because it's less coarse. I've also noticed the Giants going through rest cycles, something that the exxxxxxemplary species never does when grown in a pot.

WHERE TO GROW IT

If you live where it never freezes, you can grow crown of thorns outdoors in the ground. But you probably don't, so you'll have to grow it in a pot you can bring inside to a bright window when it gets exxxxtra cold. Mine comes indoors when the temperature drops below 40 degrees. Below 32 degrees, your plant will be injured or die.

HOW TO GROW IT

Crown of thorns is exxxxxtremely easy to grow. I've never seen a single bug or fungus on mine. All it wants is sun and well-drained soil. If the soil goes completely dry, the leaves may shrivel and drop and blooming ceases. However, soon after you water, it'll shoot out more leaves and flowers. Old flowers drop as new ones pop. Drought tolerance makes it good for arid climates, but it also does just fine in high-rainfall areas like central Alabama where Grumpy lives. Just make sure the pot drains well. Feed a potted plant with a liquid all-purpose fertilizer about every two weeks from spring through summer. It will prove your crowning achievement.

[RULE #47]

Many plants wilt in hot sun, even if the soil is moist.

So how do you know when to water? Examine your plants first thing in the morning when it's cooler. If they're wilted, water.

———

YES TO YEAST!

What is the most magnificent plant on Earth?
The giant sequoia? The live oak? Newton's apple tree?
Okra? Worthy candidates, all, but they pale in
importance next to a plant so tiny you can't
even see it. Yeast.

Yeasts are microscopic, single-celled organisms belonging to the fungus family. More than a thousand species exist. Unlike typical fungi, yeasts don't grow bigger after consuming a meal. Instead, they pop out millions of new yeasts just like themselves, because like-minded yeasts enjoy agreeable dinnertime conversations.

There are good yeasts and bad yeasts. One bad yeast, *Candida*, causes yeast infections in people. But the benefits of good yeasts far outweigh the crimes of bad ones, and the best yeasts of all are the ones people use to make beer.

It's widely speculated that the Egyptians were the first to brew beer using the good stuff, but this is false. The history of beer is far more ancient and goes back to the dawn of humanity. People blame Eve for getting us in trouble with the Big Guy by tempting Adam with the forbidden fruit. What they overlook is that, just prior to this, Adam tapped a keg of his dark, malty Edenbrew and they both quaffed several ladles. Thus, they bear equal responsibility for our plight.

The main task of yeasts in the brewing process is fermentation—breaking down the sugars obtained from grains and other things and converting them to ethanol and carbon dioxide. What a noble act this is, yielding an alcoholic and therefore germ-free beverage with a satisfying fizz. The two most important brewer's yeasts are *Saccharomyces cerevisiae* and *Saccharomyces uvarum*. The former is called a "top-fermenting" yeast as it rises to the top during brewing and is used for making manly ales. The latter, which prefers cooler

Yellow Jacket Solution

Q. We have a yellow jacket nest under our crabapple tree. How can I get rid of the insects now so they won't come back in the spring?

—Paula

A. The nest is probably abandoned, because the workers die in winter while the queen spends this time sheltered in a tree cavity or similar place. In spring, she may build a new nest there. You can use a jet-spray can of wasp and hornet killer according to label directions to kill the hive. Or you can make your own yellow jacket trap from an empty 2-liter soda bottle. Cut off its top about a quarter of the way down, turn it upside down, and place it inside the remaining bottle to act as a funnel. Securely tape together the sections, fill the bottle with several inches of apple juice or soda and two drops of liquid detergent, and place near the nest. Hungry yellow jackets will fly down the funnel into the sweet liquid and drown. Observe their demise from a very safe distance!

temperatures, is a "bottom-fermenting" yeast that settles to the bottom and is used to make lighter, smoother lagers.

While hops and malts are the chief flavorings of beers and ales, yeasts play a surprisingly important role. This is why breweries cultivate proprietary yeast strains that give their brews unique flavors and characters. Unfortunately, the current craze for sour beers and ales—copying a Belgian tradition not nearly as successful as the waffle—takes things too far, in my opinion. Sour brewers inoculate their concoctions with bacteria or let the boiling kettle cool uncovered overnight so that wild yeasts floating through the air can infect the beer. The resulting flavor is unpredictable and charitably described as "funky."

I do not like funky-tasting beers. Thus, if I ever partake of one and describe the taste as "possessing surprising notes of horse blanket, dirt, wet hay, sauerkraut, and burnt match underpinned by Band-Aids and paint thinner," you should interpret this as "I wish the person who made this abomination were standing in front of me now, so I could have him summarily flogged."

Say "yes" to yeast, but only the right kind.

YUCCA

Although yuccas are often thought of as desert plants, in fact they grow over much of North and South America. Their cold-hardiness depends on the species. For example, the gaudily yellow variegated 'Bright Edge' Adam's needle (*Yucca filamentosa 'Bright Edge'*) is cold-hardy as far north as Wisconsin. But I enjoyed it at the U.S. Embassy in Belize, Central America, just before I was kicked out of the country for dancing the "Macarena" with the ambassador's wife. What can I say? My bad.

KINDS OF YUCCA

There are dozens of species, but you can divide them

into two groups. The first, like Adam's needle and curve-leaf yucca (*Y. recurvifolia*), are stemless. They basically form a big clump. The second and larger group, including Spanish bayonet (*Y. aloifolia*) and twisted-leaf yucca (*Y. rupicola*), form trunks and grow into large shrubs or small trees.

FLOWERS AND FOLIAGE

Flowers and foliage are why you grow yuccas. On most species, statuesque spikes of white, bell-shaped, sometimes fragrant blooms stand up to 6 feet above the foliage in spring and summer. Flowers don't get much showier. The long, sword-shaped leaves are also striking and may be green, blue-green, or blue-gray and striped with cream, pink, or gold. The leaves of some species, like curve-leaf yucca and mound-lily yucca (*Y. gloriosa*), have soft tips. The sharp tips of others, such as Spanish bayonet, are potentially lethal. Cold-hardy to USDA Zone 7, it is also an excellent choice for planting around your cousin's still.

HOW TO GROW

The most important thing yuccas need is good drainage. They will rot if planted in heavy, wet soil. Yuccas prefer full sun, although I've found they'll take part sun too. Because they store water in their leaves, established yuccas need little if any water other than natural rainfall. They don't mind humid, high-rainfall areas, though, as long as the soil is porous and fast-draining. Try to keep their foliage dry. Leaves that stay wet can develop leaf spots and other fungal diseases.

WHERE TO BUY

Many garden centers carry yuccas. In Grumpy's experience, the easiest ones to find are Adam's needle (particularly 'Bright Edge' and 'Color Guard'), mound-lily yucca, and curve-leaf yucca (such as 'Banana Split'). If you can't find them locally, however, try Yucca-Do, a mail-order nursery specializing in heat-tolerant, low-water plants. Plant Delights Nursery is another excellent mail-order source.

[RULE #48]

Find out how big a tree or shrub will grow before you plant it in the ground.

Assume that if the plant tag says it grows 6 feet tall, it will grow twice that big in your yard. Many homes in the suburbs have been lost forever to shrubs planted from 1-gallon pots that grew as big as Stone Mountain.

———

YUCCA TULIPS

The continuing influx of newcomers to the South means that many people arrive here sadly unaware of some of our most cherished traditions, such as painting rocks along the driveway in patriotic colors, hoarding toilet paper at the sight of a lone snowflake falling from the sky, or drowning a Kobe beef rib eye in a sea of ketchup.

I cannot allow this horrific state of affairs to continue. So listen up, newbies. Here's a traditional spring project that's sure to win you the respect and welcome of your Southern neighbors. We're going to make yucca tulips.

First, you need a plant called yucca. While the South is home to many yucca species, my favorite for this job is one renowned for the potentially lethal, needle-sharp points on the ends of its stiff, spear-shaped leaves—the aptly named Spanish dagger (*Yucca aloifolia*). Cold-hardy to USDA Zone 7, it is also an excellent choice for growing beneath windows.

On the pretense of making Easter eggs, buy some yellow, pink, blue, and white egg cartons from the grocery store. After eating all the scrambled eggs (smothered in ketchup, of course), cut tulip-shaped blooms out of the cartons. Spear them onto the ends of the yucca leaves, being careful not to impale yourself, as copious blood loss will result in unconsciousness and failure to complete the project.

Voilà! Yucca tulips. What a striking display that lasts for months! Folks, you just don't see such creativity up North. It's one of the many things that makes living here so special.

Shucks. You're now a Southerner.

[RULE #49]

There are easy flowers for people who have never gardened before.

Start with the ones you can grow by simply scattering their seeds on bare soil and watering. Sow columbines, zinnias, marigolds, cosmos, sunflowers, and bachelor's buttons in spring for summer blooms. Sow poppies, sweet Williams, money plants, and larkspurs in fall for spring blooms.

—

ZIMPLY ZENZATIONAL ZINNIAS

innias are the Toyota Camrys of the flower border. Every year, new annuals like 'Serena' angelonia and 'Snow Princess' sweet alyssum come along, delivering more color for more weeks with less work than the flowers before them. Yet at the end of the day, one dependable old favorite on the garden center lot still begs to go home with us. The zinnia.

Say "zinnia" and the image that pops into most gardeners' heads is the big-flowered common zinnia (*Zinnia elegans*). It grows up to 4 feet tall and boasts flowers up to 5 inches across in just about every color except blue. The blooms make great cut flowers—the more you cut, the more you'll get—and butterflies love them. 'Park's Picks,' a double-flowered strain I photographed at Becky Savitz's garden in North Carolina last week, sports fully double blooms with a greenish yellow eye.

LOTS OF SPOTS

Unfortunately, as Becky will attest, when common zinnias are grown closely together and you get rainy weather, they fall victim to a variety of leaf diseases, including powdery mildew and several leaf spots. Spraying according to label directions with a systemic fungicide such as Immunox before diseases show up can prevent them, but once these rogues appear, you're pretty much left with just picking off and trashing infected leaves. Because high humidity favors these diseases, plant common zinnias in sunny, well-drained spots. Avoid wetting the foliage when you water, and don't crowd plants.

TROUBLE-FREE ZINNIAS

Insect and disease problems associated with common zinnias caused a lot of us to look for a trouble-free type. In narrowleaf zinnia (*Zinnia angustifolia*), we found it. It gets its name from its slender leaves. Unlike common zinnia, it's a mounding plant and grows about 16 inches tall and wide. The blooms are smaller, about an inch wide, but it flowers profusely. While it's not great for cutting, narrowleaf zinnia doesn't need deadheading to keep blooming either. It resists mildew and leaf spot and is much more drought tolerant than common zinnia.

Flower colors of early strains, such as Classic, Crystal, and Star, were limited to orange, yellow, and white. Then plant breeders asked themselves this question: "Is it time for a sour Belgian beer?" All agreed it was not, so they asked a second question, "Could we cross common zinnia and narrowleaf zinnia and come up with something that combines the best traits of both?"

They did. And that's why we now can plant zinnias that are more compact, disease-resistant, and drought-tolerant than common zinnias and have bigger flowers in many more colors than narrowleaf zinnias. In general, the new zinnias such as the Zahara and Profusion series, form a lower, tidier mound than Classic and Star—about a foot tall and wide. The blooms can be single or double.

IT'S NOT TOO LATE TO PLANT!

Think you've missed your chance at zinnias this year? Not necessarily. Zinnias are just about the fastest and easiest annuals to grow from seed. If you start them by midsummer, you can enjoy weeks of great color in August and September, right up until frost. Though zinnias take hot weather, they also love the fall. Look for seeds at garden centers. If they don't have them, try Park Seed, Burpee, and Renee's Garden, three good mail-order sources for all kinds of zinnias. Or go with transplants for even earlier blooms.

Zinnias like fertile, well-drained soil and as much sun as they can get. Go easy on the water, don't wet the foliage when you water, and soon you'll be singing the praises of these old favorites.

ZZ PLANT

You can't kill it in the office, and you can't kill it at home. So even if you don't know a philodendron from a Philly cheesesteak, you can grow ZZ plant.

ZZ plant is an ideal indoor plant for people who can't spell "IQ," let alone possess one, because it's their BFF in two ways. It's their best friend forever because it will probably live longer than them. And it's brain-free foliage because even that famous Darwin Award winner who mooned his parents as he flew over them in his ultralight and then lost control and crashed could have succeeded with it.

Here are all the things most houseplants need that it doesn't:

1 Bright light. ZZ plant (short for *Zamioculcas zamiifolia*—you knew that, right?) accepts very low light indoors. It'll grow under the fluorescent light in your office or the neon Corona Beer sign in your man cave. Granted, it'll grow faster and look better if it gets bright, indirect light from a nearby window. Don't put it in the hot sun, though, or you'll likely burn the foliage.

2 Frequent watering. ZZ plant grows from a large tuber that stores water, so the plant needs very little water. Let the soil dry completely between watering. Make sure excess water escapes through a drain hole but doesn't sit in a saucer under the pot. Too much water results in yellow foliage.

3 Fertilizing. Feed it maybe twice a year with water-soluble houseplant fertilizer—once, if it's growing in very low light.

4 Spraying for bugs. No insects bother it. I know you are very disappointed to hear this! If only we humans could be so lucky.

5 Humidity. Humid or dry, it doesn't care either way. This does not seem to be the case with most women and their hair.

Zamioculcas zamiifolia is native to Zanzibar. (Zorro reportedly found it there at the zoo.) It resembles a cycad (think cardboard palm—*Zamia furfuracea*), but is related to philodendron. This slow grower takes years to reach 3 feet tall—perfect for a table top. Thick, deep-green leaves that alternate up the stems are so naturally glossy they look plastic. You can buy ZZ plant anywhere they sell foliage plants.

The Grump loves ZZ plant almost as much as he loves that famous band from Texas, ZZ Top. I've written new lyrics to the tune of "Sharp Dressed Man" to honor it.

You ready? Sing!

No food

Low light

Not a problem cause I'm feeling right

Fat leaves

Thick stems

Most gardeners say I am a foliar gem

They come running just as fast as they can

Cause everyone's crazy about a tough houseplant!

INDEX

Pity the fools who don't read my blog each week.

The full richness of life eludes them.

———